Luce Irigaray

presents

International, Intercultural, Intergenerational

DIALOGUES

Around Her Work

Printed and bound by CPI Group (UK) Ltd, Croydon, CR0 4YY

Contents

INTRODUCTION   *Luce Irigaray*   1

READING — INTERPRETING — IMPARTING

Poetic Nuptials   *Judith Still*   7
                         University of Nottingham

Reading and Rethinking the *Heidi Bostic*   22
Subject in Luce Irigaray's Michigan Technological
Recent Work   University

On Faithfulness in   *Kaisa Kukkola*   32
Translating   University of Turku

PHILOSOPHY — ETHICS — POLITICS

To the Other as   *Stephen Pluhacek*   45
Other — Hearing, Listening, Michigan Technological
Understanding   University

From the Same to the   *Florinda Trani*   57
Other   University of Lecce

A Gendered Education   *Maria José García Oramas*   66
towards the Fulfillment of University of Mexico
Democracy

WHY CULTIVATE   *Luce Irigaray*   79
DIFFERENCE?

PAINTING — ARCHITECTURE — CINEMA

Approaching Painting   *Hilary Robinson*   93
through Feminine   University of Ulster
Morphology

Love in Architecture   *Andrea Wheeler*   105
                         University of Nottingham

Light, Colour and Sound in *Liz Watkins*   117
Cinema   University of Leeds

Feminine Enunciation in   *Caroline Bainbridge*   129
Cinema   University of East London

BEING TWO,   *Luce Irigaray*   143
HOW MANY EYES
HAVE WE?

FEMININE IN THEOLOGY AND PHILOSOPHY OF RELIGIONS

The Woman at the Gate: *Laine Harrington*   155
Access or Barrier to   Graduate Theological Union,
'Goddess Talk'?   Berkeley

Incarnation: The Flesh   *Anne-Claire Mulder*   173
Becomes Word   University of Utrecht

Divine Love   *Morny Joy*   189
   University of Calgary

CONCLUSIONS   *Luce Irigaray*   204

Introduction

I thank Judith Still who has welcomed the proceedings of the *Dialogues* conference in a special issue of *Paragraph*. I thank her also for helping me to get the typescript in the style of the review and in good English. I am also grateful to Heidi Bostic and Stephen Pluhacek who likewise assisted me in putting my own texts in correct English, and who helped me to prepare for the meeting. Many thanks also to Maria Bailey and Kaisa Kukkola, who gave me assistance in translating or reading my texts for the *Dialogues* conference. This took place at the AHRB Centre for Cultural Analysis, Theory and History in Leeds, with the collaboration of the Arts and Humanities Research Board and the Centre for Interdisciplinary Gender Studies. I would like to express my gratitude to them for giving hospitality to this encounter, and especially to Griselda Pollock who arranged the conference. I know that the work to satisfy my own will was considerable and that it implied more risk than that usually involved in planning a university symposium or publication. I am thus very grateful to Griselda Pollock and to Judith Still for having agreed with my proposal.

Why did I want a gathering of another kind? For a few reasons. First, I do not like repetition. And I prefer inventing something new to doing something that already exists. Furthermore I am allergic to conformism and formalism — which I consider in some way politically problematic — that is, to all that I would have to do because it is already expected, foreseeable. And just to do another symposium does not awaken great interest in me.

But there are other more decisive reasons. The thought of difference requires new practices, more based on difference itself, on dialogues taking into account the other(s), it requires new ethical attitudes.

Another motive: Our times are difficult, for all people and perhaps particularly for young people. Thus I wanted to give an opportunity to those who have dedicated a part of their time, of their lives, to my work. I know that in order to make such a choice they must have a great will and sometimes impose this will with difficulty. I know that they have run a risk because they often had to work alone in a new matter without a general consensus, without help except their own will. Thus I desired to celebrate their courage, their heart. One manner of doing that was to give them the possibility of talking about their own work, and above all of talking together about their work.

After a Ph.D., after so great an effort, many people feel tired and disappointed. For a part of them, this important work will remain the only one of this sort because they did not receive any encouragement to pursue the task of thinking. I hope that this gathering between those who have carried out such work about my thought will be an encouragement to continue on the way of thinking. And that they will support one another in this direction.

We know that a certain kind of family is today in crisis. Perhaps we can give rise to another kind of family: neither natural nor religious or ideologically political, but a family in thought. I hope something of this sort will be born thanks to the *Dialogues* conference and this publication. To succeed in this we must take the time to listen to each other and we must also reflect on the words we use. We must pay attention to the fact that we are — as in a family — in part young people and in part older people. The attention we have to pay to one another is a little different in every case.

Furthermore the people gathered here belong to different countries, cultures and languages. We compose, in a way, a multicultural family. But this corresponds to the reality of our times. And certainly we can assist the growth of our communities by living and reflecting between us.

In all families, but above all in multicultural families, the question of language is decisive. The presence of translators was thus indispensable in our gathering. Their function and their responsibility in passing on a culture, a thought, is critical and is becoming more and more important in a global perspective. Speaking only in one language is not a good way for constructing a universal democratic culture. Each culture is constructed starting from its own language. The question today is how to go from one culture to another, how to translate not only its content but also the style in which it is expressed. It is not enough to have paternalistic discourses about democracy, we must first practice democracy in respecting the culture, the thought and thus the language of each citizen, each writer, each country.

We compose also a mixed family. And this requires, in another way, a particular attention for the language we use, not only to transmit information but to communicate between us. Certainly there are more women than men among us. In order to change our manner of living the difference perhaps it would be better to be fifty-fifty. But it is not the case, and I am not sure that this is not, in the end, better. In fact the thought about difference between sexuate subjects is new, it is also difficult to establish, to put into practice. And to succeed in that, in spite of a masculine monosubjective culture, women have to prepare themselves. They have to learn how to think and to live the sharing between two, being two. This is possible thanks to a sexuate difference that constrains them to respect the man as other, not only corporally but subjectively, culturally. They have to overcome their natural identity and their natural way of knowing the other in order to respect him, and after that also her, in a transcendental manner. This is the condition on their part to reach a culture of two subjects. In fact, the culture of difference is difficult to establish because it requires a change in perceiving and living transcendence, for our own part and between us.

This publication includes four parts, as the conference itself did. They correspond to the fields in which my thought arouses most interest. In the first part, the papers approach the crucial question for our times of how to pass on a thought and a style, particularly in another language: in a poetic discourse (Judith Still), with a personal or educative point of view (Heidi Bostic), or as a work of a translator as such (Kaisa Kukkola). The second partition of the whole concerns philosophy as theory but also in its possible applications: how to hear, listen to, understand the other as other (Stephen Pluhacek, who belongs in fact to the first and the second part, as both a philosopher and a translator), how to go from the same to the other (Florinda Trani) and how to take into account a sexuate perspective to reach a more democratic education (Maria José García Oramas). In the third part are gathered texts which concern the arts: how to use artistic media in painting (Hilary Robinson), the place of love in architecture (Andrea Wheeler), some considerations about light, colour and sounds in cinema (Liz Watkins), and feminine enunciation in the cinema (Caroline Bainbridge). The last section of contributions examines the means of discovering, and partly re-discovering, the ways for feminine subjectivity to become divine, either through theology or religious studies: access or barrier to Goddess talk in our tradition (Laine Harrington), the becoming word of the flesh in incarnation (Anne Claire Mulder) and love as divine in Western or Eastern horizons (Morny Joy).

Wanting to meet the wishes of those who welcomed our gathering and to be a participant among the others, I took part myself in *Dialogues* with two texts, one after the part dedicated to philosophy and the other after that dedicated to arts: the first tries to explain why cultivating our difference(s), toward a culture based on dialogues,[1] corresponds to a task of our times, and the second considers the various ways of looking at, especially when being two.

To remain faithful to the title *Dialogues*, my own first questions to the contributors and their first answers have been kept in this publication. In the conference, two co-chairs posed questions before allowing the public to ask theirs. I regret that the available space in this special issue of *Paragraph* did not allow reproducing all the interventions and thus showing how our international, intercultural, intergenerational *Dialogues* took place. But *Paragraph* already did much in welcoming the texts that arose from our gathering. Many thanks to its Editorial Committee!

LUCE IRIGARAY

NOTE

1 In fact the text pronounced in Leeds was 'Approaching the Other as Other', now published in *Between East and West* (New York, Columbia University Press, 2002, 121–30). I thus decided to integrate in this volume 'Why Cultivate Difference', a talk which took place in the University of Nottingham, 20 June 2001.

READING — INTERPRETING — IMPARTING

Poetic Nuptials

Introduction

This paper seeks to examine the rich and polysemic expression *poetic nuptials* in the context of reading and translating the work of Luce Irigaray. While some of Irigaray's work is written in a seemingly approachable and accessible style, other texts are densely poetic and *invite* different kinds of reading relationship. I deliberately use the plural *kinds* because these poetic texts do not demand just one (kind of) reading. They can be read pleasurably even without 'full' understanding. Equally, sections, even words or expressions (such as that of *poetic nuptials*) can be lingered over at length so that layer upon layer of connotation becomes apparent, and it is the relationship *between* these connotations which is crucial. Poetic nuptials, I would suggest, can take place between text and reader or translator; they can take place within the text, between elements of the text; they can be a mode of intertextual relationship — the way in which the text stages its relationship with other texts. Poetic nuptials are an alternative to ways of reading such as critique which demand a particular distance between what become subject and object. Poetic nuptials would take place *as if* between (at least) two subjects, and lead us on to consider intersubjective relations in general outside any text in the narrow sense of the term.

Poetic nuptials between text and reader

A key question over the last few decades has been: how do we read? A number of different paradigms have been proposed including a would–be objective, professional, scientific analysis of the text, on the one hand, an empathetic meeting of like minds (often like-minded deliberately 'amateur' gentlemen) on the other hand, and, different again, a psychoanalytically-derived notion of an agonistic struggle between poet/reader as ephebe and the fantasized author-father text. This question of reading is not just of interest to University departments of literature; the expansion of the notion of text which has taken place reveals, or helps us to see, how reading is an activity which takes place not only in relation to a book, but also in relation to other minds and bodies, in relation also to the social and material world which surrounds us. Consequently this question, 'how do we read?' is crucially important: do we take an instrumental approach treating the text as object? Do we privilege an elitist clique of 'first-rate' works appreciated by first-rate minds — each endorsing the other with the stamp of approval? Do we model relationships entirely on aggression, on the competitive struggle to be first? Each of these three approaches has some value, some insight to offer, and yet if any one of them becomes absolutely predominant then much is lost.

In this short paper I'd like to suggest that *poetic nuptials*, a term borrowed from the work of Luce Irigaray, might inspire in us a more productive relationship between reader and text as between two subjects. This would surely entail respect for the text in its inevitable difference from us; I should not wish to propose some kind of union in uniformity which might lead even to psychosis or death. However, the difference between reader and text would be one which is dynamic and entails each subject searching for points of reciprocity. It may seem a strange conceit to describe a text as searching, but I would argue that (some) texts do exactly that — they seek readers who will reciprocate. Not readers who are already identical to themselves, not readers who are to be subjugated or who will seek to subjugate them, but readers who will respond to the gift of the text.

This paper will focus on *To Be Two*. *Etre deux* in French, *to be* or *towards being* two, takes up the questions which have absorbed me for many years: how to think two without a hierarchy (which would be difference without equality)? How to avoid hierarchy without letting one be established all the more firmly for being refused (which would be equality without recognizing difference)? Obviously a key inequality historically is that built upon sexual difference — and we might pose the question from psychoanalysis (and from feminism), is it the foundational difference? As Irigaray writes:

In fact, there is no rupture between intersubjectivity in the strict sense and the intersubjectivity of a collectivity, and the desired changes in the relations between man and woman, men and women, form part of a transformation which is helpful to all of our social relationships. (*To Be Two*, 23)

This suggests that changing relations between the sexes will bring about a certain change in social relations more generally.

Feminism as analysis of women's situation in a variety of spheres (work/economics, body/sexuality and so on) has necessarily involved critique of men, of masculinity, and of male power. Masculinity studies (not to be confused with men's studies — usually carried out by men and sometimes fuelled by guilt, and/or defensiveness which can become aggression), is just beginning to move from critique of men (although that work of critique is far from ended) to a consideration of how men could be, what they could become, and what a relation to men/masculinity could become. Irigaray is unusual as a serious philosopher and theorist who addresses this question — usually deemed the stuff of popular speculation (if not of women's magazines) — regarded suspiciously by feminists and contemptuously (or at least patronisingly) by many men. As Irigaray remarks:

The fact that loving relations are, for the most part, considered a sort of decadence [*déchéance*], seems to come from a tradition of the sensible which has no respect for intersubjectivity or the exchange of words between those who love each other. This tradition reduces the feminine to a passive object which must experience sensation, while man must distance himself from woman in order to protect his relationship both with the realm of the intelligible and with his God. (*To Be Two*, 23)

There is a section on the male other/lover in *To Be Two* ('He arrives', 8–16). The relationship between *je* and *lui* is described as one of *not*-knowing; there is a darkness and distance between the sexes. This reprises male philosophers' (psychoanalysts', novelists' . . .) take on feminine mystique or mystery, the dark continent of female sexuality. For Irigaray, the mystery is what lies *between* us, and *not* what is located in the feminine, such that it must be grasped, penetrated and possessed in the thirst for knowledge. Anecdotally, when I first read Irigaray, about twenty years ago, I was more struck by what the text had to say about the *feminine*. Now I am seeking out, and feel engaged by what is said about the potential *relation between* the feminine and the masculine subject. More generally, as reader, this increasing focus on the 'between two', on relationality as content, has come to mirror the structure of the reading relationship.

Re-thinking the relation to other texts

Another aspect to reading Irigaray is her staging of a relationship with other texts. This takes a number of forms — sometimes the intertextual relationship is not presented via quotation marks and footnote references, but through a textual dance with one or more partners implied. That subtle play with other texts is perhaps a more obviously poetic form of interrelating and changing perceptions. However, even within what may seem a more conventional scholarly critique of other thinkers — a pedagogical exercise which can be extremely helpful, and should still co-exist alongside more experimental forms for the benefit of those like myself who sometimes feel lost and want solid ground to rest on — there can be a thought-provoking twist. In the middle of a lengthy quotation from Levinas, where he discusses the eternal feminine as virginal, Irigaray intersperses a reference to the man, Levinas himself.[1] The reader's reception of the philosopher's meditation on the caress (where he has deployed a lexicon that overlaps with Irigaray's own) is certainly affected by the perception of the author not as a disembodied subject, but as a male.[2] The parenthetical insertion of the writer's body has an effect. It makes us re-think our reading relationship, which does *not* take place outside social and inter-personal power relations that are always sexed. The relation between body and words can be figured as a nuptial one, 'Les noces entre le corps et la parole' as Irigaray puts it in *Etre deux* (35–55) (translated as 'The wedding between the body and language' (17–29)).

Reading and Translation

Translation (in the literal rather than general sense of the word) is a particularly intimate and anxiety-ridden mode of reading. It brings the reader up close to the detail of the text. For example, personal pronouns figure prominently and crucially in Irigaray's writing. Sentences such as 'Dois-je m'éloigner de toi pour aller vers lui?' with its evocation of *je, toi,* and *lui* are not unusual, and require the reader to think carefully about what or whom these shifters designate. The English translator loses a certain amount of nuance simply in the almost inevitable rendering of *tu/toi* as you.[3] Both intimacy and a relation to the divine co-exist in the French term, but are lost in the more neutral English version, which also covers formal you and plural you (*vous*) and can cover one (*on*). Thus the key inter-subjective relation, between *je* and *toi* is made less wittingly amorous and playful — a mode which should deliberately spill from the literally intersubjective to the civil and political domain. The archaic *thou* is another possible alternative for the translator, but ever-greater distance from contemporary English makes it a risky choice these days.

There is endless play on grammatical gender in Irigaray's work as befits a feminist who has developed a specialism in socio-linguistics. In the 'Prologue' to *Etre Deux* there is a panegyric of praise to *elle (la terre)*, and an exploration of the loving relationship between *je* and *elle*. While a simple interpretation would see that *she* denotes Mother

Earth, the repetition of *elle* across pages has a powerful and complex effect on the reader.

Je deviens elle, devenant également moi. Je la respecte, en me respectant. Je l'aime en m'aimant. Elle est dans et hors de moi. Certes je ne peux l'étreindre, mais elle est là. Elle m'entoure, elle se diffuse en moi, elle m'illumine, elle me réconforte, sans rien en échange. (16)

I become her, becoming also myself. I love her, loving myself. She is within me and outside of me. Certainly I cannot embrace her, but she is there. She surrounds me, radiates in me, illuminates me, comforts me, without a gift in exchange. (5)

While rendering *elle* as *it* in English would surely lose the point, rendering *elle* as *she/her* makes the effect much clumsier and heavy-handed. A feminine or masculine noun often appears to be the result of a conscious choice on Irigaray's part — she plays with *l'univers* (masculine) or *le monde végétal* (ditto), but returns to *la terre* (feminine). This grammatical play is almost impossible to transpose into English. Conversely there are moments where English insists on a sexed person's relation to the object (*his* or *her* object) which is veiled in French in which the gender of the object itself (*son univers* or *sa terre*) is marked instead.

Translation in the literal and professional sense is a task carried out by only a small minority of readers. However, translation in a more general sense affects all readers. The transposition of words from writer to printed page, and from printed page to reader, always involves a kind of intersubjective translation.

Nodal expressions

I should now like to turn to certain particularly dense and thought-provoking expressions in Irigaray's work. These are words which may not seem so difficult to translate from *French* to *English* because our two languages have a degree of shared antecedents, shared history — but which may be far more difficult to translate metaphorically from Irigaray's writing into our own. Irigaray often selects terms, such as 'virginity' which have had a difficult or complicated history; and sometimes her choice seems more provocative in a different linguistic and cultural context, or simply outside the context of her own texts where they are carefully explained or judiciously deployed. I shall briefly evoke a select series of figures: poetic nuptials again, two lips, gift, virginity, and caress.[4]

There is a tendency of words that we should note — they seem to have a habitual, relatively fixed primary meaning; but then slip sideways, metonymic associations accumulate; and finally move *heimlich/unheimlich* towards an anonymous meaning. This mobility of words is something to be celebrated, but also to be carefully observed lest in 'translation' from one text to another, an expression comes to mean *only* all that it did *not* originally. One key question to consider is that of the relation between the literal and the figural — are these meanings exclusive? Or if co-present does one have to predominate? Do we have to decide which takes precedence? Can they flicker in and out? Can there be *noces* between two meanings? The literal and the figural also play between the opposition so familiar to us between body and mind, between material and spiritual/intellectual. Can poetic nuptials suggest something about a sensual-emotional continuum, which might be a different way of thinking the body-mind dichotomy? Irigaray's work evokes a *sensible-transcendental*. How do these various oppositions *or* relationships correspond to the distinction between literal and figural?

In 'Plato's *Hystera*' (*Speculum*, 241–364), Irigaray suggests that the history of philosophy and of metaphysics, has involved a denial of material origin. The foundation of male philosophy lies in a metaphorical transposition of the woman's body, and specifically her reproductive organs, in the Platonic myth of the cave. Thus a desire to read Irigaray's work, and specifically the references to the female body, as pure metaphor would seem to play into the hands of the enemy. Biological references have to be taken seriously, literally, or else we end up once again de-materializing the body in favour of an intellectual structure. Nevertheless, I would argue that we always read and hear — including in relationship to the body — on multiple levels, and that these different levels interact. Reducing the text to one meaning can only be a strategic gesture.

Let us turn first of all to a dictionary, one of the tools of the translator's trade. In the Oxford English Dictionary we find that *poetic* has a first meaning of 'Belonging or proper to poets or poetry'. The sixth meaning given is 'Making, creative; relating to artistic creation'. The definition of *poem* includes the restrictive sense of verse (and yet the definition of a prose poem is a poem without verse), but also has the expanded sense of any literary text, or indeed of the epitome of the literary or aesthetic. The etymological sense (from the Greek) of poetic as *creative* introduces the issue of the economy of (re)production — at various points on the chain: vegetable, animal, human, divine. The economy of (re)production brings together the two terms poetic and nuptials.

Nuptials means both marriage and wedding. In the OED you can read over the slippage between these two meanings. In a French dictionary (the *Petit Robert*) it is made evident and taken further: *Noce* or *les noces* has a primary meaning of marriage. The second meaning is defined as: 'Ensemble des réjouissances qui accompagnent un mariage' (The celebrations which accompany a marriage). The third 'by analogy' is 'a party to celebrate a wedding anniversary'. The fourth meaning refers to the wedding *guests*, the participants or 'wedding party' in that rather different sense. The fifth meaning given is a popular or informal one: 'Partie de plaisir, de débauche, généralement accompagnée d'excès de table et de boisson. — Vie dissipée, consacrée à la débauche, au plaisir. *Faire la noce*' (Party, particularly dissolute and generally accompanied by excessive eating and drinking. — Dissolute life, devoted to debauchery and pleasure. *Live it up*).

We can note the complicated relation between the singular and the plural in the French. *La noce* can err towards the pejorative and individualistic sense of debauchery although it does not have to. Even if *faire la noce* involves a collection of individuals, there is no union. *Les noces* introduce the conceit that nuptials are plural because they involve at least two. The amorous underpinning of nuptials for us today is important in the context of Irigaray's work, in which loving relations are revalued and esteemed relevant not only in the field of intersubjective relations in a narrow sense, but in social relations more widely. The insistence on a culture of two subjects, one other to the other, makes the term *nuptials* particularly pointed. It is, however, illustrative of the problem of de-contextualizing Irigaray's vocabulary, or of re-contextualizing it to mean only the negative social connotations it has acquired. This is the danger of snipping out short quotations in order to critique a thinker who has, at times, such a radical approach to the use of language. The celebration of marriage has a very troubled history for feminism, which is acutely aware of the way in which the marriage market has functioned (and can still function) as a homosocial economy that reduced women to objects circulating between men. Irigaray has herself written a key essay, 'Women on the Market', on this very subject. Thus she is not using the term in ignorance of its social and political origins (the appropriation of woman-object by man-subject), but rather reclaiming it, redefining it as a *fête* or a celebration (wedding), and also the act (marriage) of the coming together *towards* union of two subjects. Perhaps unsurprisingly, each of the terms I have picked out links to, and overlaps with, each of the others — and so I shall pass on to the gift.

Gift. The importance of an other economy in the relation between *je* and *toi*, and beyond, cannot be over-stated. The rejection of mine and thine as founding commerce is repeated in Irigaray's work as if a mantra. Mine and thine, possessive individualism, is the necessary pre-condition of workaday life as we know it. Alongside the market economy in which most of us function, and in which women have had to demand a range of 'equal rights', there is private, domestic existence — which, historically, has also often functioned econom-ically and involved exploitation of women. Again, Irigaray's work shows that she is very well aware of this, and of the need for legislative intervention in both spheres. However, she also suggests something different: the potential *fête* of amorous relations. Intersubjective rela-tions can be modelled not on the market, nor on fusion, but on the exchange of gifts. Gift exchange assumes the existence of two different partners: donor and recipient. It also assumes dynamic reciprocity. There are numerous examples of the rejection of possessiveness and appropriation, and of the celebration of giving, in Irigaray's writing.

This first example refers to language in a double sense:

Nous nous parlons dans toutes les langues, oublieux de la nôtre, connaissant l'autre. Nous sommes attentifs au sens au-delà du véhicule — jamais tien, jamais mien, inappropriable. Nous restons présents à nos sens qu'aucune possession n'aveugle. (*Etre Deux*, 25)

We speak to each other in all languages: forgetting ours, knowing another. We are attentive to the meaning beyond the vehicle of language: never yours, never mine, inappropriable. We remain present to our senses, unclouded by any possession. (*To Be Two*, 10)

Sens, senses and meanings — the play works a little better in French where the noun is written and pronounced the same in both the singular and the plural although it can be *sensed* in English too. The abandoning of the possessive mode enables us to sense the other's senses in the many languages available to lovers.

Between us is something which will never be mine or yours. Would a vertical transcendence not rob of us of this third dimension beginning from which we approach each other as different others? Others in flesh and spirit. If the third dimension is found in the beyond, we become images-of, reduced to two dimensions, with a bit more [*un en-plus de*] subjectivity and with a bit more or a bit less of [*un en-plus ou un en-moins de*] the object: phallus or baby (. . .)

I want to live in harmony with you and still remain other. I want to draw nearer to you while protecting myself for you. (*To Be Two*, 13)

En-plus has the sense in French of surplus value, that which can be extracted as profit because human labour produces more than it is paid for (and valued at) in a market economy. It is important to note the vocabulary of economics alongside that of psychoanalysis or philosophy. Our familiar two-dimensional self images, which leave aside that third possibility of a different encounter, fear castration and seek profit to shore themselves up. This masculine economy entails the accumulation of objects to stand in for the phallus, the transcendental signifier — and notoriously the child can be one of these objects.

To be two would allow us to remain in ourselves [*le demeurer en soi*], would permit gathering, and the type of safeguarding which does not restrain, the kind of presence which remains free of bonds: neither mine nor yours but each living and breathing with the other. It would refrain from possessing you in order to allow you to be — to be in me as well. (. . .) To be irreducible to one another can assure the two and the between, the us and the between-us. And from where would the need for appropriation arise, if each allows the other to return to his or her to be?

Consuming does not produce one's existence. Instead, difference can protect this existence: I am if you are, to be together with you allows me to become. The two, this two, is the bit more [*l'en-plus*] which is indispensable if I am to be. Closing myself up in consumption, in possession, in production, does not make me one. What makes me one, and perhaps even unique, is the fact that you are and I am not you. (16)

The *demeurer en soi*, being at home in, and with, ourselves, brings us to the next term selected, that of virginity. Before moving on, I'd just like to note that in the last quotation we see that (sexual) difference *gives* us each our own subjectivity. This sexuate subjectivity is brought about by a gift; whereas, in our market society, we are accustomed to the false notion that identity comes about through what we consume, through what we produce or through what we possess.

Virginity. This has proved to be a controversial term to invoke — 'get thee to a nunnery', but what does it mean in context? Should it be understood as you irreducible to me, as against a relationship which involves possession, which involves you becoming mine? Should it be related to *repos*, understood as a kind of peace with, and in, yourself, a respite?[5] Irigaray refers to the privileged time-space of *fête*, which is outside the quotidian (work), just as the gift is outside the market. The use of this expression, virginity, evokes the need for a *bodily* (sexuate) *subject* in order to be able to consent freely to a relationship, to 'touch one another in intersubjectivity' (26).

Caress. A caress suggests 'deux sujets qui se touchent', *not* just a man touching a woman (or the 'eternal feminine' to which Levinas alludes), and *not* a relationship mediated by an instrument (bodily or not). A caress need not *only* be understood literally although it might be understood literally *as well*. It can be a 'gesture-word', 'an offering of consciousness, a gift of intention and of word addressed to the concrete presence of the other, to his natural and historical particularities' (*To Be Two*, 26). It stands against the market which is a violence which does not respect intersubjectivity.

Two lips. Penis-phallus-psychoanalytic signifier-coherence/unity-power: how do we understand the relationship between the elements in this chain of terms/concepts? Vague association, metaphor, metonymy, synecdoche, real link? Much energy has gone into the feminist critique of the phallus and of phallic power, which *could* have taught us something about the subtleties of the imbrication of literal and figural, of body and word. Nevertheless, Irigaray's introduction of 'ce sexe qui n'en est pas un' notoriously met a storm of hostility from some feminists and from some men, accusations of biologism and/or essentialism, of having tried to perform a simple reversal of positive and negative terms while leaving the matter of hierarchy unquestioned ... The complexity of the relation between literal and figural necessarily involved in Irigaray's thought-poems was embraced by some readers, but met with an angry refusal from others. The refusal to see the penis anywhere in the phallus on the part of some masculine critics could be said to be another ruse to retain masculine power, just as the denial of difference can be an effective way of maintaining inequality under the guise of egalitarianism (something Rousseau already pointed to in his *Discourse on Inequality*). And yet any insistence on invoking the reality of the female body (alongside much which complicates that literal reality), is greeted with such terror ...

The textual demand that we should be 'faithful to the reciprocity in touching-being touched, itself a matter of perceiving or of speaking' (*To Be Two*, 23) is a good example of the complication (or stepping beyond, into the imaginary and symbolic realms) of literal reality which co-exists alongside a powerful evocation of embodied relations. What is the meaning of *touch* here? Is it sense (and in what

sense?) — sensual, sensation, signification? Being moved is important — both an emotional and an intellectual shift.

Last words

To return to the question of modes of reading: we can read *inter*
and think of burial, and so death, or we can read *inter* and think of
the *between* which enables creation, poetic creation, (re)production.
We can read *inter* and think of the relationship between burial,
death, mourning and creation, poetic creation, (re)production ... In
French we have the related, albeit different, play between *entre* and
antre.[6] *Entre*, a key word for Irigaray, is repeated incessantly in her
analysis of Plato's *Republic* VII, a founding text for philosophy and for
metaphysics. For example: 'Entre ... Entre ... Entre l'intelligible et
le sensible. Entre le bien et le mal. L'Un et le multiple. Entre tout ce
que l'on voudra' (*Speculum*, 306) ('Between ... Between ... Between
the intelligible and the sensible. Between good and evil. The One and
the many. Between anything you like', 246–7). All these relations
between, in particular between the outside and the inside, are turned,
dichotomized, into philosophical oppositions by the forgetting of the
vaginal passage *between* the interior (also *ventre* or womb) and the
exterior in the Platonic myth of the cave (*antre*). Poetic nuptials is a
term for a different thinking of relationality, not an oppositional one
which claims that no encounter is possible. It is also, in perhaps less
comfortable ways, a tool for remembering the literal female body.

JUDITH STILL
The University of Nottingham

NOTES

1 'It [and I wish to add: this is man's caress]' (24). In the French version this
   reads: 'La caresse (et j'ai envie d'ajouter: celle de l'homme Lévinas, L.I.)' (48).
2 Irigaray has written extensively on Levinas before, both in 'The Fecundity of
   the Caress' and in an article 'Questions to Emmanuel Levinas'. In other words
   this is an ongoing dialogue on her part at least. Irigaray's work on Levinas
   has attracted some attention: translations of her essays have been included
   in volumes of essays on his work, and Tina Chanter, amongst others, has
   addressed the issue of the relationship between Irigaray and Levinas. Kate Ince
   puts forward the view that Irigaray could be more generous to Levinas and
   that his subject is explicitly an embodied one. However, she agrees that it
   is only ever a male subject, that his notion of voluptuosity fails to establish
   a relationship with his notion of the Other feminine, and that the only

relationship which (according to Levinas) can be established is with the son. I am grateful to Alison Martin for drawing this article to my attention.

3   In the unusual case of *Etre Deux* the translators were in fact working from an Italian original. I shall continue to refer to the French as this is the more general case with translations of Irigaray. The two languages Italian and French share a pattern of sexing objects and not possessive pronouns.

4   Many others could have been chosen including, for example, mucous.

5   See *To Be Two*, 27, and contrast the account of Levinas, 25.

6   See for example: 'De cet *entre* deux "mondes", modes, modalités, mesures, de répliques, représentations, regards, notamment du soleil, du feu, de la lumière, des "objets", et de l'*antre*' (*Speculum*, 305, my italics) 'Of the "go-between" path that links two "worlds," two modes, two methods, two measures of replicating, representing, viewing, in particular the sun, the fire, the light, the "objects," and the cave' (*Speculum*, 246).

BIBLIOGRAPHY

Chanter, Tina, *Ethics of Eros: Irigaray's rewriting of the philosophers*, New York and London, Routledge, 1995.

Ince, Kate, 'Questions to Luce Irigaray', *Hypatia*, 11, 1996, 122–40.

Irigaray, Luce, 'The Fecundity of the Caress: A Reading of Levinas, *Totality and Infinity*, "Phenomenology of Eros"' in *An Ethics of Sexual Difference*, London, Athlone, 1993 (185–217), translated by Carolyn Burke and Gillian C. Gill from the French *Ethique de la différence sexuelle*, Paris, Editions de Minuit, 1984.

Irigaray, Luce, 'Questions to Emmanuel Levinas' in *The Irigaray Reader*, edited by Margaret Whitford, Oxford, Basil Blackwell, 1991, 178–89, translated by Margaret Whitford from the French 'Questions à Emmanuel Levinas', *Critique*, 522, 1990, 911–20.

Irigaray, Luce, *Speculum*, Ithaca, New York, 1985, translated by Gillian C. Gill from the French *Speculum*, Paris, Editions de Minuit, 1974.

Irigaray, Luce, *To Be Two*, London and New Brunswick, NJ, 2000, translated by Monique M. Rhodes and Marco F. Cocito-Monoc from the Italian *Essere Due*, Turin, Bollati Boringhieri, 1994. The French version was published as *Etre Deux*, Paris, Grasset, 1997.

Irigaray, Luce, 'Women on the Market' in *This Sex Which Is Not One*, Ithaca, New York, Cornell University Press, 1985, 170–91, translated by Catherine Porter with Carolyn Burke from the French *Ce Sexe qui n'en est pas un*, Paris, Editions de Minuit, 1977.

Luce Irigaray's questions

I appreciate the efforts Judith Still made to clear some misunderstandings about my work. I would like to give some help myself with such an end in view. It is not possible to change a language in a day, and we can hardly wish for that. We are ourselves structured and permeated by a certain language from the very beginning of our life. And we are also born into a family, a country, a culture which speaks this language, thinks and communicates through it, etc. Thus the language represents an important part of ourselves, of our affective and historical environment.

For example, to remove a word like 'virginity' from our vocabulary runs the risk of leaving a kind of hole in our subjectivity, a hole which could little by little undermine its constitution for ourselves, and also in the relations with the others. What to do then? 'Virginity' is a key-word in the definition of feminine identity. But this word, which in fact concerns the woman, serves to define her from a masculine point of view, and in order to structure the exchanges between men. It was thus indispensable to give back to the woman a word which has served to alienate her. I define 'virginity' as psychological autonomy and integrity, safeguarded by the woman herself. Virginity no longer alludes to the part of the female body which will prove to a man that he is the first one who makes love with this woman. Virginity rather signifies a capacity of the woman herself to be autonomous and to keep herself free and whole in relation with any one. Including her readers, which is particularly difficult!

When I use 'nuptial', I also intend to take this word away from institutions which subdued love to patriarchal rules. 'Nuptial' refers to happy and reciprocal love between two persons, love in which either body or soul, spirit, take part independently of any institutional context. And, alluding to the 'two lips', I try to give back to the woman that which only she herself can feel of this part of her own body. The purpose is always to restore meaning and life to words which have too often lost them because of their neutral and arbitrary meaning.

It is also on my part an attempt to overcome the dichotomies, among others between natural and metaphorical, literal and figurative etc. These belong to a masculine culture in which body and spirit are maintained separate. My intention rather is to pass gradually from life itself to its words — kind of flowers in a way — and this for the life of nature but also for my life, your life ... Our manner of talking brings death because it presupposes a separation from life, from body in order to designate them through language. Then we can only speak about them and not speak them. How to become capable of speaking nature, body, love? This is a crucial question for me. In such a perspective the problematic of the 'gift' is not really appropriate because it generally refers to an object. Now the question rather is that of giving oneself through words and of welcoming the other in the same way, while remaining each one ourselves. I am also afraid that the vaginal mediation will not be sufficient here: we must use negativity to safeguard a space between us, a space which does not belong to one nor to the other.

I would also like to insist on the fact that I choose certain words because they are beautiful, materially beautiful: for their sound for example. I know that this aspect of a text is difficult to translate. But I regret that most translators do not care enough about it, because it represents a part of the meaning.

My question to Judith would be: Have you some suggestions to make about the manner of speaking life, body, love, soul ... without using a language which duplicates them in an arbitrary way, but rather transmits an experience of their own existence, growth and so on?

Another question: my work, especially my latest books, would like to express a relation between two subjects without reducing them to a unique subject, who holds a unique discourse about nature, world, others. How to translate or impart such a relational content conveyed by my texts? How to express this 'between two' which does not take place in occidental logic except between polarities of a unique unity? How to speak the quest of two subjects for meeting, loving each other and holding a dialogue?

Judith Still's response

I should like to thank Luce Irigaray for these gifts: the benefit of more commentary on some of these key terms; her impossible questions which make us think; reminding us of the importance of onomatopoeics — and the oral–aural pleasure we can derive from savouring a word in our mouth and feeling its delicate vibration in our ear. Language always touches our senses as well as arousing our intellects, and the attempt to render and harmonize affect with precise or indeed obscure and multi-layered meaning in translation makes the translator's task both acutely painful and pleasurable. When Joanne Collie and I translated *Passions élémentaires*, we would spend hours at the kitchen table with a bottle of wine, bowls of dips and pitta bread amidst the piles of paper, dictionaries, and, of course, our sacred text. We would take it in turns to read aloud French, then our different English versions, sometimes close to tears, sometimes furiously debating, sometimes laughing hysterically and sometimes embracing and shouting 'yes' at each other if we thought for a moment that we had come anywhere near a version we could be happy with. An intellectual collaboration, an exchange of gifts, an emotional experience and a labour of love: rolling words around your tongue, letting them fall from your lips to have them reverberate in another's labyrinthine inner ear echoes your hopes for further passionate encounters between the text and other readers.

Reading and Rethinking the Subject in Luce Irigaray's Recent Work

Motivated by the importance of reflecting upon the challenges and opportunities that present themselves to whoever reads, teaches or translates Luce Irigaray's work, these remarks will have a threefold focus. First, I would like to offer some thoughts on approaching her texts as a reader, as a teacher and as a translator, and on encountering the thinking and writing subject expressed in this work. Second, I will discuss aspects of Luce Irigaray's theorization of the subject. Finally, I will sketch out some suggestions along the lines of 'Where do we go from here?'.

Approaching Irigaray's Work, Encountering the Subject

Luce Irigaray's work calls for an other way of reading, of approaching the text as subject-reader or as subject-translator. As the reading, teaching, translating subject meeting these works, one must adopt a mode of being that is attentive to breath. The rhythm of these works resembles in some ways the rhythm of poetry. They require an openness like that needed to encounter another culture. The reader is invited to an other way of thinking, an other way of reading, different from the exclusively cerebral way of reading in which most of us in Western universities have been trained. A passage from *Between East and West* devoted to the encounter with the other provides insight into the experience of a first encounter with Luce Irigaray's work:

The state that springtime, certain landscapes, and certain cosmic phenomena provoke in us, sometimes takes place at the beginning of an encounter with the other. It is in the first moments of drawing near to one another that the other moves us the most, touching us in a global, unknowable, uncontrollable manner.

The continuation of this same passage is an apt description of what often occurs when one relies exclusively upon the academic way we have been taught to read and interpret:

Then, too often, we make the other our own — through knowledge, sensibility, culture. Entering our horizon, our world, the other loses the strangeness of his or her appeal. The presence of the other included us in a certain mystery, communicating to us an awakening that is both corporeal and spiritual. But we reduce the other to ourselves, we incorporate the other in turn: through our knowledge, our affection, our customs. (123)

Luce Irigaray's texts call upon us not to reduce them to something previously known. They challenge us to read without translating in the impoverished sense, that is, without interpreting according to well-worn schemas of thought. This challenge is especially acute when one reads in translation. And, of course, this means that the work of the translator herself or himself is especially fraught with danger. My experiences reading, translating and teaching Luce Irigaray's work have highlighted for me both the difficulties of translating and the importance of helping to bring this work to a wider readership.

Whoever reads Luce Irigaray's texts with respect and care encounters a thinking and writing subject invoked through these works who resembles the subjectivity described in the texts' most hopeful moments. This subject is respectful, attentive, and spiritual. The speaking subject here cares for nature, cultivates breath, and uses language with care. There is no clear boundary between what we could call the theory of the subject described in these texts and, on the other hand, the living subject that is expressed in them. The words of the texts are not the lifeless, technical work of a disinterested sage, but rather the living expression of a way of being. Keeping this is mind, I turn now to some specific aspects of Luce Irigaray's theory of the subject.

Rethinking the Subject: Practices, Relational Identity, Gender

Luce Irigaray's work has always demonstrated a concern with thinking the subject.[1] Her account of the subject represents a radical departure from the Western philosophical tradition, and constitutes a critique of certain philosophers. I would like to focus, however, on some of the positive moments of her recent work, in which she poses questions that are crucial today, including: How to approach the other as other? How to cultivate identity while building community? Stated briefly: How to be two?

Luce Irigaray's recent books, and particularly *Between East and West*, show that the answers to these difficult but important questions lie in practices — not just in an intellectual exercise, but in a way of being in the world, a way of being toward the other. Rather than dwelling exclusively in the ether of abstraction, Luce Irigaray offers specific ways of cultivating subjectivity in one's daily practices, here on earth.

This focus on everyday rituals that are central to a good life includes attending to one's spiritual life, especially through the way of breath. A communion with the natural world of air, the practice of purposeful breathing also creates a silence that cultivates awareness of both self and other. This silence is foreign to our world of incessant talk. In *Between East and West*, one encounters the following observation:

Breathing and speaking use breath in an almost inverse manner, in any case for the majority of people. From this point of view, it is interesting to note that people who do not breathe, or who breathe poorly, cannot stop speaking. It is their way of breathing, and notably of exhaling in order to draw another breath. Frequently, they also paralyse the breathing of whoever takes corporeal and spiritual care of his or her breath, of the breath of others. To remain silently attentive to breathing comes down to respecting that which, or who, exists and maintaining for oneself the possibility to be born and to create. $(50-51)^2$

In one particularly memorable example of a practice, Luce Irigaray describes Buddha's act of contemplating a flower without picking it (*I Love to You*, 24–25, 139–40). This caring encounter contrasts sharply with our habit of picking the flower, of appropriating the other. Just as we can learn to appreciate the flower's beauty without tearing it up by its roots, we can learn to acknowledge the other without consuming him or her.

Closely linked to the cultivation of practices is an idea at the heart of Luce Irigaray's thought on subjectivity, namely, relational identity. The very style of her texts is a teaching on relational identity, on the way to be toward and with the other. In a 1996 interview entitled 'Thinking Life as Relation', Luce Irigaray offers the following remarks as part of her response to a question about what is meant by 'relational identity':

According to the traditional logic, identity refers to self-identity, to identity to the same. It designates a reality which is if possible fixed, not subject to change, not modifiable by the event nor by the other (. . .) Relational identity goes counter to this solipsistic, neuter, auto-logical ideal (. . .) Relational identity considers the concrete identity which is always identity in relation. As such, it is always metastable, becoming (. . .) The fact of being a woman, and of having to always realize my own gender more perfectly, provides me with an anchoring in an identity which must not for all that be fixed and unchanged (. . .) When I speak of relational identity, I designate that economy of relations to the self, to the world and to the other specific to woman or to man. This identity is structured between natural given and cultural construction. (353)

The importance of relational identity results in part from the impossibility of thinking the subject in isolation from intersubjectivity. As Luce Irigaray writes in the introduction to the Italian edition of *L'Oubli de l'air*, entitled 'From *The Forgetting of Air* to *To Be Two*': 'Life is never simply mine, because it is always already received from the other and presence to the other' (311). Elsewhere in this same article, she writes: 'Strangers we are to one another, irreducible to the same Being. Being, then, is split in two, or, rather, is held in two and in the relation between' (313). Cultivating relational identity means unlearning the tendency to reduce the other to the same. It means approaching the other while respecting our differences.

This respect explains the curious 'to' in the title 'I Love to You', a preposition that 'is the site of non-reduction of the person to the object' (*I Love to You*, 110). This word 'safeguards a place of transcendence between us, a place of respect which is both obligated and desired, a place of possible alliance'. It signals the non-reduction of the other to 'a factual thing or to an object of my love' (*To Be Two*, 19). Inserting the preposition in the habitual expression 'I love you' calls our attention to the inseparability of language and meaning, to the way syntax encourages objectification. As Luce Irigaray writes: 'Objects as such, whether concrete or abstract, sensible or mental, are not necessary for perception. I can perceive another living being while still respecting him as subject' (*To Be Two*, 40). That is, it is possible to learn to approach the other without reducing the other to an object of my perception. We may approach one another while remaining subjects.

Luce Irigaray's work attends to relational identity not only with regard to private intimacy between two, but also with regard to public life, to the cultivation of a new civil society. The attention to both of these levels is a unique and rich aspect of her thought. While theorizing the between-two on the most intimate level, for example, in her work on the caress (*To Be Two*, 25–29).[3] Irigaray attends as well to subjectivity on the public plane. She asks, in other words, how to cultivate relational identity, while building a bridge between singularity and community.

To borrow a phrase from Margaret Whitford, part of Luce Irigaray's project is to 'rethink the social contract' (*Luce Irigaray*, 2). Luce Irigaray's work offers the hope that a new conception of subjectivity, love, relational identity, and spirituality may help us to refound society as a whole. Discussing *I Love to You* in the interview 'Thinking Life as Relation', she remarks:

The fact that I approached the problem [of the intersubjective relation] beginning with the political level is not an accident. It is on this level that masculine philosophers have at times spoken of the relations between individuals. But it was a question then of relations between individuals defined in the sociocultural organization of the world of between-men: the city, the nation, even the religious group. It was never a question — except in an abstract manner? — of the relation between two individuals here and now present one to the other (. . .) Personally, I consider that the civil relation must be founded upon a real rapport between two concrete individuals (. . .) I wrote *I Love to You* because of necessities which presented themselves to me: how to engage in politics with a man in respecting our differences, of gender first of all, then of culture, of language, of education, etc. *I Love to You* corresponds to a [brief] treatise of political philosophy that aims toward a democratic organization of civil community. (354)

More recently, in a chapter of *To Be Two* entitled 'Each Transcendent to the Other', Luce Irigaray has discussed the slogan 'liberty, equality, fraternity', in a subtle challenge to the legacy of Enlightenment philosophers. There remains much to be said about the tools that Irigaray offers us for rethinking subjectivity and reason as foundational concepts in modernity. As women contemplate the failed promise of the eighteenth-century revolutions and seek various solutions, including the much-discussed debate on parity in French politics, it is time to rethink all of our modernist commitments, not the least of which is the ideal of a universal, neuter human subject. As we examine the legacy of excluding women from democracy in Western nations, attention to both public and private concepts of subjectivity must inform our attempt to reclaim what Ernst Bloch has called the 'undischarged utopian potential' of the 1789 Revolution, and its proclamation of liberty, equality and fraternity.[4]

While the Western philosophical tradition has long thought subjectivity starting exclusively from a male subject, Luce Irigaray's theorization of gender and subjectivity together enables us to think female subjectivity without trying to assimilate women to a masculine model, a model that is reflected in this talk of 'fraternity'. The subject in the Western tradition is, she writes, 'subjected to mediations proper to the masculine subject, and thus not really universal or neutral'. Once we realize this, we discover 'that nature as human nature is *two*: masculine and feminine, and that it requires a double subjectivity, a double 'being I,' in order to be cultivated' (*Between East and West*, 98). In this way, we come to recognize 'the other gender as irreducible to me, to mine' (*Between East and West*, 102).

Each gender has a specific relational identity, which is both natural and cultural. This difference results in part from women's and men's experience with the mother as belonging either to the same or to the other gender, and is reflected in different ways of language use. Women's speech, for example, tends to privilege the intersubjective relation. Affirming that men and women have different subjectivities does not mean that we reduce them to a simple 'biological destiny'. Rather, it entails a realization that men and women are '*culturally different*' (*Between East and West*, 129).

Thoughts for the Future: Where do We Go from Here?

Thoughtful attention to Luce Irigaray's theorization of the subject, including practices, relational identity, and gender, should cause us to rethink every aspect of our lives, a crucial task for today's world. Upon encountering these texts, we must ask: Where do we go from here? What are we called upon to do? There can be no single blueprint that all may follow. Indeed, any single prescription or announcement from on high would mask our individual and collective responsibility to forge new paths. Luce Irigaray has resisted the tradition of following such pronouncements in her reading of the Annunciation. Rather than conceiving of a God who announces to Mary that she will have his son, we can imagine God inviting Mary to share breath, to join in the creation of a new life (*I Love to You*, 123–24, 140–41; *To Be Two*, 54). Each person must respond to these questions based on his or her own lived situation. As a teacher, I see it as a matter of entering into relation with students and with the texts in my classes. As a reader, I feel a responsibility to allow the texts to speak to me, to allow their unique breath to circulate. As a translator, I must respect this breath, and not attempt simply to encode words into another language, as if some sort of equivalence were possible. As a human being who is a woman, my daily life may be influenced by this new vision of the subject. Rather than seeking to minimize the importance of my gender, I need to seek the possibilities it presents to me. In relation with the other, I must cultivate the necessary space and silence. The teachings of the texts are not something to be forgotten when leaving campus or closing a book. These works ask to influence us beyond the sphere of our academic intellectual inquiry.

I have said that for Luce Irigaray, the answers to some of the most difficult questions that we ask as subjects, both in private relationships and in public life, lie in practices. To this I would like to add that it is a matter, first, of learning to ask the right questions, of attending to the blind spots in our thought that are caused by the lack of culture in the feminine and in the masculine.

The world has not yet seen more than a glimpse of the possibilities that Luce Irigaray offers to us. What would our culture look like if we respected the other as other? What kind of civil society could be constructed upon the recognition of our singularity, as men and as women? These texts demand that we rethink, from top to bottom, the way in which we understand the constitution of our identities, in intimate relationships as well as on the level of civil society. One manner of cultivating the necessary reflection is to organize public dialogues, with the aim of sharing the possibilities presented by this work with increasingly wider audiences. Offering a new way of thinking the subject, and indicating possibilities for fostering speech and action in both private and public spheres, Luce Irigaray's work is a challenge and an invitation.

HEIDI BOSTIC
Michigan Technological University

NOTES

1 See, for example, the section entitled 'Toute théorie du "sujet" aura toujours été appropriée au "masculin"' in *Speculum*, 165–182, translated by Gillian C. Gill as 'Any Theory of the "Subject" Has Always Been Appropriated by the "Masculine"' in *Speculum*, 133–46.
2 On this topic, see also Luce Irigaray, *I Love to You*, 122.
3 See also Luce Irigaray, 'The Fecundity of the Caress: A Reading of Levinas, *Totality and Infinity*, "Phenomenology of Eros"' in *An Ethics of Sexual Difference*, 185–217.
4 Ernst Bloch, *The Principle of Hope*, vol. 1.

BIBLIOGRAPHY

Bloch, Ernst, *The Principle of Hope*, Vol. 1, Cambridge, Massachusetts, MIT Press, 1986.
Irigaray, Luce, *Between East and West, From Singularity to Community*, New York, Columbia University Press, 2002, translated by Stephen Pluhacek from the French *Entre Orient et Occident, De la singularité à la communauté*, Paris, Grasset, 1999.
Irigaray, Luce, *An Ethics of Sexual Difference*, Ithaca, New York and London, Cornell University Press-Athlone, 1993, translated by Carolyn Burke and

Gillian C. Gill, from the French *Ethique de la différence sexuelle*, Paris, Editions de Minuit, 1984.

Irigaray, Luce, 'From *The Forgetting of Air* to *To Be Two*', in *Feminist Interpretations of Martin Heidegger*, edited by Nancy Holland and Patricia Huntington, University Park, Pennsylvania, The Pennsylvania State University Press, 2001, 309–315, translated by Heidi Bostic and Stephen Pluhacek from the French original.

Irigaray, Luce, *I Love to You, Sketch for a Felicity Within History*, New York-London, Routledge, 1996, translated by Alison Martin from the French *J'aime à toi, Esquisse d'une félicité dans l'Histoire*, Paris, Grasset, 1992.

Irigaray, Luce, *Speculum*, Ithaca, New York, Cornell University Press, 1985, translated by Gillian C. Gill from the French *Speculum*, Paris, Editions de Minuit, 1974.

Irigaray, Luce, *To Be Two*, London-New York, Athlone-Routledge, 2001, translated by Monique M. Rhodes and Marco F. Cocito-Monoc from the Italian *Essere Due*, Turin, Bollati Boringhieri, 1994. The French version has been published as *Etre Deux*, Paris, Grasset, 1997.

Pluhacek, Stephen and Heidi Bostic, 'Thinking Life as Relation: An Interview with Luce Irigaray', *Man and World*, 29, 1996, 343–360.

Whitford, Margaret, *Luce Irigaray, Philosophy in the Feminine*, London-New York, Routledge, 1991.

Luce Irigaray's questions

I encountered some difficulties in posing a question to Heidi Bostic. And I asked myself why. I found that it results in part from the fact that Heidi's speech is in some way a discourse of praise. I have often said that we must return to this kind of discourse, perhaps the first one that allows us to be two, and furthermore to compose a community.

Saying 'thank you', for example, we begin to recognize the other as another subject. But we have become unaccustomed to words of praise. And I was first obliged to reach anew this kind of talking in order to ask my question. It is also particularly difficult because words of praise, at least in our culture, are generally non-reciprocal. Someone gives praise and someone receives it: they don't give praise to one another. We must discover or re-discover almost everything in order to reach a discourse of praise between us.

I have also understood that a praising discourse implies — at least as its horizon — a global subject, and not a fragmented subject, if praise is real and not formal. In fact, Heidi Bostic's text is a discourse which considers the human subject in its totality. And I think that this way of approaching individual subjectivity is necessary in a world that claims it is becoming global. If globalization progresses without allowing a subjectivity to be global, it corresponds to a machine that will reduce humanity at best to a part of itself, at worst to nothing.

Thus cultivating the individual as global is necessary for humanity in order to resist globalization. And it is also necessary to pursue the becoming of humanity as humanity.

In my opinion only the difference between man and woman and the cultivation of their relation can open a way to a global status of individuals. I am not talking here only about sexual difference in a limited sense, but about the fact that subjectivity is constituted differently by man and woman and that they live in two worlds foreign to one another.

I would ask Heidi: How and why did you discover this dimension of my work? Or, how have you discovered, for your part, the necessity of considering the individual as global: body, affectivity, thought . . .?

Another question: How will you impart such experience, such knowing, in particular to your students?

Heidi Bostic's response

Insofar as I have been able to understand something of Luce Irigaray's texts, it is thanks to two factors: time and relationships. I have been reading her works for over ten years, and my first encounter with them was a great revelation — it allowed me to think about my sexuate identity in totally new ways. Since then, I have had frequent, even daily conversations about her work, across the lines of sexual difference, in various contexts. Being open to the texts means taking time as one reads them, respecting the words of the other, not trying to force them in one direction or another. Carrying out an interview with Luce Irigaray, together with Stephen Pluhacek, and translating the interview into English is one example of a relation that has deepened my understanding of her work. The opportunity to participate in reading groups across disciplines has also been very important. Such dialogues call upon us to question and to explain, without simply speaking and learning 'among ourselves'. These dialogic relations have been decisive, and provide a model for teaching Luce Irigaray's work.

Transmitting this understanding to students is also a matter of both time and relationships. In a course, it is important to take enough time to read the works carefully, to use the available time well but also to abandon any hope or goal of mastery in one semester. This also involves helping students to view Luce Irigaray's work in relation to the long philosophical tradition and the specific philosophical texts she analyses. It is a matter of working with and of learning from the work, while avoiding appropriation. In an Anglophone context, teaching these works is often a matter of translation, and it is important to bring the French text to bear on the discussion. I think this question would be a good one to pose to the students themselves: How to teach Luce Irigaray's texts? This could help students to seek an appropriate context for listening to the work, and suggests that they, as future teachers, will participate in the transmission of this work, that the task does not simply end with them.

On Faithfulness in Translating

Faithfulness is probably the most common criterion when evaluating a translation. There is a great variety of opinions as to what it means to be faithful, and to what should one be faithful. For some it is transmitting 'the message' of the original text while for others it is evoking the 'same' feelings and provoking the same 'effects' on the readers of the translation as on the receivers of the original text. For a long time this clear-cut division of views was not discussed. Fortunately, since the birth of translation studies, attention has been paid not only to this major issue but also to more subtle and detailed questions. For example, what is the message and what are the same effects (see Amparo Hurtado Albir, *La notion de fidélité en traduction* and Lawrence Venuti, *The Translation Studies Reader*).

In my MA thesis I wanted to make a good (that is to say, faithful) translation of Luce Irigaray's texts 'Un mystère qui illumine' (*Etre Deux*, 183–98, translated as 'A mystery which illuminates', 103–12 in *To Be Two*) and 'Quand nos lèvres se parlent' (*Ce sexe qui n'en est pas un*, 205–17, translated as 'When our lips speak together', 205–18 in *This Sex Which Is Not One*). My goal led me to ask different kinds of questions about faithfulness and fidelity in translation. I just could not proceed without rethinking what I had been told about the work of translating.

How to identify the message?

The translator should find the message in the text, or define and decide what the message of the text is. It has been said that if the meaning of the text is not clear, the context will clarify and help in the decision-making of the translator.[1] The most important task for the translator is nevertheless the comprehension of the source text. While trying to find a context for Luce Irigaray's texts which could help me, some unexpected problems arose.

Luce Irigaray is a well-known philosopher whose thinking is widely commented on and used in different fields of the academic world in Finland. As a student, I got acquainted with her work in several of them: in philosophy, in women's studies, in literature, in cultural history and in French. Each of these disciplines seemed to have a quite different view of Luce Irigaray's work and they seemed even to disagree about her message. As my further approach was to show me, those disagreements were linked to the secondary literature on Luce Irigaray and the different ways of interpreting her thinking. Inside each discipline a different Irigaray was living, and she did not communicate with the other Irigarays. What could that fragmentation mean for the context, which is supposed to help the translator? Was the right Luce Irigaray the philosophical one? The literary one? The feminist one? None of those? All of them?

In my opinion the primary context should be Luce Irigaray's own work. But, what then happens if I, as translator, know only the literary interpretation of her thinking, or the philosophical one? Does it not also influence my further reading as a pre-existing knowledge? Does it not determine my view of her work? How can I, as translator, take it into account?

So, I was affected by some interpretations of Luce Irigaray's work but I still wanted to be a faithful translator. I kept on reading her and more or less abandoned all the other material, that is, the secondary literature. A whole different world of thinking opened up to me. And it had very little to do with the one that I had met previously. I thought that it was a solution to part of my problems: not to take as guidelines one of those 'Finnished Irigarays', not to make my translation measure up one of those images. I wanted to move the idea of fidelity into my process of translating. It was a way of considering my 'contamination' by other readings. I tried to keep them in the background — not to let them determine my interpretation but not to ignore them either.

Translating as a process, the product of which is a translation, can be divided into several stages. Simplifying, one could say that they are: 1) reading/ interpreting, 2) understanding, 3) reformulating (see Amparo Hurtado Albir). One could go on saying, still presenting simplifications, that: the first step includes such things as classifying the text by its function and/or by its nature, the second would consist of linking the text with encyclopaedic knowledge, creating the meaning of the text,[2] and the third one would then be adapting the 'idea', the 'message' to the norms and rules of the target language. These stages are not successive in time nor in the work of the translator.

What was the problem with Luce Irigaray's texts? First of all the traditional functional division did not work. I could not decide whether the texts were informative or expressive, metalinguistic or poetic, scientific or lyric. That kind of division did not make any sense. That also meant that I did not have model-texts or norms which I could have taken as guidelines for my Finnish translation.[3] In the same way that I had already abandoned the idea of forcing my translation to a certain mould of Luce Irigaray, I abandoned the categories of text-types. Luce Irigaray has made something radically different and there were no examples or pre-existing models for it. I then limited my work to the reading of the texts and what I actually found in them.

The Problem of translating gender

Now I shall give a few concrete examples of the difficulty of translating gender from one language to another. The quoted examples are from 'Un mystère qui illumine', translated by Monique Rhodes and Marco Cocito-Monoc as 'A mystery which illuminates'.

In this text, Luce Irigaray specifies the gender, giving both the feminine and masculine versions: *lectrices — lecteurs, certaines — certains, toutes — tous, chacune — chacun* ('readers', 'some' — 'certain', 'all', 'everyone'). In some cases, but not in others, this is possible also in English, for instance by using suffixes of the type actor-actress. Suffixes are often used when French thoughts are translated into English, even if they are not usual, and the creation of new words has then been seen as one of the translator's ways of using her or his power in the target language. Some notions may even stay in French in the final version (see Sherry Simon, *Gender in Translation*, 106–8). The result can be suitable, and comprehensible to readers but it can also bring unwanted, even derogatory connotations to the text. In the English translation, *lectrices et lecteurs* become 'female and male readers' (*To Be Two*, 103) but *toutes et tous* and *chacune et chacun* become just 'all' or 'everyone' (107) without any specification in gender.

I do not claim that one should try, in the name of fidelity, to make up inadmissible sentences or words. In the original, the specification of two different groups is everywhere in the text, and in that I see something that should be respected. If we take into account why Luce Irigaray writes that way, then the result can be different and extremely interesting. In 'Un mystère qui illumine', she reminds us of her reasons: two different subjects, two different subjectivities. Simultaneously she speaks and explains what/why she is speaking so. Translating these two aspects, two levels is challenging and only the explanations can easily be transmitted, not the way of speaking which is explained.

Does the impossibility of making both levels visible in Finnish mean that the language is unable to express some of Luce Irigaray's thoughts? Is there no space for two subjectivities — no place for Luce Irigaray's thinking — in this language? I do not think so and, fortunately, some further question have been asked in several languages but not (yet) in Finnish.[4] The Finnish language has often been described as egalitarian and sex/gender neutral. The arguments are for the most part that: Finnish nouns are not gendered as in French, Italian or in German. That is to say that the gender of the speaking subject is not marked in adjectives nor in past participles and that there are not even different pronouns for s/he. Therefore defining the space of two different subjectivities can be difficult, but further research could reveal interesting things.

However, a translator needs immediate solutions. One of those could be a translator's preface or footnotes where she or he could explain this difference to readers. Footnotes are often used but are not always the best means (see Louise von Flotow, *Translation and Gender*, 35–48). They add to the text a metatextual, explanatory level and this changes the nature of the text.

I do not believe that Luce Irigaray's aim in her text is to teach her readers French, to explain the French way of excluding/including the feminine. She wants to speak directly to them, all of them, to women and to men and then — taking into account their difference — say something which they could understand. To what should I be faithful? If I include all Finnish readers in the Finnish way, I will not specify their genders. If I translate Luce Irigaray, I should do otherwise.

About the choice of good words

The second problem also deals with inclusion/exclusion, this one on the level of vocabulary. In her text Luce Irigaray uses such notions as *l'identité, identique, le sujet, la subjectivité, le discours* ('identity', 'identical', 'subject', 'subjectivity', 'discourse'). They all have a good and suitable translation in Finnish ('identiteetti', 'identtinen', 'subjekti', 'subjekti-ivisuus', 'diskurssi'). The problem is that these are acceptable, scholarly words with their own specific use. They are also often such recent loan-words in Finnish that their use and meaning cannot be found in dictionaries. They are more abstract concepts than living words. Furthermore they cannot be understood without special knowledge of other language or of certain scientific domains. So by choosing the word which might seem to be the best one — for instance, 'diskurssi' to translate *le discours*—, I exclude some readers, even if they could resort to a dictionary.

Moreover for the words already cited, we also have good 'Finnish', comprehensible translations ('samuus', 'yhtäpitävyys', 'tekijä', 'puolueellisuus', 'keskustelu'). There is no linguistic—or any other kind of—link between these two translation possibilities: *le sujet* as 'subjekti' or 'tekijä'. These are two completely isolated paradigms between which the translator is supposed to choose. By that choice s/he also determines the potential public, the people who can understand the text. In my opinion, the original text does not define, does not exclude a specific public. To what should I then be faithful? A potential publisher certainly has his or her idea of Luce Irigaray and, according to that, s/he can impose on me choices, exclusions. It is certain that if Luce Irigaray is considered as poet,[5] the acceptable translation will be different than if she is seen as a philosopher, at least in a traditional Occidental context. In any case I should bear in mind that Luce Irigaray's texts in French can be read outside of academies or universities, and my translator's sense of fidelity tells me that it should be the same for the Finnish public.

On cultural or linguistic specificities

The third problem that I want to explore here is situated on a completely different level of text than the previous ones—even though it has its repercussions, for instance on vocabulary. The question is that of the Finnish way of expressing 'seeing'. In this respect, English and French are quite similar. It is good to bear in mind that Finnish is a Finno-Ugric language whereas French and English are Indo-European languages. This viewpoint might be even more pertinent with respect to other texts of Luce Irigaray but it has helped me a lot when structuring my own thoughts.

I shall give some examples related to 'sight' and 'seeing', which I consider to be of great interest when we take into account Luce Irigaray's critique of sight-centred Western culture and philosophy. First:

Il ne reste donc qu'à s'approcher de cette aporie et peut-être élaborer une phénoménologie non seulement de ce qui existe, de ce qui apparaît, mais de ce qui n'existe pas et ne peut pas apparaître. ('Un mystère qui illumine', *Etre Deux*, 185–6)

There remains nothing else to do but to approach this aporia and perhaps elaborate a phenomenology not only of what exists, what appears, but also of what does not exist and what cannot appear. ('A mystery which illuminates', *To Be Two*, 104)

There are quite good translations in Finnish for 'appearing' ('ilmetä') and for 'phenomenon' ('ilmiö') but 'phenomenology' is, once again, a scholarly word ('fenomenologia') which does not mean anything to a great number of Finnish-speaking people. It is different in French and in English because the root of the word belongs also to the common language. In this sentence I must probably give both the 'Finnish' and the scholarly translation.

The next example, also from *To Be Two*, is:

J'exposerai des vérités qui seront seulement apparences, et non au sens de l'apparaître de la vérité. (186)

I would expose truths which will only be appearances, and not with the meaning of appearing of truth. (104, translation amended)

I should probably keep on using the same stem of the verb 'to appear' ('ilmetä') in order to derive the noun which expresses 'appearance'. Unfortunately the semantic field of that derived noun ('ilmentymä') does not correspond to 'appearance' and cannot be used. I should choose another word. And there it gets complicated. The vocabulary, which is so rich in sight-centred tradition, is not that important in Finnish. A mere glimpse at the dictionary reveals that words related to sight are not only fewer but that the relations between them are not the same than in French. Because of this the translation of words like: *voir, (s')apercevoir, percevoir, concevoir* ('see', 'to catch a glimpse of'/'notice', 'perceive', 'conceive') can be extremely delicate.

What is the question of faithfulness here? Is there any? Is my kind of interpreting too problematic? Is this kind of deep level problem something that I, as a translator, should take into account? How should I do it? With 'Un mystère qui illumine' ('A mystery which illuminates') problems are not impossible to solve but 'Quand nos lèvres se parlent' ('When our lips speak together') demands already more reflection. In my opinion, if a difference on an implicit level of thinking and writing exists, then it too is a part of the text that I have to translate. I do not have any answers, only further questions.

What do I propose as a conclusion to the vast question of faithfulness in translating? I can only say that, for a translator, it means several things: global decisions, ways of searching for information, concrete choices of structures, words and word-endings, consideration for cultural particularities. Above all it would be a humble attitude: a translator should never pretend to have the right answers, to know before reading. Instead of having as a goal to make a translation that could fit into something already existing, a certain image of Luce Irigaray in Finland, I have to be responsible for my attitude in my reading and in my translating.

KAISA KUKKOLA
University of Turku, Finland

NOTES

1 On the construction of sense, see Catherine Kerbrat-Orecchioni, *L'implicite* and *L'énonciation*; on the translator's decision-making, see Wolfram Wilss, *Knowledge and Skills on Translator Behavior* and 'Decision-making in Translation'; on the notion of fidelity, see Amparo Hurtado Albir, *La notion de fidélité en traduction*.

2 On different skills used in the interpretation of what is implicit in the text, see Catherine Kerbrat-Orecchioni, *L'implicite*, 151–298.

3 I do not want to ignore the translations of some of Luce Irigaray's writings in Finnish but I did not want to imitate Pia Sivenius (*Sukupuolieron etiikka* and 'Onko tieteen subjekti sukupuolitettu' in *Naisen tieto*) or Kaija Anttonen ('Sukupuoli, joka ei ole yksi' in *Kielletty hedelmä*).

4 See Luce Irigaray *Sexes et genres à travers les langues, Thinking the difference* and *I Love to You*.

5 I would have used the word poetess, if I had not been warned of its negative connotation.

BIBLIOGRAPHY

von Flotow, Luise, *Translation and Gender, Translating in the 'Era of Feminism'*, Suffolk, University of Ottawa Press, 1997.

Hurtado Albir, Amparo, *La notion de fidélité en traduction*, Collection 'Traductologie', no. 5, 1990.

Irigaray, Luce, *Ethique de la différence sexuelle*, Paris, Editions de Minuit, 1984; translated into English by Carolyn Burke and Gillian C. Gill as *An Ethics of Sexual Difference*, Ithaca, New York and London, Cornell University Press-Athlone, 1993; also translated into Finnish by Pia Sivenius as *Sukupuolieron etiikka*, Tampere, Gaudeamus, 1995.

Irigaray, Luce, *Etre Deux*, Paris, Grasset, 1997; translated into English as *To Be Two* by Monique Rhodes and Marco Cocito-Monoc, London-New York, Athlone-Routledge, 2000, from original text in Italian: *Essere Due*, Turin, Bollati Borighieri, 1994.

Irigaray, Luce, *J'aime à toi*, Paris, Grasset, 1992; translated into English by Alison Martin as *I Love to You*, London-New York, Routledge, 1996.

Irigaray, Luce, *Parler n'est jamais neutre*, Paris, Editions de Minuit, 1985; translated into English by Gail Schwab as *To Speak is Never Neutral*, London-New York, Athlone-Routledge, 2001; one chapter 'Le sujet de la science est-il sexué?' has been translated into Finnish by Pia Sivenius as 'Onko tieteen subjekti sukupuolitettu?' in *Naisen tieto*, editor Sara Heinämaa, Helsinki, Art House, 1989.

Irigaray, Luce, *Ce sexe qui n'en est pas un*, Paris, Editions de Minuit, 1977; translated into English by Catherine Porter with Carolyn Burke as *This Sex Which Is Not One*, Ithaca, New York, Cornell University Press, 1985; one chapter 'Ce sexe qui n'en est pas un' has been translated into Finnish by Kaija Anttonen as 'Sukupuoli, joka ei ole yksi', in *Kielletty hedelmä*, Helsinki, KSL, 1984.

Irigaray, Luce, *Sexes et genres à travers les langues*, Paris, Grasset, 1990.

Irigaray, Luce, *Le temps de la différence*, Paris, Biblio essais, Livre de Poche, 1989; translated into English by Karin Montin as *Thinking the Difference*, London-New York, Athlone-Routledge, 1994.

Kerbrat-Orecchioni, Catherine, *L'implicite*, Paris, Armand Colin, 1998 (first edition, 1986).

Kerbrat-Orecchioni, Catherine, *L'énonciation, De la subjectivité dans le langage*, Paris, Armand Colin, 1999.

Simon, Sherry, *Gender in Translation, Cultural Identity and the Politics of Transmission*, London-New York, Routledge, 1996.

Venuti, Lawrence (editor), *The Translation Studies Reader*, London-New York, Routledge, 2000.

Wilss, Wolfram, 'Decision-making in Translation', *Target* 6:2, 1994.

Wilss, Wolfram, *Knowledge and Skills on Translator Behaviour*, Amsterdam-Philadelphia, John Benjamin's Publishing Company, 1996.

Luce Irigaray's questions

Kaisa Kukkola has evoked the problem of gender in language. It is a difficult and complex question and its relation with subjectivity is not simple. For example, French and other Romance languages are said to be gendered languages, which means that all the nouns have a gender. But the relation of this gender with masculine or feminine subjectivity is not clear. Sometimes it is different between two Romance languages. For example, 'la mer' (the sea) is feminine — she — in French, and masculine — he — in Italian. In order to understand the connection between a noun and its gender it is necessary to undertake historical studies and thus discover why and how a noun has become masculine or feminine. The feminine is not always negative. It depends on the epoch. The most recent times, our times, are the most unfavourable to positive connotations for the feminine.

Now I can already say that sexuate connotations exist in languages in which the nouns are not gendered through an article and a grammatical gender. Thus in a way all languages are gendered. With regard to subjectivity, I can add that English is perhaps more gendered than French because the connection between subject and complement is gendered, contrary to French. We say 'She has finished her Ph.D.' in English, and 'Elle a fini son doctorat' in French. The gender agreement is thus determined by the subject in English, and by the complement in French. The connection of possession, but also of activity, is gendered in English and not gendered in French (See, for example, *Je, tu, nous, Toward a Culture of Difference*, 67–74).

But only in a way. Because this connection of possession can become gendered, for example, through syntactic use. The masculine subject, more than the feminine subject, uses the connection of possession with the complement. But a French man cannot say that he looks at 'his' wife like an English man can, because in French the possessive will be in the feminine.

I could add that the possessive does not serve the feminine subject to indicate one's own property in French. Rather, it serves to create a tie with another subject: 'Elle a noté son accent', 'Elle lui a rendu son livre' ('She noticed his or her accent', 'She gave back to him or to her his or her book').

In this perspective, one can say that English is gendered in a masculine way. It insists on the connection of possession or property more than French or the other Romance languages do. The reason is probably that it was constituted later.

But the most relevant factor when considering how a language is gendered is certainly generative structure. A masculine and a feminine subject do not produce discourse in the same way. And this specific production does not depend only upon apparent gendering. It is concerned with the manner of connecting together subject, verb, complements, for example. But also with many other things.

Now I shall ask Kaisa my question. Many people have said to me that Finnish is a language that is not gendered. Personally, after all the analysis carried out on language production, I think this is not possible. Thus I would ask you — and we have already discussed this together — to indicate some marks of gender in Finnish discourse. And also to show through a few examples if the development of Finnish is favourable to feminine subjectivity or rather to masculine subjectivity, as I fear.

Kaisa Kukkola's response

The gender in Finnish language is not visible, at least not in the same way as it is in several Indo-European languages. This explains why Finnish is often considered as neutral. But it is above all differently gendered. A few examples allow us to think so.

Even though neither nouns nor adjectives are sexuated, sometimes people imagine a particular gender. For instance if a union between a cat and a dog is imagined — in children's books of fairy tales —, the cat is always a woman. Nevertheless cat is not feminine nor dog masculine. This kind of collective consensus becomes visible particularly during French classes.

There are also some names of profession which are in fact masculine, like *puhemies* (spokesman). Instead of creating other words for women, Finnish often uses the ending *-henkilö*, which means 'person'. That is to say that man stays man: the word used for him is the 'man'-ending one, whereas woman is designated as 'person'. She can enter the professional world as woman only by becoming person, thus neuter.

One other thing: the word designating human being — *ihminen* — is said to be gender-neutral because there exists another word for male-human, contrary to English and French. Nevertheless, if I say that a human being has periods — *ihmisellä on kuukautiset* — or that a human being is pregnant — *ihminen on raskaana* —, someone always objects to me that it should be woman — *nainen*. In fact, the word is gendered even though it is supposed to refer to human in general, both woman and man.

Finnish feminists, moreover, are quite keen on gender-neutral language. But there is very little linguistic research especially on the deep level of discourse to support such an attitude. In spite of this, any consideration about sexuation of language comes up against their claim to neutral and egalitarian language.

PHILOSOPHY — ETHICS — POLITICS

To the Other as Other — Hearing, Listening, Understanding

I. Prelude

I would like to begin by stepping back, by respecting that nearness that does not efface the space that separates us while drawing us together. To respect this nearness I aim not to speak *on* or *about* Luce Irigaray, to make of her an object of study, but to speak *to* her, to speak *with* her. I hope to continue a dialogue begun some time ago — to listen faithfully to the other, to seek understanding in her words, and to venture some words of 'my own'. My hope is not to appropriate or to master a discourse, but to share in the birth and growth of a dialogue, of a speaking between us. Thus, I begin as I believe we must, by attending to the call of another, in this case to the words of Luce Irigaray. I quote:

It is in the first moments of drawing near to one another that the other moves us the most, touching us in a global, unknowable, uncontrollable manner. Then, too often, we make the other our own — through knowledge, sensibility, culture. Entering our horizon, our world, the other loses the strangeness of his or her appeal. The presence of the other included us in a certain mystery, communicating to us an awakening that is both corporeal and spiritual. But we reduce the other to ourselves, we incorporate the other in turn: through our knowledge, our affection, our customs. At the limit, we no longer see the other, we no longer hear the other, we no longer perceive the other. The other is a part of us. Unless we reject the other.

The other is inside *or* outside, not inside *and* outside, being part of our interiority while remaining exterior, foreign, other to us. Awakening us, by their very alterity, their mystery, by the in-finite that they still represent for us. It is when we do not know the other, or when we accept that the other remains unknowable to us, that the other illuminates us in some way, but with a light that enlightens us without our being able to comprehend it, to analyze it, to make it ours. The totality of the other, like that of springtime, like that of the surrounding world sometimes, touches us beyond all knowledge, all judgment, all reduction to ourselves, to our own, to what is in some manner proper to us. In somewhat learned terms, I would say that the other, the other as other, remains beyond all that we can predicate of him or her. The other is never this or that, that we attribute to him or her. It is insofar as the other escapes all judgment on our part that he or she emerges as *you*, always other and non-appropriable by *I*. (*Between East and West*, 123–4)

There are a good number of lessons to be learned from this beautiful and illuminating passage from *Between East and West*. I will limit myself to what I believe are the most significant lessons that might be drawn from it. In doing so, I hope to convey some of what I have begun to learn from reading and translating the work of Luce Irigaray. What I wish to say is far from being comprehensive or exhaustive, and, in some manner, I hope that it is rather obvious. But our experience shows us that the obvious and the near at hand are often the first to be passed over, neglected, or forgotten. Laying aside our habits is never easy. For to lay aside our habits is to lay aside our very being. We have, indeed we *are*, the habit of gathering together that which is disjointed and disparate, of giving it form. Thus, it is no easy task to let things lie in their proper dispersion. And yet, that is what I would like to do.

II. *Closure and Economy: Approaching the Other as Other*

Perhaps we must start where we are — although this is not always easy to do.[1] For where we are is not where we want to be nor where we perceive ourselves to be. Nevertheless, here we are — closed in upon ourselves even as we seek to escape; hiding behind great barriers that have been erected around us, that we ourselves have helped to erect; limping along, alone and without the energy or the will to break out of our little worlds.

Perhaps we must start when we are — although this too is not easy to do. For when we are is perhaps not when we want to be nor when we perceive ourselves to be. Nevertheless, now we are — carrying the heavy load of this history upon us, occupied with these historical concerns; lifted by the hopes of some future; standing in this moment, although perhaps fleeing or chasing another time.

It changes little, perhaps nothing, if we are content — or take ourselves to be content — with where we are or when we are. For if our contentment itself is unavoidably a restricted, economic contentment, our 'joy' or 'happiness' is as burdened as our suffering. Even in our contentment we are closed in upon ourselves and carry the load of history upon us. Indeed, these are most often the very conditions of our 'contentment'. We are content when the world leaves us alone, or when the world rewards our efforts. We find happiness in the accomplishment of some project, or in the passing of some event.

And all too often, perhaps always, our joy is bought at the expense of others.

In our suffering and our joy, we are confined within economy. We start from economy and return to economy. Economy—the gathering together within a systematic unity of the disparate and the different, as well as their arrangement and ordering according to some scheme—precedes, sustains, and directs our lives. We live within economy. Our lives are saturated with the economic. The houses in which we live, the relationships we sustain therein, the friendships we pursue beyond, between, and within their walls—even the love we give as well as the love we are offered—are dependent upon or the result of such gathering. We ourselves are economic beings. We have been gathered together—a collection of physical and historical elements pulled together across space and time; a unique nexus of biology and genealogy. We gather together—pulling together various elements across space and time. Our biological, psychological, and sociological identities are the results of such a gathering.

In gathering together, we move ceaselessly, relentlessly, toward closure. This movement toward closure is a restriction. Around this restriction, some semblance of interiority is established and sustained. The name 'habit' can be given to this establishing and sustaining of interiority around restriction. Habits are always economic, setting up little economies. These economies are constituted through the restriction of diachrony. In each case, a radical diachrony is seemingly tamed, channeled, given a rhythm. Diachrony is seemingly forced to repeat—which is to say that there is no longer diachrony. This restriction of diachrony can be given the name 'forgetting'. Habits are a form of forgetting.

The dream of such forgetting is the reduction of the other to the same, the elimination of alterity. Yet such reduction is bound to fail. For it feeds on that which it seeks to eliminate. There is something desperate in this reduction—as there is in all violence.

Regardless of the impossibility, not to mention the undesirability, of gathering all beings within a systematic unity, of economizing being(s), the attempt is made over and over again to reduce the other to the same. This gathering takes various forms—war, patriarchy, matriarchy, consciousness, egology, representational structures—which must be brought into question. And from this questioning a new way of living and thinking can perhaps be discerned.

There is much that has not been forgotten or covered over — that continually surges forth in and around our lives. It surges forth even in being forgotten or covered over — even in our habitual ways of living and thinking. Even in our habits we are surrounded by mystery and can be awakened by surprise. If there is any hope, it may be that it is situated here. This is no utopian hope. Nor is it a project. It is not directed toward some future to come. Rather, it welcomes the mystery and surprise that surge forth continually.

Despite the pervasiveness and seeming naturalness or inevitability of economy and the economic, as a *gathering* together within a systematic unity, economy comes to be. It is not (a) given. Yet how does there come to be an economy? How is economy established? In what way does there come to be the gathering within which economy would take place?

III. *Sharing-Opening-Dwelling*

Life is shared before it is offered or given — which does not in any way diminish what is thus shared. More past than any memorable past, this sharing was neither accepted nor received. Rather, it was imposed, not as the law is imposed, from on high, but as a mystery that simultaneously envelops and opens. Neither a threat nor a persecution, this sharing was (an) open(ing). It was without obligation. It did not ask for repayment. It was an open hand extended — but one that could not be refused. Thus, this sharing was the beginning of an openness toward ..., an openness to ... — but it was also an opening by....

This sharing is a sharing of flesh, of blood, of breath — of life. And yet it is not reducible to an exchange of matter, a working upon that which is sensible. Sharing is not reducible to physical overflowing. The sensible, matter, is always already spiritualized in sharing. Sharing creates a between that not only precedes the between of extended space and the between of chronological time — it makes them possible. Sharing is the opening of space-time — an opening that is not accomplished once and for all, that is not accomplished at all. Rather, sharing opens space-time.

This sharing is the first dwelling—dwelling here is not a mode of maintaining oneself, nor is it a site of power, of being-able-to ... Rather, it is a relation to the other before it is a site, a physical space, situated in the world. Sharing-dwelling would open the world, the very possibility of the site, of being there. Being there presupposes this sharing from which it survives, from which it lives on. As the passive openness to the other, dwelling is not something 'I' can do or accomplish. The possession often associated with dwelling would be superfluous in sharing-dwelling. Thus, there is in this dwelling neither host nor guest. No one has priority over the other. But there is not yet symmetry or equality either.

There is a subtle economy of/in sharing—perhaps even a sublime economy. Sharing is not a reversible relation whose terms can be read from left to right or from right to left. It does not constitute a system or the unity of a system. The relation of sharing cannot be totalized, grasped from the outside. Sharing precedes—and makes possible?—equality and justice. Equality and justice can be said to live on sharing. This sharing does not imply symmetry, nor does it imply asymmetry.

Sharing points the way toward a new understanding and experience. It is not a question of how the same can enter into relationship with an other without immediately divesting the other of its alterity. There is a relation to the other—an other who is never neuter—from the very beginning. It is thus a question of how sharing comes to be forgotten, fractured, distributed in an economy of the same. Sharing is the forgotten experience from which we live. How is the other divested of her alterity? That violence—which is perhaps the only violence—is the mystery.

Sharing is not to be thought on the basis of giving/receiving or on the basis of exchange. It precedes these possibilities. Sharing is not a gift from one to another. It is not an exchange from one subject to another. In sharing there is not a $1 + 1(+1)\ldots$. The plurality of sharing is not constituted of such unities. There is not a collectivity in sharing, but rather a community—even if it is a community without community.

With giving/receiving or exchange, the other disturbs the being at home with oneself. This is not the case with sharing—in which being at home is first made possible. Sharing precedes any recovery (of identity) that would take place across/through exchange. Such sharing cannot be represented or thought, although it can perhaps be experienced. Perhaps it is the only experience.

What is it to be open? To be open is not (yet) to adopt a stance toward the other. To be open does not depend upon any action or decision (by a subject). To be open is imposed — prior to any decision, to any action, to any possibility. Yet this imposition is not a threat, nor is it an obsession or a persecution. It is a sharing. I, the subject, am open to the other. I am opened by the other. Every subject, every stance presupposes being open. This being open would be a 'Yes!' prior to every no, to every negation. To be open to/by the other is to be surprised; is to be infinitely passive before the other.

With sharing-opening-dwelling, love is possible — it is not (a) given, but becomes possible. This is quite difficult to discern: within the closure of economy, sharing is taken as giving, opening becomes restricted, dwelling becomes appropriating, and love is entered as a contract (between symmetrical parties). Giving, closure, appropriation, and contract are also possibilities of sharing-opening-dwelling. The gathering of all beings within a systematic unity also becomes possible within sharing-opening-dwelling. Yet love too becomes possible.

IV. Hearing, Listening, Loving

Within the closure of economy, everything and everyone is cloaked in anxiety and fear. Even our yearning, our 'hope,' is mediated by the economic. This results in an inability and/or an unwillingness to hear, to listen, and to understand. Lacking the ability or willingness to hear, to listen, to understand, communication and community, if they are possible, become restricted. Love, community, and communication are thus understood and pursued as forms of fusion — a fusion that is contradictorily coherent.

To hear is not yet to listen, and to listen is not yet to understand. Only a finite being can hear. For to hear you, I must not be the whole. Furthermore, I must be open to you. Hearing presupposes an opening toward ..., an openness to.... But to be open is not yet to show hospitality, to welcome the other. It is possible to be open to the other, to hear the other, without yet welcoming the other, listening to the other, seeking to understand the other.

To cultivate listening requires that we do more than hear a message in terms already established by society or coded by language. It involves a recognition and respect of the other—listening to the words of the other as something unique, irreducible to my preconceived ideas of the other, as something unknown, and perhaps even unknowable.[2] Thus, in listening we neither expect nor hear some information from the other. Rather, we cultivate a relation of indirection and of respect toward the other. Such a listening allows the other to come, to cross the threshold, and prepares the way for the unexpected. To accomplish this requires a rhythm that differs from any rhythm made possible in the closure of economy. It requires a multiple rhythm, a rhythm of intersection *and* distance.

To listen is not yet to understand. Nor is understanding reducible to comprehension. To comprehend often amounts to grasping and appropriating, to claiming to know you in advance—and thus to not really needing to listen to you. Understanding is never an accomplished act. To understand you is to remain committed to listening to you, to remain open to your irreducible alterity.

There is to be love between us. (How) is this possible?

There is to be love between us—that is, distance in proximity. There is to be between us a nearness that does not efface the space that separates us while drawing us together. There is to be between us listening and speaking (which will come first? for whom?). Listening and speaking—does that not presuppose openness, hospitality, welcoming of the other. (How) is this possible?

Yes, love is a welcoming of the other, hospitality. But to welcome the other is not yet to love.

There is to be love between us—that is, a home. This is not a site of immanence. It is not a domesticated safe haven. The hearth is the curved space-time of joint solitude, of the outside drawing near. I am at home means that I am at risk—(even) in the warmth of proximity.[3] To be at home is to welcome the other, to be welcomed by the other. It is something I can never do alone.

V. Concluding Remarks

To conclude. While we find ourselves in the closure of economy, there is a more primordial sharing-opening-dwelling (which is aneconomic) that 'lies under' this economy. If we could become more open toward this groundless ground of sharing-opening-dwelling, we may find that love is possible. But this will require cultivating a relation of indirection. I hope to have participated in such a cultivation here. I have been touched in a global, unknowable, and uncontrollable manner by (the words of) Luce Irigaray. And I have attempted to be faithful to her (words). Her presence has included me in a mystery, communicating to me an awakening that is both corporeal and spiritual. I hope to have been attentive to her (words), and not to have strayed too far from their intention. Thus, it seems only fitting that I close as I began, by again receiving her words and listening to them. This time, they are from *I Love to You*: 'Without a doubt, we approached, maybe even passed by, one another. Your retreat reveals my existence, as my withdrawal is dedicated to you. May we come to recognize the intention here as a pathway leading indirectly to us' (*I Love to You*, 150).

STEPHEN PLUHACEK
Michigan Technological University

NOTES

1 Despite the weight of overwhelming evidence granting a certain inevitability, if not necessity, to starting where we are, I would like to suggest that perhaps things are not so simply. Indeed, it may well be that this 'we', this here where we are, is a *telos* to be investigated rather than an *arche* from which to set out.
2 See Luce Irigaray, *I Love to You*, 115–19.
3 For one never knows what the other might expect, ask, or demand.

BIBLIOGRAPHY

Irigaray, Luce, *Between East and West, From Singularity to Community*, New York, Columbia University Press, 2002, translated by Stephen Pluhacek from the French *Entre Orient et Occident, De la singularité à la communauté*, Paris, Grasset, 1999.

Irigaray, Luce, *I Love to You, Sketch for a Felicity Within History*, New York-London, Routledge, 1996, translated by Alison Martin from the French *J'aime à toi, Esquisse d'une félicité dans l'Histoire*, Paris, Grasset, 1992.

Luce Irigaray's questions

We lack the words in Western philosophy to express our emotions. Nevertheless, they take part in wisdom, and also in truth. I learned this from the Near or the Far East. I have perceived that the Buddha, for example, is not without emotions but has become able to use them with wisdom, what is more, as a way to wisdom.

That implies not renouncing feeling and loving, as we Westerners often think about Buddha, but becoming able to feel and to love without being attached or dependent with regard to any object or any fusional, undifferentiated state. In this case, to feel and to love — and to share, which goes with feeling and loving — become an opening of a space which in fact belongs to no one but to the two who have opened this space.

This space is in some way a home which exists but in which we will never live together, although it is necessary for living together in a lasting way, that is, for dwelling. This space belongs to us as a space between us, a space in which to be, to become, to love, to exchange, to create, to share voluntarily even if this sharing remains without any object.

This space opened by the two will exist but no one can make it their own property, no one can dwell in it alone, except perhaps sometimes to rest a little, to restore oneself a little.

This space corresponds to the creation of a transcendence opened between us. Now we cannot appropriate transcendence, even or above all horizontal transcendence. It remains between us, unless it no longer exists.

I think that the Eastern tradition — not only through texts but also through practice — has taught me how to try to renounce passion and attachment in order to open a transcendental space between us. Perhaps this task will be our task after creating bridges between the Eastern and Western traditions.

I will then put to Stephen my first question. He has demonstrated an interest in sharing, and in the transcendental — he is a philosopher —, but also in the traditions of the East. Thus I would like to ask him: How do you think we can transform the primitive sharing, about which you have spoken, into a sharing of the transcendental? I am not referring here to transcendence in a past way, that is to say to a transcendental being which or who would exist outside of our own being, of our human capacities, but to a transcendental that we establish between us in order to become finally human.

A second point. To reach this possibility of a transcendental relation between us, we must also renounce the kind of feeling that the Western tradition has left us, has in a way fabricated for us. And we have to return to an education of the senses, of the perceptions that we have neglected, disparaged and finally forgotten. We need a new culture of perceptions or of senses (see my *To Be Two* and 'Being Two, How Many Eyes Have We?') to be able to renounce possessing the other in any way, to renounce any regressive return, without pain but rather in order to become more happy, in order to discover bliss.

We must learn how to look at one another, how to listen to each other without appropriating the other or losing ourselves.

For example, you have translated some of my texts, in particular *Between East and West*, listening to me, to me as subject and not only to words already transformed into objects. It is perceptible when reading your translation. But I imagine it was also necessary to listen to yourself. And I know through our exchanges about this translation that you have also listened to yourself. How did you listen to the two? Is it possible to listen in the same way when we are present, bodily present, to one another? How can we introduce this listening-to into our manner of teaching, which too often has constrained young people to conform to teachers, to repeat their words and even their manner of living?

A final question for the moment: How can we put together, or put together again, looking at the other and listening to the other? This is another thing that our teachers, in particular in philosophy, have forgotten to explain to us. Probably because they generally spoke about relations with objects, with something in some way already dead, and not about relations with other living beings. If this happens, teaching is often confined to a moral discourse. But we then lose the most important spring of happiness, of bliss, and the way of becoming human.

Stephen Pluhacek's response

It is, unfortunately, rather easy to cover over the space opened by and between two. While I can guard against this covering over, it is not within my power to prevent it. Thus, to be graced by an other who is able and willing to cultivate this space is truly to be given a gift — indeed, perhaps it is the first gift or the only gift. I can only hope that I am able and worthy to receive it.

I hesitate to respond immediately or directly to your words, to your questions. For such questions do not simply call upon a cognitive capacity or an intellectual subtlety. I believe they call upon me in my very being. Thus my response cannot be merely verbal or simply written. And yet that is the context in which I am called to respond.

So my response here will be only a beginning — and I would like to point out in advance that it will be too abstract.

I have been blessed with good teachers and favourable circumstances. So it is somewhat easier — and, of course, more appropriate — for me to respond to the question of how *I* listened to the two rather than to the more general question of how to listen to the two. There is then already a recognition of limits; a non-appropriative relation to the other, to others; a letting-be. I recognize that I am not the whole, that you are irreducible to me, and that for me to listen to you entails cultivating that which is proper to me as well as helping you to cultivate that which is proper to you. In doing so, a relation is established, or perhaps re-established, in which the wonder and mystery of one to the other might engender a space between. I propose calling such recognition, such relation, humility. This would be a first condition for my listening to the two. This humility is not mine, does not come from me, but is granted to me — although in order to be received it often calls for the laying aside of certain habits. This laying aside of habits would be a second condition for my listening to the two. These are the habits through which I keep the other at a safe distance, which may be either far away or quite close. In the forgetfulness of habits, the space between the two is covered over and there is a neglect of self, of other, and of the relation between the two. Yet even in my habits I am surrounded by mystery and can be awakened by surprise. But this requires patience — which I would call a third condition for my listening to the two. One way in which such patience might show itself is in a cultivation of silence, within myself and between myself and others. Within such a silence there can be the space-time of joint solitude. While there is a tendency to fill a void or a silence between us, I must learn to step back and allow the space between us to be and to become if I am to hear, to listen and to understand.

I do not think it is possible to listen in the same way when we are present, bodily present, to one another. The cultivation of this presence requires different strategies of indirection. Bodily presence often seems to call for a more immediate response — within which it is more difficult to safeguard that space between in which we can love and share and create. Despite this tendency, the bodily presence of the other can and should serve as a reminder of the negative that prevails between us, a negative the cultivation of which might allow us to put together (again) looking at the other and listening to the other.

Finally, in response to your first question, I would venture to say that transforming a more primordial sharing into a sharing of the transcendental entails the progressive development or cultivation of listening and its conditions. Perhaps love is another name for the sharing of the transcendental to which we aspire. Love, distance in proximity, is impossible without the cultivation of listening and its conditions. And such cultivation is not unrelated to a cultivation of the breath, or to the cultivation of new ways of seeing and listening and touching, as well as new ways of speaking.

From the Same to the Other

In a multi-ethnic, multiracial and multicultural society like ours, we cannot but discuss the theme of difference, we cannot but talk about the other. The blending of races, of cultures and of customs has become an integral part of our daily lives. For this reason, it is necessary to learn to value differences, to learn that they must not be refused, negated or simply integrated but, on the contrary, they must be welcomed as an advantageous counterbalance to uniformity.

Our Western tradition, however, is founded on the logic of identity, of similarity, of symmetry. What has always been favoured by the symbolic order characterizing our culture is sameness. And difference has invariably aroused fear; consequently, the issue of otherness has always been evaded. Even when it has been dealt with, it has not been correctly formulated, as the other has nonetheless remained other in relation to the omnipotent model of the one: it has not been seen as another being, different but possessing equal dignity. Therefore, diversities have often been thought of in a hierarchical way.

Openness to the other as different from the self then does not correspond at all to the Western subject's mental habits. Attracted by sameness, he has in fact been taught to rule on, to dominate, to exorcise differences. Imbued with a type of culture characterized by the model of a unique subject, used to thinking on the basis of the distinction between 'subject' and 'object', he has not yet reached a culture founded on otherness, on the relation with the other as such. This above all is what Luce Irigaray criticizes and analyses in her books and in particular in her *Speculum, An Ethics of Sexual Difference, I Love to You, Democracy Begins between Two*.

Since our age is one of generalized mingling, we are obliged to reconsider our relationship with the other. We must learn to meet the other recognizing his/her equivalent value, but with a radical respect of all the differences between us.

The most universal difference

The most universal of differences is undoubtedly the sexual one. Humanity is in fact primarily made up of men and women. Gender duality crosses all races, all cultures and all traditions. It is therefore to be supposed that respect for gender difference may ultimately lead to respect for all other manifold, secondary differences. But, since the desire for the same has dominated and guided our culture, Luce Irigaray believes that it is impossible to tackle the issue of gender difference without also taking into account the question of sameness.

Man, in fact, in his persistent longing for what is identical to himself, has finally included woman's otherness, altering her identity in such a wanting. In his perennial quest for the same, he has raised himself as the model for mankind, and has reduced woman to being an image of his own self. The masculine has absorbed both in himself: the feminine has been annexed to the masculine universe. Woman thus has lost her own real and independent identity, or has anyway acquired an identity which is incompatible with her gender, because it is defined according to the masculine identity model. At best, she has been simply considered as the other of the same, that is, an other only defined in relation to man. She has equally remained trapped within the range of the same, in her being hierarchically submitted to man. The logic of the same is then a system that negates differences. Luce Irigaray regards it as the most dangerous philosophical, cultural and symbolic construction man has ever contrived because it reduces the subject to one. This one appropriates the other by assimilating it and making it similar with itself. The other as such is no longer respected, particularly in its primary difference, the gender difference.

It is therefore essential to define an identity for both woman and man, which is appropriate to their own gender: a sexuate identity. It is absolutely impossible to identify the female gender with the male one, nor must women passively accept such a destiny, if they do not want to lose or reduce their own identity. Man as well as woman must become aware of their gender identity. They must each identify with their own gender, and thus they must realize that they are partial.

In particular, man must learn that he is not the whole, that he is not the model for humanity, because humanity is composed of two different beings: woman and man. He must remember that on his way, around him, he cannot always meet the same, that he shall often meet the other too. At the very least, he shall meet the other of gender difference, woman.

Man and woman must thus start from being faithful to the gender they belong to. But they must also be able to recognize the other as irreducible to the same. Obstacles of fusion, of appropriation and of submission will then be overcome.

The subjects are two, not one only

Woman can in no way be represented or identified by using the same terminology as that applied to man. She is neither the 'non-man' nor the same as man. She is not even a man, thus she remains a 'same' which is lacking something (a penis, perhaps?). It is illegitimate to reduce female sexuality to the categories elaborated to explain masculine sexuality, because this would nullify the existing differences between genders. Woman would in this way be deprived of an autonomous representation, she would not be defined in her effective and genuine otherness. Her otherness would at best be described from the male subject's point of view and, as a consequence, man would always and in anyway remain the source and the creator of her identity. She would be without an identity independent from that of man, without a definition of her otherness deriving from her own point of view.

It is therefore both desirable and indispensable that a unique subject will not be alone to speak. That is, that only the male subject defines both himself and the other half of humankind.

We need a culture of two subjects, man and woman. Otherwise, woman would remain a simple object in relation to the defining subject who has always been man. Deprived of her own subjectivity, she would live in an inauthentic situation, characterized by dependence and submission. Therefore it is necessary to recognize the existence of two human subjects, man and woman, and to consider them as 'different without hierarchies', as Luce Irigaray writes in her *I Love to You*.

Woman cannot and must not 'undersell herself by being satisfied with man's considering her as an equal'. By so doing, women themselves would destroy differences, they would neutralize feminine identity, foregoing an identity appropriate to their gender. They would move towards the destruction or, in any case, the devaluation of feminine gender, favouring 'the eternal return of the same', and their own assimilation to the other half of humankind, men.

For this reason, Luce Irigaray believes that it is an ethical necessity to reconsider, theoretically as well as practically, the role historically assigned to woman. We must give place to a thought different from the one which has always characterized our Western tradition. We have to realize a revolution in the way of thinking, by trying to have access to 'the thought of sexual difference'. A way of thinking, this one, which shows that it is open to the plurivocity in which reality expresses itself, a plurality that first of all manifests itself in the duality of male and female. No more oneness, then, but duality of subjects, first, and then also plurality of subjects.

Philosophical thought itself should be based again starting from the existence of two different subjects, overcoming the logic of the one, of the same. It would undoubtedly be a source of unprecedented fecundity if woman were assuming the role of a different subject. 'Difference', here, is not simply 'diversity'. 'Diversity' refers to multiple differences — race, generation, culture, religion . . . — and also to many people who share these particularities. Sexual difference, the most basic and universal of the differences, distinguishes two persons the one from the other not only in accordance with a distinctive feature — for example a sex, as it is too often affirmed — , but because they correspond to different subjectivities.

Man and woman are truly different from each other, in every aspect of their lives. In *Democracy Begins between Two*, Luce Irigaray maintains that men and women are more different than Blacks and Whites or Catholics and Muslims. They are in fact not only biologically and morphologically different, but they also think, perceive, react, feel desires and judge according to different modalities. They communicate and speak in different ways, and they relate to the other differently. Recognizing all this means attributing to both genders their effective reality; it means considering the other as real otherness, as completely other, without trying to submit the different to the same.

The difference between man and woman is undeniable: to conceal it would be to hide reality, to violate truth. But, in order not to forget the other, it is necessary to remain two; it is essential to do away with the 'nostalgia for the one', for the same; it is necessary to recognize that we are limited by the presence of a different other, who is irreducible and unknowable in his or her totality. The attraction of man to woman is rather to be related to the very fact that they are different and that they will never be able to know each other completely. The one remains a 'mystery' for the other: the mystery of a difference which cannot be reduced to the same. This mystery ought to be respected as otherness, without submitting it to oneself. This mystery can be approached without confusing or cancelling one's self but, on the contrary, preserving one's different identity, thus remaining 'two different beings' capable of entering into a relation with each other.

We can then attain not only a thought which concerns subjectivity, but also and mainly inter-subjectivity. In this way, it is possible to show the sterile 'repetition of the same' and work to dynamic and fertile relationships, by restoring their respective identity and dignity to both halves of humankind, both being endowed with 'equivalent values', despite their differences.

Necessary changes to cultivate feminine identity

Luce Irigaray, however, maintains that if we want the thought of sexual difference to be fruitful, we have to reinterpret everything. It is primarily necessary to reassess our *culture*, because we lack a culture of sexuality as well as a culture of the feminine. It is also indispensable to provide woman with her cultural identity, that would allow her to treasure 'her being a woman' and that would make her leave a cultural context which is both unique and male. A mono-sexuated culture, in fact, prevents not only the recognition of difference, but also inter-subjectivity. However, our cultural universe has so far been monopolized by man; it is about time, therefore, that women were as involved as men in the production of culture.

It is equally important for women to use a *language* appropriate to their gender, as our language is on the whole better suited to a male society. It is indispensable for them to have access to a new language or, at least, to another use of language. Language must serve not only to inform, but also and mainly to communicate, to listen to and hold dialogues. Then the language becomes a meeting place for the manifestation of differences, rather than a source of division and rupture.

Changes to the *legal order* are furthermore required. The existing law is better suited to men than to women, because man has always been regarded as the model of the citizen, whereas woman has had to be content with an equality of rights which do not correspond to her real needs. Since there exist two different human beings, man and woman, only a legal system suited to each gender, and not simply to the male one, can confer a real civil identity on both male and female citizens. Rights relevant to women must therefore be formulated, because requesting the same rights as those enjoyed by men is tantamount to an abolition of differences. The law must instead take into account the fact that women are not the same as men; this is the reason why it is essential to formulate what Luce Irigaray defines as equivalent 'sexual rights'. Thus rights which possess an equivalent value but which are nonetheless necessarily different because 'specific', that is appropriate to each of the two genders, in conformity with the reality of their relative needs. Such a legal system would oblige citizens to respect the existence of the other, it would safeguard differences between subjects, in particular gender difference.

Another modification we need to bring about concerns the *economy of our relations*. Our culture has in fact educated us to take possession of whatever is near, and our relations are consequently subordinated to the object, to the logic of having. It is instead fundamental to learn to renounce all forms of possession, in order to respect both subjects in a relationship, without reducing one to the other. The persons would then remain two in the relation, without one of them supplanting the other or identifying with the totality: in fact, this would only lead to a loss of identity for both. We ought then to reach a 'we' made up of two different human beings, who must be able to meet even if they remain always two, without ever absorbing the other within the same.

However, we constantly tend to look for the same even in our love relations. We ought therefore to change our models, even where love is concerned, so that it does not become appropriation of the other, or reduction of our beloved to a simple object of desire. Love must also be lived in 'two', without a division of roles between the 'loving' and the 'loved' one. There must then be a new interpretation of love, which can acknowledge differences without masking them, which can respect the other in his/her subjectivity and grant him/her equivalent dignity. Only such a vision of love, which is in a particular way analysed by Luce Irigaray in her *I Love to You* and *To Be Two*, can make possible a relationship that avoids the fusion of the two lovers and safeguards a distinction between the two.

In conclusion, it is good to remember that the basic trait of each and every person is not banal sameness, but their difference. It is everywhere present, and it is the principle of life itself. Since gender difference is the most particular and, at the same time, the most universal of real differences, it represents the key that can lead to a peaceful coexistence of all other differences. The desirable modifications in the relations between men and women are thus part of a programme of radical change which must involve and improve all social relationships. The man-woman duality can and must become the basis for every plurality. The acknowledgement of such a duality represents the gesture which will allow the respect for all the different ways in which otherness can manifest itself, be it in terms of race, culture or religion. This acknowledgement represents the path we must necessarily walk to get to a new community, and to humanize our entire society.

It is true that man really is a peculiar creature: difference terrifies him. Instead of joyfully welcoming the challenge and the surprise that divergence brings with itself, he generally seems to be afraid of it. As a consequence, he avoids it or tries to evade what is by him considered as an obstacle, by activating lethal mechanisms such as fusion, subordination, assimilation, reduction of the other to himself or to his. For this reason, Luce Irigaray rightly affirms that only a new interpretation of difference can re-open the repetitive circle of the same, break up this historical vicious circle, teaching us to respect the other as other, such as the other presents itself. Similar cultivation of difference(s) will distance ourselves from the violence of the reduction of the other to the same, and help us to benefit from the richness of the two, and then of the plural, enjoying the fruitfulness of the encounter with the different other.

I am however convinced that to remain oneself is the most wonderful present each of us can make to himself or to herself, and that the most marvellous gift we can offer to the other is to let him or her be who he or she is.

FLORINDA TRANI
University of Lecce

BIBLIOGRAPHY

Irigaray, Luce, *Democracy Begins between Two*, London–New York, Athlone–Routledge, 2000, translated by Kirsteen Anderson from the Italian *La democrazia comincia a due*, Torino, Bollati-Boringhieri, 1994.

Irigaray, Luce, *An Ethics of Sexual Difference*, Ithaca, New York and London, Cornell University Press-Athlone, 1993, translated by Gillian C. Gill and Carolyn Burke from the French *Ethique de la différence sexuelle*, Paris, Editions de Minuit, 1984.

Irigaray, Luce, *I Love to You*, London–New York, Routledge, 1996, translated by Alison Martin from the French *J'aime à toi*, Paris, Grasset, 1992.

Irigaray, Luce, *Je, tu, nous, Towards a Culture of Difference*, London–New York, Routledge, 1992, translated by Alison Martin from the French *Je, Tu, Nous, Pour une culture de la différence*, Paris, Grasset, 1990.

Irigaray, Luce, *Speculum*, Ithaca, New York, Cornell University Press, 1985, translated by Gillian C. Gill from the French *Speculum*, Paris, Editions de Minuit, 1974.

Irigaray, Luce, *To Be Two*, London–New York, Athlone-Routledge, 2000, translated by Monique M. Rhodes and Marco F. Cocito-Monoc from the Italian *Essere Due*, Turin, Bollati Boringhieri, 1994. The French version has been published as *Etre Deux*, Paris, Grasset, 1997.

Luce Irigaray's questions

Perhaps the man of whom you speak is above all the man of the Western tradition. It would be important to make this clear. Certainly men of all cultures must resolve the problem of the relation with the mother, with their own birth, and also the problem of their own incapacity of engendering in themselves or of making love in themselves, as women do. But in some cultures the way of dealing with this question leads to valorizing the woman in her difference and to seeking how to enter in relation with her in an appropriate manner.

Now this is not the case in the Western tradition. And to avoid resolving the difficulty, Western man has constructed a culture of men and of between-men, without the participation of women as subjects. This way of treating the problem of the relationship with the mother has imposed a logic of the identical, of the same, that excludes difference(s).

This is the first point of my remarks. The second will concern a problem of method. You speak about the respect of the other with words that evoke above all a moral law: we must respect the other. Such a strategy will not really open another world, a world constituted by a subject who is different. In the perspective of a tradition with only one subject, we remain in moral law to relate to others. And men today do so, which gives our times a moral emphasis that is not very pleasant and that belongs to patriarchal condescension. We are not yet here entering a new culture, a culture of difference in the sense that I would give to this utterance.

In my opinion, you speak too little about the change of method necessitated by the consideration of the other as other. Now, it is a very important aspect of my thought, above all in the most recent books that you know. But many people have not yet understood them very well. Thus I will briefly explain my methodological strategy. Instead of remaining in a purely critical attitude, in a simple criticism, I have used a new dialectical method. I have displaced the negative at work in criticism in favour of a more radical one. With a more philosophical approach also. If criticism often concerns a culture that is already defined, already constituted as object in a way, the negativity we must use to recognize the other as other concerns the subject as such. The gesture is thus more radical and it is also different because it questions the constitution of subjectivity itself. It affirms that no 'I' can exist without a 'you'. This 'you' can no longer be or remain an absolute 'I', a God of my gender for example. It must be a subjectivity on my level, but radically different. This situation exists in reality in sexual difference. Here I can even be negativized as 'I', still remaining 'I' because of desire and love to 'you'.

Sexual difference in the Western tradition has appeared as a space of return in a nature without consciousness. In fact it is rather a reality which constrains us to pursue the becoming of consciousness, that leads to a new stage of the development of humanity. But without enacting this stage, the human as such does not exist.

In connection with these remarks, I would ask Florinda: do you know any cultures in which sameness has not been the most important paradigm for defining identity? And also: How do you realize the passage from duality to plurality, that is, from the other to others?

Florinda Trani's response

1. No. I do not know a culture wherein sameness has not been the most important paradigm to define, or to found, identity. I think that this characterizes the entire Western culture. But thoroughly studying the problem, certainly it would be possible to discover some examples which could correspond to your question.

2. I think that admitting and welcoming plurality is the consequence of acknowledgement of duality. Who is capable of approaching the other as such, is also capable of approaching any otherness. However, we always have to begin with the acknowledgement and the respect of the other who is completely different: the other who belongs to a different gender. Such a difference is that which we can the least overcome and thus accepting the duality of genders becomes the base to admit every possible otherness. The first step must be to modify our habits of thinking, our ethical and political habits, and this could happen thanks to the diffusion of the powerful 'thought of sexual difference'. Every other with whom we succeed in constructing and keeping a real duality becomes a ring of a long chain which constitutes plurality.

A Gendered Education towards the Fulfillment of Democracy

1. The Construction of a Truly Democratic Society from a Gender Perspective

An education at the service of people's freedom, as Paulo Freire conceived it early in the 60s in his famous book *Education: The Practice of Freedom*, requires the construction of new methods and programmes designed for people's empowerment. In this way, education will become a privileged tool able to provide people with the capability they need to act freely and with responsibility in their lives. In Freire's view, this is the only manner in which education can contribute to constructing truly democratic societies where full citizens can relate to each other in freedom.

Moreover, from a gender perspective, that is to say, from a perspective that considers women's emancipation and gender equality — or rather equivalence — crucial in constructing just and equitable societies, democracy should be considered not only, as Luce Irigaray argues (Interview with Maria José García Oramas, 'Luce Irigaray y la Construcción de una Cultura Democrática Fundada en la Diferencia'), a matter of economics or an act of formal politics such as the nomination of representatives through elections, rather it should promote people's emancipation and their active responsible participation in civic life.

In Irigaray's words, it is imperative that we 'refound democracy' from a human perspective, that is to say, placing at the centre of people's needs their human rights, and not just their goods or property. The basis of this process will be the equitable organization of the civil community founded on civic respect and love between citizens, able to relate to each other through all forms of difference(s) in a more just and fecund society (see *Democracy Begins Between Two*).

Because *Democracy Begins Between Two*, it must be founded again between two, that is to say, starting by transforming the everyday relation between the sexes. Irigaray's aim is to conceive a new model of human liberation and social relationship towards civic responsibility, love and happiness for all. In this way, democracy becomes a way of living, of thinking and of acting, individually as well as collectively.

She says:

> It is imperative to develop new bonds between citizens. The basis of this social network is the relationship between men and women in the respect and tolerance of their differences at all levels: from the most intimate to the most political and cultural. The fundamental bonds are, at the same time, the respect of sexual difference as the more universal and a form of interaction in daily life. It represents, by itself, the most primitive articulation between nature and culture (. . .) The person who is able to respect difference(s) between men and women will not meet any difficulty in respecting other differences because the instincts of possession, of exploitation, rejection and contempt will already be educated starting from the elemental instincts. ('Luce Irigaray y la Construcción de una Cultura Democrática Fundada en la Diferencia', 5, my translation)

Democracy can become a concrete reality for humanity only through the development of educational and political actions centred on the citizens themselves. Luce Irigaray proposes three strategies: 1) the formulation of civil rights according to the specific subjectivity of both men and women; 2) the transformation of actual cultural paradigms (such as language, religion, and cultural images) founded in masculine values; 3) the design and development of alternative educational models able to promote feminine values and to recognize women's contributions to cultural life.

Regarding the formulation of specific civil human rights for each of the sexes, Irigaray argues that even today women do not have a civil identity. Thus, they continue to live under the guardianship of men — either fathers, husbands, politicians or political representatives — , so that their social identity is solely related to their biological and natural condition, and not to their singularity as feminine subjects. If social institutions — from the State to the family, and in particular religious and educational institutions — continue to conceive women as subjects without the capacity for autonomy or civil responsibility, they will never participate in civic life as full citizens.

To transform this reality, Irigaray considers that it is imperative to promote the formulation of civil regulations for women, not equal but equivalent to those of men's, that is, human rights related to the specific necessities and conditions of each one of the sexes. Among others, a woman's legislation would include:

> — the right to physical and moral inviolability, that is, to a civil identity guaranteed by a positive law which does not force each woman to defend herself in each case only via the criminal justice system against rape (which is considered as a crime

not as rape), battery, incest, pornography, involuntary prostitution, particularly in the public use of representations of women's body and speech;
— the right to voluntary motherhood without Church or state leaders exercising, either directly or through institutions, real power over a woman, and that includes financial or ideological power;
— the right to culture, that is, to languages, religions, sciences, and arts appropriate to female identity;
— a preferential and reciprocal right for mother and child(ren), particularly as guarantee against violence and economic poverty, but also to assist mothers and children in inter-cultural marriages which lack suitable legislation. (*I Love to You*, 132)

As it is beyond the scope of this paper to describe in detail Luce Irigaray's strategies for action (for this subject see, for example, *Je, tu, nous* and *I Love to You*), I will simply discuss one of them related to the design and development of alternative educational models able to promote feminine values and to recognize women's contributions to cultural life.

2. A Model for the Education to Citizenship Founded in Difference(s)

As I have already mentioned, the development of alternative educational methods is a strategy relevant to the construction of a new democratic culture. In Irigaray's view, this task demands the incorporation of feminine values in programmes which, for centuries, have been based only on male ones. Otherwise, education will continue to respond to men's necessities and not to women's necessities.

Luce Irigaray (see 'Luce Irigaray y la Construcción de una Cultura Democrática Fundada en la Diferencia') says that today's educational programmes encourage children and adolescents to become competitive and efficient citizens, emphasizing the subject's formation towards 'having' more than 'being', in relation to others. Rather, it should teach them to live in relation with others in order to develop their relational identity, as this is a vital element in promoting the mutual understanding between citizens, particularly between the sexes.

In this way, a masculine-centred education helps to create a society formed from $1 + 1 + 1$ neutral and abstract individuals, disconnected from each other. Instead, if educational programmes included feminine values — such as the ability to establish relationships with the other(s), the respect for nature, for health, for felicity, the capability to take care of the natural environment, of shelter, the interest for dialogue, for arts, etc. — , they would be enriched.

Founded in a new paradigm based on the promotion of relational identity, on the tolerance and the fecundity of difference(s), Irigaray has designed a new educational method, already being successfully applied in Italy, in the Lombarda and Emilia-Romagna regions (see *Chi sono Io? Chi sei tu?* and *Progetto di Formazione alla Cittadinanza per Ragazze e Ragazzi, per Donne e Uomini*) with the following objectives:

1) To raise consciousness, from childhood, of the relevance of the differences between the genders, through innovative scholarly programmes and methods;
2) To teach the respect of oneself and of the other, beginning with the recognition of the sexually same or different other, key to the possibility of living within all forms of diversity: either related to gender, or to culture, tradition, race, nation, etc.;
3) To develop relational attitudes among subjects at the different stages of their scholarly life, but also between teachers, and between parents;
4) To balance, in the programmes, values related to masculine subjectivity and these related to feminine subjectivity. (*Progetto di Formazione alla Cittadinanza per Ragazze e Ragazzi, per Donne e Uomini*, 7. My translation)

2.1 An Experiment with Mexican Youngsters

Based on Irigaray's theory as well as on her educational activity in Italy, I have designed a method of education to citizenship for Mexican youngsters to serve as an alternative programme able to contribute to the construction of a new democratic culture in my country, Mexico. The objective is to help Mexican youngsters to construct their own relational identity according to their specific needs, either as women or men, promoting, at the same time, democratic values in their daily lives such as tolerance to difference(s) and mutual understanding.

I have considered that these objectives can be better achieved by the creation of small consciousness-raising groups because, in my view, the group is not only the primary reference for young people but also, in itself, a powerful tool for developing the relational identity of their participants. I will come back to these arguments later in my paper. Firstly, I would like to give a brief overview of the reality of Mexican youngsters today in order to contextualize the educational programme I intend to propose.

Mexico is largely a young people's country. Indeed, out of its around 95 million habitants, half of them are under 22 years of age, and around 16 million are young people between 15 and 22 years old; 48.6% are men, and 51.3% are women. In the throes of a severe economic crisis since 1982, this young population confronts difficult living conditions: more than 40% of the population live in conditions of poverty, and almost 26% in extreme poverty (Sergio Aguayo, *Almanaque Mexicano*, 201).

Young people are specially vulnerable to this structural crisis because, for them, living in conditions of scarcity implies a lack of opportunities for an integral development in terms of economic growth, and ultimately in terms of their possibility for a better future. It is not only that these minors need to start work earlier in life and mainly in the informal sector, but also that poverty carries with it an increase in social and cultural problems such as violence, drug abuse and delinquency, problems that have a strong impact on young people.

More importantly, networks of solidarity and family bonds, an ancestral strategy for survival among the country's population, have been eroded. Consequently, elders, women, young adults and children, the most vulnerable sectors of our population, are without protection. As a result, social problems such as maltreatment, domestic violence, lack of attention and care tend to increase. This results in Mexican youngsters confronting the challenges of their everyday life and future fearfully or with apathy and indifference.

These problems affect young men and women differently. In a country with a strong patriarchal structure, women experience the new complexities of their cultural environment not only in the midst of a critical national situation but also within a family context marked by a traditional male culture. Thus, they suffer the contradictions between their own expectations and values and those of their families. For most young Mexican women, their parents do not encourage them to develop professionally but, on the contrary, expect them to be good wives and care givers. These women also continue to be vulnerable to sexual harassment and to unequal treatment either at home or at the workplace. It is estimated than 40 to 50% of Mexican women are exposed to domestic violence (202).

In the field of education, women's discrimination continues as well because, even though young women have increasingly been participating in the labour market, they are now becoming the head of their families. Indeed, nowadays, one out of every five households are sustained by a woman alone, and when men are at home still 93.6% of the girls and women continue to perform all domestic work (*Diario de Xalapa*, 10 May, 1999).

Given this reality, it is clear enough why Irigaray's ideas become relevant in the Mexican context in the sense of the need to develop new models of education for our people to be able to contribute to a development of a better quality of life, especially in the case of young women. An innovative model centered on the education to citizenship will empower both men and women and will allow them to participate in civic life as full citizens introducing, at the same time, democratic values into the whole community. As I have already mentioned, I conceive this alternative educational model within the confines of small consciousness-raising groups having young participants and an adult facilitator. I will proceed now to describe this model.

2.2 The Group Design and the Protocol of the Sessions

I think that the small consciousness-raising group permits the analysis and discussion of themes and provides a forum for the incorporation of tasks which relate to the individual as well as to the group as a total entity. Through face-to-face relationships, in the equal-horizontal domain with the other members of the group and in the non-authoritarian-vertical one with the adult facilitator, the members of the group relate to each other learning to see themselves and to see the other(s) in innovative ways.

Thus, following Irigaray's ideas, this process of learning is neither neutral nor abstract, rather it implies relation with the other for a mutual understanding in civic life. The development of self identity can only be achieved with others. It is, therefore, a relational process. Irigaray says: 'Cultivating one's natural identity would signify becoming more and more able to elaborate a universe of relations both faithful to the self and capable of communication with the other, in particular with the different other, belonging to a gender other than mine' (Stephen Pluhacek and Heidi Bostic, 'Thinking life as relation: An interview with Luce Irigaray', 354).

From this perspective, the small consciousness-raising groups function as alternative spaces for an education to citizenship, where youngsters can elaborate this universe of relations, so as to learn to act freely and with responsibility in their lives. Because the group permits experimentation, the participants can find new ways of peaceful coexistence between them, so that this experience can affect their families, their schools and communities.

Coming back to Freire's argument, the democratic organization of civil community will be constructed by a process of education for free responsibility starting, as Irigaray conceives it, from respect, recognition and love between man and woman, cementing a living civil society (355).

At the present moment, I have not yet started the activities of the groups with Mexican youngsters. I am now designing the programme I envision. So I will finish my paper by describing the protocol of the group sessions I aim to organize. The group will function around a task that concerns both the individual and the group as a whole. The objective is to aid the self-awareness of proper identity and of the difference linked to sexuated identity while filling gaps in the communication between the sexes. It is a task for finding, together, responses to the questions: Who I am?, Who is the other?, and also to discover together how to sustain these questions throughout life (see 'Thinking Life as Relation', 356). The adult coordinator will function not as a leader or as another participant but as a facilitator of the group's dynamic. He/she is there to guarantee a climate of respect, tolerance and mutual acceptance through which the group can function better and the learning process can be achieved.

As Irigaray has set it up in Italy, this method takes place in a mixed group, through the development of diverse activities, including the composition of sentences of relational significance, conversation between the sexes, and invitations to do things together. In Veracruz, Mexico, where I live, I also intend to set up small groups having 8 to 10 participants and involving an equal number of female and male participants. I will work with groups of youngsters, of parents and of teachers as well. With each of them, I will facilitate 10 sessions within a fixed arrangement of schedules and places, in order to guarantee the optimal performance of the group.

Participation will be voluntary and the invitation will be extended through local schools and community organizations. The sessions will start with an instigator theme or task, that is to say, with a facilitator's proposal for action, either in the form of a theme to discuss, or of an activity to be developed in the session.

These generator themes and tasks will include, among others:

1) Relational identity: learning to relate to myself, to the same other(s) and to the different other(s);
2) Communication among us: women with women, men with men and women with men;
3) Learning from our differences: sexual difference, cultural difference, racial difference, generational difference, etc.;
4) Feminine and masculine values;
5) Living in couples:
   — Sexual relations,
   — Love and happiness between two,

— Constructing together a new civil community starting between two;
6) Our human rights:
— Equivalent civil rights for men and women,
— Civic action towards our equivalent human rights.

Final Remarks

I truly hope that the method of education for liberty and responsibility I am proposing will contribute to the improvement in the living conditions of the young people of my country. I certainly know, in advance, that it will not change the country's reality as a whole, as it is only a small strategy for action, but it represents my personal contribution to Mexican Democracy. I believe, as Luce Irigaray does, that the construction of a new democratic culture requires precisely the action of each one of us, citizens of the world, in our own communities and starting with our daily relations. It is up to us, especially to us women, to do it if we truly expect to live in a more just and fecund society.

MARIA JOSÉ GARCÍA ORAMAS
University of Veracruz, Mexico

BIBLIOGRAPHY

Aguayo, Sergio, *Almanaque Méxicano*, Editorial Grijalbo, Mexico, 2000.

Diario de Xalapa, 'Las Mujeres en México', Xalapa, Veracruz, 10 May, 1999.

Diario La Jornada, 'El Trabajo Femenino', Mexico, 25 March, 1999.

Freire, Paulo, *Education, The Practice of Freedom*, Writers and Readers, London, 1976, translated from the Portuguese *Educacão como Prática da Liberdade*, Editora Paz e Terra, Rio de Janeiro, 1967.

García Oramas, Maria José, 'Luce Irigaray y la Construcción de una Cultura Democrática fundada en la Diferencia', Interview, *Periódico La Jornada, Suplemento La Triple Jornada*, Mexico, 5 March, 2001, 5–7.

Irigaray, Luce, *Chi sono io? Chi sei tu? La chiave per una convivenza universale*, Biblioteca di Casalmaggiore, 1999.

Irigaray, Luce, *Democracy Begins Between Two*, London-New York, Athlone-Routledge, 2000, translated by Kirsteen Anderson from the Italian *La Democrazia Comincia a Due*, Torino, Bollati Boringhieri, 1994.

Irigaray, Luce, *I Love to You, Sketch for a Felicity within History*, London-New York, Routledge, 1996, translated by Alison Martin from the French *J'aime à toi*, Paris, Grasset, 1992.

Irigaray, Luce, *Je, tu, nous, Toward a culture of difference*, London-New York, Routledge, 1993, translated by Alison Martin from the French *Je, Tu, Nous, Pour un culture de la différence*, Paris, Grasset, 1990.

Irigaray, Luce, *Progetto di formazione alla cittadinanza per ragazze e ragazzi, per donne e omini*, Rapporto di consulenza su incarico della Commissione per la realizzazione della paritá fra uomo e donna della Regione Emilia Romagna, Bologna, 1997.

Irigaray, Luce, *Thinking the Difference, For a Peaceful Revolution*, London-New York, Athlone-Routledge, 1993, translated by Karin Montin from the French *Le Temps de la différence, Pour une révolution pacifique*, Paris, Librairie Générale Française, Livre de poche, 1989.

Instituto Nacional de Geografía e Informática, INEGI, *Los jóvenes en México*, Mexico, 1995.

Pluhacek, Stephen and Heidi Bostic, 'Thinking life as relation: An interview with Luce Irigaray', *Man and World*, 29, 1996, 343–60.

Luce Irigaray's questions

I would like to express my joy about the use of my work in order to educate young people towards a democratic citizenship. Here, I will recall why I have undertaken such a gendered education with Italian young people.

As you know from the book I recently published in English, *Democracy Begins Between Two*, I made efforts to obtain rights for women, young people and immigrants from the European Parliament. I did this in collaboration with Renzo Imbeni, who has now become Vice-President of the European Parliament. We did not obtain satisfaction, in spite of a great interest in our proposals, because our 'Report about Citizenship' was not approved by the majority. The perspective was too new, and not already past, as some people imagine about my work. Even the women were suspicious about our text, since they required only economic rights and not civil rights. Now this is not the appropriate way, in my opinion. Discrimination against women results from their lack of civil identity. And we must pass through civil rights to obtain economic rights, as Maria José García reminds us with reference to my books.

Instead of lamenting and becoming discouraged, I decided that it is necessary to educate young people for the future because older people do not understand anything or understand too little about these new political and cultural perspectives. Thanks to a grant from Regione Emilia Romagna (Italy), I had the possibility to begin this education to citizenship with young people. I went to schools and started the work. The first time, I gathered about fifty linguistic samples from mixed groups, above all of boys and girls or adolescents, but also of parents and teachers in order to compare their answers, their attitudes, their citizenship with that of young people. All the people were very enthusiastic, especially the children, adolescents and parents. The problem was a little more difficult with the teachers. And I have understood through their answers that the teachers have learned to efface sexuate identity and difference, because of a training appropriate to a neutral culture, to an abstract culture and discourse. According to them, to consider difference and identity as sexuate represents a sort of cultural regression. But it was obvious that, for them, this sort of education entailed a loss of identity, above all of relational identity for women, and also a growth of aggressivity and of individualism. The children, in fact, demonstrate a more ethical behaviour than the adults, in particular than the teachers. And it is a pity that their education does not take account of their relational capacities, in particular those of the girls. I have noticed that because of this lack of consideration of their relational identity, girls and boys return into themselves in a regressive way. To open new possibilities of entering into communication, they must often use violence, especially the male adolescents. But they do not find again a harmony between body and affectivity, body and mind, body and soul. They have lost the passage provided by desire, by attraction between them which could conduct the one to the other with loving and trust.

It is thus very important to educate young people to be conscious of their sexuate, and not only sexual, identity, and of their difference(s). It is very important to give them the means of relating to one another without violence in order to construct a society that is more democratic, more civil and more happy. If this seems difficult and, according to many people, useless in France, I hope that it would be possible and fruitful in Mexico.

I would ask Maria if she thinks there are possibilities in Mexico for such a gendered education of young people that we still lack in France. And why?

Next, I would ask her if it is really fitting to mix a clinical approach with a civic formation. I think that it is difficult to mingle the two in a public place or in a collective context, and that young people need active and creative education more than a clinic approach, or even clinical help. It seems to me that this civic formation will little by little cure a society which is responsible for the various difficulties of the young. It is in this way that I have also begun to assist drug addicts.

The idea is to give back to young people the possibility of helping themselves and each other. This is the possibility of discovering their own energy, and of cultivating their own desire. Our culture, our education have not provided for that, on the contrary. But we can do little for young people outside of this way.

Maria José García Oramas's response

I consider that today it is possible to foresee the development of alternative models to the formation of citizenship for Mexican young people due to different reasons:

First, as I mentioned in my text, Mexico is largely a young people's country so that the programme I intend to develop aims to provide them with the necessary tools they need to act as a generation able to construct a different country in the way you define it, that is, a society more democratic, more civic and more happy.

Second, today Mexican young people are living an important democratic transition. After being ruled for almost eighty years by presidents belonging to a one single party named the PRI, Partido Revolucionario Institucional (Institutional Revolutionary Party), we have now a President in turn, who has been democratically elected and who belongs to a different political party, the PAN, Partido de Acción Nacional (National Action Party). This peaceful and legal democratic transition has been possible, among other reasons, thanks to young people voting for a political change.

Finally, I want to mention that this transition to democracy is happening on different fronts, not only through the participation in political parties but also inside social movements coming from the civil society. One of them, the EZLN, Ejército Zapatista de Liberación Nacional (Zapatista Army of National Liberation), a social movement which aims at the recognition of indigenous peoples' traditions and human rights, is developing its political discourse focusing on the importance of difference.

Rather than starting from an egalitarian discourse, what is interesting is that the participants of this movement intend to be incorporated into the nation's project — it is clear that they accept to be part of the country — but only if their differences, as regards their culture and tradition, are taken into account. And again, they conceive difference in the same way you do, that is, arguing that the basis for the construction of a democratic country needs to be founded in the recognition of the nature of contemporary Mexico as multi-ethnic and multicultural.

As regards the second question, I agree with you in considering that a project for democratic formation to citizenship certainly needs to be applied through a programme which intends to give the population the possibilities of helping themselves. However, this is not very easy when people have lived within an authoritarian context, as it is the case for the young people of my country. Thus, when I am considering to develop my programme using small consciousness-raising groups, what I am trying to do is to set up with them a truly democratic place, and not at all to display a therapeutic one with a clinical approach—although perhaps I gave that impression at first. Certainly, I employ aspects of the group dynamics approach which have already been successfully applied with young people by different Latin American authors who are therapists. My intention is to partly apply their method to the problem of difference, particularly of sexuated identities of men and women.

Why Cultivate Difference?

Toward a Culture of Two Subjects

The question of difference between the sexes is often reduced to a biological difference, or a social difference based on stereotypes.

Before attempting to show that this difference is not simply one or the other, I would recall that, considering sexual difference in this manner, we consider men and women as two separate entities whose characteristics or specific features are analysed in a comparative way. And generally in order to restore the one, the same.

The ideal thus seems to reduce the human species to only one gender, furthermore to an individual that would become neutral with regard to sexual identity. What is removed, what is denied, is difference itself, difference between the two genders. But sexual difference is the most universal one and denial in this case risks becoming a denial of difference elsewhere.

If we look at sexual difference as composed of two separate entities that we could compare, then we forget that sexual difference corresponds first of all to a manner that human beings have of entering into relationship, the one(s) with the other(s).

The attraction between man and woman, men and women, risks remaining an animal instinct if we do not take care of the possibility of sharing speech between them. Now generally language — in any case in the West — is a code elaborated taking into account masculine subjectivity. The linguistic code is not really neutral. Yet it would be necessary to give masculine and feminine subjects an equal opportunity to talk.

What Does the Generation of Language Reveal about Sexual Difference?

But if we listen to boys and girls, to men and women, beyond the difference of the way of talking determined by the linguistic code, we discover differences which come from their respective subjectivities. In fact, the subjectivity of each sex is characterized by a specific world. How can this be apprehended? I attempted to do this through an analysis of the language produced by girls and boys, women and men. I gathered and interpreted a wide corpus obtained from mixed-sex groups — of different languages and cultures, different socio-cultural backgrounds and different ages. It became obvious that *girls and boys, men and women, live in different worlds based on specific relational identities.*

I will explain myself by giving an example of the work accomplished. When mixed-sex groups were asked to make up sentences using words such as: I . . . you, I . . . her/him, with, together, to share, to love, etc., I noticed that girls and boys, women and men gave very different responses.

I could not have imagined such a difference before doing a research project of this kind. However, I had felt that the difference between the sexes was not simply biological or social. What was its nature then? I came to the conclusion that the difference between the sexes was above all a difference in relational identity.

I will refer here to the final part of the research, which was undertaken with children, adolescents and adults, and in which they were asked to make up sentences using words that express the process of forming relations.

As it turned out, subjects used these words very differently depending on whether they were male or female. Looking at the responses from a sample group of 8-year-old Italian children, I observed that:

— girls in their sentences favoured relationships between people, particularly between two people, and of a different sex;
— boys, for their part, favoured subject-object relationships and, when they did evoke a relationship between people, it would involve a subject among a group of others like them, of the same gender. The only allusion to the other sex would be to the mother, therefore to someone of a different generation — a response not found among the girls in this sample group.

So, given the word 'with', a girl would make up the sentence: 'I speak with Marco', and a boy: 'I hit the ball with a racquet', or sometimes: 'I play basketball with him' or 'with them' (boys, as indicated by the context). For the word 'together', a typical girl's wording would be something like: 'Gianfranco and I will have a baby together', and the boy's: 'I always play together with him' or 'with them [boys]'. With 'to love', a girl would write: 'I love Paolo so much' and a boy: 'I love basketball'. With 'to share': 'I share with Dilan even though I've never really known him', would be written by a girl, whereas a boy would write: 'I share the computer with my mum'.

It is also possible to observe that cues implying a relationship between two elicit positive responses from girls and negative ones from boys: 'You and I like the same things', or 'I hate you'. And with cues such as 'I . . . he' or 'I . . . she', girls would give a positive response if the question is about the two different sexes: 'He and I love each other', and boys a negative response: 'She and I hate each other'.

I could go on for hours — or even days — discussing this research that I conducted in collaboration with other researchers, men and women. I would refute at the outset any claim that we are dealing here with girls who are already alienated. Such an objection assumes that the ability to relate to another must be valued as inferior to an ability to relate to an object. Or that to favour the group is better than favouring the other. Or indeed that to prefer difference to sameness is the consequence of alienation and that it would be better to prefer sameness. Such an objection fails to recognise that little girls are more aware and creative than little boys, particularly because they have a more developed aptitude for relational life.

Next I would like to demonstrate that the characteristics that I have cited exist among adolescents and adults as well. And that these tendencies are not specific to a given culture. Hence for the word 'with', 16–17 year-old French teenagers made up the following sentences:

The girls:	— I will always live with you.
	— I am going out with you tonight.
	— I am going to see a film tonight with my friend.
The boys:	— I have my sauerkraut with beer.
	— I go to the supermarket with my trolley.
	— I like chips with mayonnaise.

Among adult women, there would always be more instances of: 'I am going to go on holiday with my children', or 'I am going for a walk with my children'; and among adult men: 'I am going to see the match with my friends'.

I could equally recall the other cues presented to the sample groups by myself and other researchers, and explain how I came to examine the relational aspect itself.

I could also show you that the languages in which sexual difference is less marked are not particularly conducive to the development of female subjectivity, as is sometimes claimed.

If you wish to find out more about this research on the sexuation of language, I suggest that you refer to *I Love to You* or to collective works, which unfortunately have yet to be published in English: *Sexes et genres à travers les langues, Le sexe linguistique* and *Genres culturels et inter-culturels.*

Each Gender Belongs to a Specific Relational Identity

You can observe that sexual difference is not only a biological or a social difference. It represents another way of entering into relation with oneself, with the world, with other(s). Thus the difference of identity between masculine and feminine subjectivities appears as a relational one. The relational identities of the boy and the girl, of the man and the woman, are not the same. And it is not appropriate to claim that the relational identity of the girl results from an alienation as has been said to me. It would signify — as already partly observed — that intersubjectivity is not as good as a relation between subject and object. And that the relation between two subjects is not as good as the relation between one individual and a group of peers. And, further, that a vertical and hierarchical relationship is better than a horizontal relationship. Now, this is not true. The problem is that some of these characteristics belong to masculine subjectivity and the others to feminine subjectivity. And that the Western tradition is constructed starting from masculine subjectivity. The values of feminine subjectivity are still unknown and not yet cultivated. But we can, we must, change that to attain a more just and more accomplished culture.

How can we explain the differences of subjectivity between male and female? We can say, for example, that it is not the same to be born a girl from a woman — that is, from a person of the same sex — or to be born from a person of a sex that is different, as is the case for a boy. Neither is it equivalent to be able, or not to be able, to engender as the mother. Or even to engender in oneself or outside of oneself. And, furthermore, to make love in oneself or outside of oneself.

These features determine two worlds that will be different and that cannot communicate with one another before first being conscious of this or these difference(s), and having found means of respecting each other.

In fact, we imagine that we communicate if we share the same needs, or if we belong to the same world, the same culture. We communicate then in a third one but not between us. And it is not possible that a common third still exists between us, man and woman. This is true between different cultures or traditions, but first of all it is true between us, between our masculine and feminine subjectivities.

The only third that we could have in common is nature itself, a nature not yet entirely marked by a culture. The natural world can be this third, but it can also be a place of life, both natural and spiritual, and a place of intimacy, prior to and after all family links. Nature is also a place to welcome the other(s). For all these reasons it is a shame to destroy nature.

Approaching the Other Through a Negative Path

What happens when in nature another comes to me? It seems that the new thing occurring with this other is *invisibility, unknowability.*

You, therefore, allow me to see the invisible. The invisible is here. You are visible and invisible. In you, the invisible appears but also remains collected, quiet, calm. It appears and subsists ... It is not necessary to enter the beyond in order to enjoy it: it is enough to contemplate you, to think of you. It is like a sky which gives itself and withdraws, near and distant, always other ... I who am visible to you must also maintain a certain reserve. Within the intention of appearing to you, there must also exist the intention of remaining invisible, of covering life and love with the shadow of a mystery. The eyes are a bridge between us, the gestures express a will, but this shows itself by hiding itself ... Thus, I am clothed even when naked. My body is never reduced to a simply naturality: the desire to love remains a cloth woven both by me and by you, of earth and of sky, of night and of light, of shadow and of sun. And so to infinity. (*To Be Two*, 47)

Looking at the other, respecting the invisible in him, opens a black or blinding void in the universe. Beginning from this limit, inappropriable by my gaze, the world is recreated. I inhabit it, but the whole of its truth is not mine. And since it is not completely known to me, it remains sensible and alive. Suspending judgement allows us to be. We can remain together if you do not become entirely perceptible to me, if a part of you stays in the night. (*To Be Two*, 8)

Never knowing you, only love consents to such a night. Between those who love each other, a veil subsists. In solitude, perhaps advancing with a lamp is necessary, but in love? ... Does such a night correspond to blind faith or to respect for what I will never know? And is it not this unknown which allows us to remain two? ... The maintenance of a mystery safeguards each of us. We remain blind to one another, perceiving each other through touch, even distant. Without knowing any violence, we are waiting for the word addressed to us. ... Leaving both of us to be — you and me, me and you — , never reducing the other to a mere meaning, to my meaning, we listen always and anew to each other so that the irreducible can remain ... For you, for us, between darkness and light. Being in the light always offends. Modesty requires a bit of mystery, a silence over what is known, a withdrawal: to respect you and leave obscurity between us. (*To Be Two*, 9)

What happens in fact is *negativity*. I cannot see or know the other as other and, to welcome him or her, I must use the negative in a daily empirical way but also in a cultural way. To allow a relationship with the other as other, a dialectical process is necessary, but it is different from the Hegelian dialectical process. Its purpose is not to assume the all into the absolute perfection of a world appropriate to a unique subject. It is rather to maintain the duality of the subjectivities and of their own worlds. Thus negativity is insuperable here. And this insuperable negativity is a necessary means or method to reach an intersubjective philosophy, that is a philosophy that takes account of relationship between subjects, in particular between two subjects who are different instead of between individuals who belong to the same group, the same culture, etc. In fact, being able to be with the other as other requires renouncing being (as) the other. As I repeat so many times in *I Love to You* and in *To Be Two*: 'You who will never be or become me or mine, I love to you'. I love to what you are, to what you want. But in order to love to you, I must renounce being or becoming identical to you or the same as you and making you mine. We live in a different world in which the relation with oneself, with the other, with the universe is not the same.

Approaching you as such requires not appropriating you in any way. It is through a negative way that I can move toward you, renouncing knowing you in order to preserve a global perception of you.

So you can become and remain a mystery that illuminates me with a light different from the light of reason. The Western tradition, which did not take into consideration the relationship between subjects as different, in particular as sexually different, does not know this kind of light that can illuminate, remaining also perceptible by the senses.

Perhaps we can find some allusion to this light in the discourse of mystics or about mystics. But it alludes to a relation with God who always remains invisible, only invisible, and who moves back — if it is possible to say so — when the mystic approaches him.

With the other, the process is different. The other constantly has some effect on me, the other communicates with me every day. He or she does not move back when I attempt to reach him or her. And to preserve the two, I must construct and respect a limit between us, a double limit in fact: my own limit and the limit of the other. Neither of us is the whole. The limit leads each one back to their own self through a coming and going from the outside to the inside, from the inside to the outside of the self. Such a limit helps me to return to myself, in myself. Neither I nor the other corresponds to the absolute:

neither I nor you. So we remain two 'I's and two 'you's, and we escape the sharing of 'I' and 'you' between masculine and feminine subjectivities.

As I have already shown, generally the 'I' is privileged in masculine discourse, and the 'you' in feminine discourse. *To approach one another in a negative way with respect for each other's difference(s) leads the man to a greater consideration for the 'you' and the woman for the 'I'.* So the dialogue between them is facilitated. And the subjects, both the feminine and the masculine, can correct their own stereotypes.

It is then possible to say that man and woman are destined for one another thanks to differences which are not only biological or social but linked to their relational identity. To deny these differences is once more to deny feminine subjectivity its own existence. And such a tendency probably results from the superiority of feminine subjectivity in relational life. In the Western tradition, the particularities of masculine subjectivity are privileged and it is difficult for a subject of this tradition to recognize that feminine subjectivity could be in some way higher than masculine subjectivity.

Other Ways Toward a Culture of Two Subjects

What are the other ways, the other methods to reach a culture of two subjects? I have already talked about negativity as a manner of respecting the other as other. I can also speak about the necessity of *listening to* and of being capable of *keeping silent*. There are two manners of being attentive to the other as such.

The capacity of acquiring or constructing the totality of knowledge, the totality of discourse, is often considered an accomplishment in our culture, and even the accomplishment of our culture itself. To succeed in constructing a culture of two subjects, we must instead acquire the capacity to remain silent in order to listen to the other as other, and to his or her truth which will always remain strange for us, unknowable by us. Our culture lacks a cultivation of silence as it lacks an education of relationship with the other as other. I would like to recall a few sentences about this necessity of being silent and of cultivating the capacity of listening to the other:

Thus, *I am listening to you* is not to expect or hear some information from you, nor the pure expression of a sentiment (a naive aim of psychoanalysis sometimes). *I am listening to you* is to listen to your words as something unique, irreducible, especially to my own, as something new, still unknown. (. . .) I am listening to you, as to another who transcends me, requires passing to a new dimension. I am listening to you: I perceive what you are saying, I am attentive to it, I am attempting to hear your intention. Which does not mean: I understand you, I know you, so I do not need to listen to you and I can even prescribe a future for you. No, I am listening to you as to someone and something I do not know yet, with a freedom and an availability safeguarded for this moment. (. . .) I am listening to you not starting from what I know, I feel, I already am, nor according to what the world and language already are, thus, as it were, in a formalistic manner. I am listening to you rather as to the revelation of a truth not yet unveiled — yours and that of the world revealed through and by you. I give you silence where the future of you — and perhaps of me, but *with* you and not *as* you and *without* you — can emerge (. . .). This silence is not hostile or restrictive. It is an available attitude that nothing or no one occupies, or preoccupies — no language, no world, no God. (. . .) This silence is the condition for a possible respect of myself and of the other within our respective limits. It also presupposes that the already existing world, including in its philosophical or religious form, is not considered as complete, already manifested or revealed. In order to be able to keep silent and listen, listen to you, without presupposing anything, without making hidden demands — to you or to myself —, the world must not be sealed already, it must still be open, the future not prescribed by the past. To really listen to you, all these conditions are indispensable. And moreover, I do not consider language to be immutable. Otherwise, language itself controls, orders, and hinders freedom. (. . .) Listening to you presupposes that, for a moment at least, I would be capable of putting aside all these obligations. That nothing and no one imposes any constraint upon me, not even what my body is saying, my inertness, my fatigue. (*I Love to You*, 116, 117, 118)

Beyond the cultivation of our capacity to remain silent and to listen to the other, we must learn *a different manner of speaking* to him, or to her.

The discourse we generally use is an informative discourse. It serves to transmit information, not to communicate between us. Moreover we generally confuse communicating something with communicating between us. Well, these two ways of speaking do not use the same language.

To communicate something from one to the other, we must participate in an identical linguistic code, an identical culture. We communicate then in a third that is common. Certainly we pass on something new to one another, but this information is a piece of a global discourse and context that is known by the two. It is the reason for our mutual comprehension. This does not yet signify a comprehension of the other as such. I could give as an example the difficulties that we have in understanding the message of someone who belongs to a language, a culture, a tradition which are different from ours. But in this case we can imagine that the problem concerns only the third. We have not yet considered how to communicate with another subject. Now the emphasis is put on the difference of subjectivity and not on the difference of information being passed on.

To communicate with another subject without reducing this gesture to passing on some information, we must change our way of talking, our use of words — we must be attentive to use words that in themselves conserve life and pass it on instead of passing on only information. We must use a language that remains breathful, alive, sensible. Thus we must attend to the quality of the words we choose, of the tone of voice, but also to the use of syntactic choice. The intransitive verbs preserve more the duality of subjects. If I say: I love you, there is a risk that 'you' will become an object. On the contrary, if I say 'I love to you' — that is: I love to whom or what you are, to your desire, etc., — we remain two subjects. To protect the duality of subjects requires also privileging interrogative transformation rather than negative and above all rather than imperative transformation. For example: 'Will you please discuss this problem with me?' leaves to the other the possibility of saying 'yes' or 'no', that is, it invites the other to generate their own discourse.

Another example: to favour dialogue, we can use prepositions like 'with', 'to', 'between', or adverbs like 'together' and privilege verbs which allow a common action such as: 'to go for a walk', 'to converse', 'to discuss', etc.

Thus in order to enter into a culture of two subjects we must pay attention to our manner of talking, and always maintain a place for the other as subject in our discourse.

More generally speaking, we must *change our manner of being in touch with the other*. This is true not only at the level of talking but also at the level of looking at the other or of listening to the other. This is true *also at the level of touching as such*. For example in the carnal relation with another subject.

When Western philosophy talks about touching, its discourse generally remains appropriate to a traditional masculine subjectivity. I would say that it is then a question of:

— a relation between subject and object,
— a relation of appropriation of the other, in particular of the feminine, that becomes an object among other objects,
— a relation of competitiveness with peers,

— a relation in which looking at and touching are gestures which
serve to dominate, to possess,
— a relation without dialogues and reciprocity between the one who
touches and the one who is touched,
— a relation in which consciousness falls asleep rather than awakens.

All of this can explain why carnal love appears as worse and finally
as guilt. And it is in fact, if it does not respect the two persons, the
two subjects in their own subjectivity.

I would give an example of the way in which a Western philosopher
considers the carnal relationship:

For Jean-Paul Sartre, the body of the other is a 'facticity', a fact, a present
objective reality, which is there beside me. As such, the other is that which I can
see and touch. But the other is more than facticity, the other is consciousness:
of-itself, for-itself, consciousness of the world even. . . . Given that consciousness
is transcendent with respect to the body — as Sartre and the majority of Western
philosophers think — , the other exists beyond what is perceived as a fact. (. . .)
How, then, to desire others and enter into carnal relationships with them? In
Being and Nothingness, Jean-Paul Sartre maintains that the only possible means is
to 'enchant' them. It is a matter of making the consciousness of the other descend
into the body, of paralyzing liberty in the facticity of a body. The consciousness of
the other must be 'coagulated' in their body — 'as one says of a coagulated cream
or mayonnaise' — so that the for-itself of the other could surface in their skin,
that it could extend itself throughout the entire surface of the body, and that,
touching this body, I finally touch the other's free subjectivity. (. . .) In this way,
I can 'possess' the other and, according to Sartre, there is no accomplishment of
desire without possession. (*To Be Two*, 17–18)

I would propose an alternative to this manner of entering into carnal
relation with an other. I take the example of the caress in *To Be Two*:

The caress is an awakening to you, to me, to us (. . .) The caress is a reawakening
to the life of my body: to its skin, senses, muscles, nerves, and organs, most of
the time inhibited, subjugated, dormant or enslaved in everyday activity, in the
universe of needs, the world of labour, the imperatives or restrictions necessary
for communal living (. . .) The caress is an awakening to intersubjectivity, to a
touching between us which is neither passive nor active; it is an awakening to
gestures, to perceptions which are at the same time acts, intentions, emotions.
This does not mean that they are ambiguous, but rather, that they are attentive
to the one who touches and the one who is touched, to the two subjects who
touch each other (. . .) The caress is an awakening to a life different from arduous
everyday existence, and a call to a return to you, to me, to us: as living bodies, as
two who are different and co-creators. The caress is an act and work which are

common, irreducible to those dedicated either to individual or collective needs
... The caress is a word-gesture which goes beyond the horizon or the distance
of intimacy with oneself. It is so for the one who is caressed or touched, for
the one who is approached within the sphere of his or her incarnation, but also
for the one who caresses, for the one who touches and accepts distancing from
oneself for this gesture. (*To Be Two*, 25–26)

The caress is also praise. An homage of feast, of evening, of spring, for what I
perceived, sensed and experienced of you during the day, the week, the winter
(...) The caress is also an invitation to rest, to relax, and to perceive, think and be
in a different way: more quiet, more contemplative, less utilitarian ... The caress
is a gift of safety. It is a call to return to yourself with a possible rediscovery of your
virginity, here and now, thanks to me, thanks to us. Your virginity understood not
as a simply physical or phantasmatic thing which is lost or preserved, violable or
inviolable, always beyond, not only of the present but also of the future. Virginity,
as your repose with yourself, in yourself, you irreducible to me, irreducible to the
common of a community ... Rather than violating or penetrating the mystery of
the other, reducing his or her consciousness or freedom to passivity, objectuality,
animality or infancy, the caress becomes a gesture which gives the other back to
himself, or to herself, thanks to the presence of an attentive witness, thanks to a
guardian of incarnate subjectivity. (*To Be Two*, 27)

You can observe that in my text, in my perspective:

— the persons remain two, furthermore the caress is a way to
   remain two,
— the two can remain different and, moreover, difference itself helps
   to remain two or to return into being two,
— the caress leads to an awakening of consciousness for each other:
   the carnal relationship is then a way to become more aware, more
   attentive in particular to intersubjectivity,
— through the caress, that is, through a corporeal gesture, the subjects
   approach each other instead of appropriating one another,
— the two subjects make each other fecund through a carnal way,
   but not only physically, also culturally, spiritually.

To reach a culture of two subjects, we need a *culture of breathing*.
Breathing is the first gesture of life, both natural and spiritual. We lack
such a culture in our tradition. Because of this lack we usually remain
dependent on each other. Thus we are part of one single entity and it
is difficult to reach being two. Cultivating our own breath would help
us each to become autonomous and to be able to be two. In this case,
to love does not mean a risk of losing our own identity. It is a way of
finding it or finding it again if we are attentive to remaining two.

One final thing. For a culture of two subjects, *the way of talking must remain poetic*, that is, an actualization of a present relationship between two. Thus a *poietic* language, a language which creates something new and does not communicate only something that already exists.

LUCE IRIGARAY
Centre National de la Recherche Scientifique, Paris

BIBLIOGRAPHY

Irigaray, Luce, editor and contributor, *Genres culturels et interculturels, Languages*, 111, 1993.

Irigaray, Luce, *I Love to You, Sketch for a Felicity within History*, New York-London, Routledge, 1996, translated by Alison Martin from the French *J'aime à toi, Esquisse d'une félicité dans l'Histoire*, Paris, Grasset, 1992. Quotations from the published translation have been modified by the author in the present article.

Irigaray, Luce, editor and contributor, *Sexes et genres à travers les langues*, Paris, Grasset, 1990.

Irigaray, Luce, editor and contributor, *Le sexe linguistique, Languages*, 85, 1987.

Irigaray, Luce, *To Be Two*, London-New York, Athlone-Routledge, 2001, translated by Monique M. Rhodes and Marco F. Cocito-Monoc from the Italian *Essere due*, Turin, Bollati Boringhieri, 1994. The French version has been published as *Etre Deux*, Paris, Grasset, 1997. Quotations from the published translation have been modified by the author in the present article.

PAINTING — ARCHITECTURE — CINEMA

Approaching Painting through Feminine Morphology

It is interesting to note that, when it comes to painting, some feminist critiques have simply enacted a reversal upon the formalist/modernist emptying of all meaning other than 'the engagement of the artistic self with the processes and procedures of painting' (Pollock, 'Painting, Feminism, History', 142). They empty paintings by women of all meaning other than that discerned in their images, thus leaving aside all examination of the use of materials.

I want to examine the possibility of the concept 'morphology' (as Luce Irigaray uses it) and in particular the morphology of the mucous, for reading certain material practices in art, and to account for the play of a *morpho-logic* as prior to, while also allowing for, the production of a syntax in the Symbolic which is appropriate for women. It would be easy to capitalize mucus by capitalizing paint, to understand 'paint' as a metaphor for mucus. Instead, I want to try to arrive at an understanding of Jenny Saville's use of paint as one site of mediation within the morpho-logic of the mucous.

Although the term 'morphology' is indeed from the Greek *morphé*, meaning 'form', and is used in the field of biology, it does not automatically imply an anatomical reading. In biology it does not refer to deterministic analysis of forms in themselves, but to a method of discerning patterns of *relationships between* forms. For example, plants-women and plants-men would be familiar with this usage: flowers as superficially dissimilar as buttercups and delphiniums are in the same family, as they share a morphology. 'Morphology' is also used as a term within linguistics where it names a method of studying the component parts of words and of language. So while there is a biological implication in the use of the term 'morphology', to reduce it to the anatomical is to restrict its possibilities. Furthermore, we are always also in the realm of linguistic structures.

Luce Irigaray made it quite clear early on that for her morphology is not a matter simply of anatomy: 'I think we must go back to the question not of the anatomy but of the morphology of female sex' ('Women's Exile', 64). She later reiterated such an affirmation: 'It is more a question of breaking out of the autological and tautological circle of systems of representation and their discourse so as to allow women to speak their sex' ('The Poverty of Psychoanalysis', in *The Irigaray Reader*, 96–7, translation modified). And she has spoken elsewhere of the necessity to 'find our body's language' (*This Sex Which Is Not One*, 214).

So when I propose a morphological relationship between women and the ways in which they signify in the Symbolic (that is to say, their uses of language, gesture, image, etc.), I am looking for forms of signification which are appropriate, a syntax in the symbolic which is appropriate to women.

In this context, 'morphology' names the site of a discursive and dynamic relationship between a subject's empirical living in the body and in the Symbolic, a relationship which does not go in one direction, but is circular. The way the subject *understands* the body is significant in determining an appropriate syntax in the Symbolic; and in turn the subject understands — or reads — the body through the Symbolic syntax. The subject then 'sees' anatomy according to the signifiers of that syntax. In this way the morphological relationship helps the two areas co-define each other, in a process of Derridean *différance*. So it is a matter of both elements both differing from and deferring to each other, and continuous play which produces identity. Morphology, in the site where it is, a spacing between body and signification, is an instance of *différance* at work or play. It is a producer of gendered subjectivity. Indeed, in that very space between body and language, and coming before any distinction between the two, it is productive of structure and transformation in the relationship between them. What is necessary is the deployment of a morphology appropriate to women: the morphology in play between women's bodies and their language will be productive of an appropriate syntax in the Symbolic, and thus of appropriate symbolic, and therefore cultural, representations of women's bodies.

The terms that Luce Irigaray uses most often in order to mediate the play of women's morphology are initially those of 'the lips' and, increasingly through the writings of the 1980s, 'mucus'. Women's morphology produces a site for itself in these terms: this is *not* the lips of the mouth, *not* the lips of the genitals, but at the same time *both* the lips of the mouth *and* the lips of the genitals: 'the lips', as a term, is the site of a play between them. The lips are at least two in at least two ways: both in the play between the (not)mouth and (not)vulva, and also in the internal morpho-logic of such (non)references.

Women's morphology, in its play between women's body and language, is the place of the birth of the imaginary: *women's morphology,*

which has its own material practices, is the necessary precursor to the distinc-
tion of a Symbolic syntax appropriate to women. And without this syntax,
women remain in a state of immediacy — that is to say, with no appropriate mediation, and thus without access to their subjectivity, since
subjectivity is entwined with signification. Luce Irigaray expresses
this threading very clearly in 'When Our Lips Speak Together', in
language which is an attempt to write of and through the morphology
of women:

If we don't invent a language, if we don't find our body's language, it will have
too few gestures to accompany our story. We shall tire of the same ones, and
leave our desires in latency, unrealized. Sleep again, unsatisfied. And fall back
upon the words of men — who for their part, have 'known' for a long time. But
not our body. (This Sex Which Is Not One, 214)

And the only way to mediate what would otherwise be an immediate,
distanceless proximity — two lips touching without mediation — , is
through the morphology of mucus. The morphology of the mucous
is that which mediates a woman to herself, and also mediates her,
in her difference and specificity, to her lover. It is the mark of her
sex, and it is the mark of mediation. The lips are, morphologically,
a threshold; ajar, but touching, not closed; but rather, mucous: the
site of mediation.

The realization of the morphology of the mucous is crucial for
woman–woman relationships, for woman–man relationships and for a
woman's relationship with herself — it is her self-mediation through
an appropriate symbolization. Luce Irigaray has stressed how important this is:

However, it is possible that the mucous corresponds to something that needs to
be thought through today. For different reasons and imperatives:
— Any thinking in the feminine has to think the mucous.
— No thinking about sexual difference that would not be traditionally hierarchical
is possible without thinking the mucous. (*An Ethics of Sexual Difference,* 110,
translation modified)

What I am trying to present here in my reading of the morphology
of the mucous is a morphology that allows for both the relinquishing of
control and the presence of the subject demanded by intersubjectivity
and attentiveness. Recalling the flowering of the subject that was the
Buddha's gaze upon the flower, Luce Irigaray evokes the potential of
the mucous: 'The flesh of the rose petal — sensation of the mucous
regenerated. Somewhere between blood, sap, and the not yet of

efflorescence. Joyous mourning for the winter past. New baptism of springtime. Return to the possible of intimacy, its fecundity, and fecundation' (*An Ethics of Sexual Difference*, 200). And this 'return to the possible of intimacy' can be found in the way the mucous marks the limits of the subject as it performs a mediation between subjects.

Luce Irigaray describes how articulating the limits between women is problematic. What is necessary, then, is a site of a 'third term' between subjects — a site that is neither of the two subjects (and which will thus prevent each woman reducing the other to herself), but which is not abstract: what Luce Irigaray describes as a 'sensible-transcendental'. This is a transcendental against which each woman can measure herself, which transcends the individual subject woman, in order that she can recognise her own limits as a subject and avoid reducing the other subject to being her object. This complex move is developed by Luce Irigaray in 'The Limits of the Transference'. In short, the two subjects have to produce a (non)object — a third term — between them:

How are they constantly to make greatest and smallest meet? And above all, move from one qualitative to another? A difficult energetistic question, especially when there is no object, no comparison between the two poles. They must become creations. Art *objects*? In that way two subjects can advene one to the other, and an alliance between the two becomes possible.

This is not so much a problem of mastery as the question of a creation allowing participation in the *jouissance* of the object or its cocreation: a useful work because it marks, without destruction, the limits of energy, of the flesh and of the body, of desire and its possibilities. The creation or elaboration of the *object* becomes an architectonic of the body, of a life and a death that does not kill the other. ('The Limits of the Transference' in *The Irigaray Reader*, 112–13)

Without the morphology of the mucous in play this would be impossible. The (non)object that is created is something more like a fluidity of creation itself: the work of creating a subject is a co-creation in the analytic scenario. This must start not from the premise that one woman is the subject and the other is her object, but that both are potentially subjects in a relationship of intersubjectivity. This consideration reminds me of the passage in *Je, Tu, Nous*, concerning the exchange of small hand-made objects between mother and daughter in order to create a space of mediation (48–9).

Once the patterns of the morphology of the mucous are recognized, they can be worked for elsewhere. I should like to suggest that this understanding of Luce Irigaray's exploration and use of the morpho-logic of the mucous can be used to great benefit if we look for its patterns in practices of art-making.

Certain questions present themselves at this point. How, at present, can we work simultaneously with and against the structures and tropes of the Symbolic currently provided by our culture? How does one produce the element of mediation, the third term, the appropriate syntax in the Symbolic, and its representations? How do we represent ourselves without reproducing, to ourselves or to others, a phallomorphic representation, 'woman'?

This is where I think we need to attempt to locate a morphology which can account for a mediation through materials, an enunciation which is legible and productive of discourse, in an appropriate Symbolic syntax. Thus, the task for us upon reading Irigaray's work is to realize, to make real, the morphological play between the language that is spoken and that which is said within that language—both of these being contiguous. This would then allow us to approach, develop, and be attentive to the motifs within that speech, without returning to them as metaphor or phallomorphic objects.

The play of morphology, including its play through the media of the artwork, precedes the distinction of the Symbolic syntax appropriate to women. The motifs and representations occurring within that syntax, that which we wish to say in it, cannot be anticipated in advance, nor can the degree of contiguity between the two. Continuous vigilance regarding the play of morphology in the structure of the Symbolic is required. In a constant multiple movement we have to work with and through the language, material and representations to hand, back to their informative morphology, and return again to language.

What is at stake here is the morphology informing both our making of artworks, and how we represent the representational practices of art to ourselves. This returns us to the materiality of art making, and to the problem of approaching a medium and working with it as that element of mediation—the third term, the gift/object of co-creation—in which enunciation in the appropriate syntax in the Symbolic is possible. Thus, 'representational practices' in artworks are in an interdependent and discursive relationship with the practices and processes engaged with by the artist in her use of materials. The materials, therefore, must be recognized by the artist and the audience as an element in a discourse productive of representations—if you like, a crucial set of signifiers among others in artworks.

I will now discuss this in relation to particular artworks: paintings by Jenny Saville. Lucien Freud's work has frequently been evoked in relation to Saville's work. However, there are crucial differences at the level of the usage of materials that I think can be read as morphological differences. Freud's paint work, particularly in his painting of skin, may look creamy from any distance, but it is also usually shiny, with a hard, repulsing surface, giving us phallomorphic closure and rigidity in the shiny paint surface. In his painting of limbs and bodies, large brush strokes (though usually small on the face) while 'molded' in effect, often appear to work against the architecture of skin, muscle and bone. It is an activity which displays a fear or hatred of, or revulsion from, flesh, and which certainly resists intersubjectivity or any mediation of the other's subjectivity. In that close-up activity of painting, I extrapolate Lucien Freud interrogating his models visually, delineating the object on canvas — the over-production of the object at the expense of subjectivity. As Luce Irigaray asks, 'is the memory of touching always disguised by senses that forget where they come from? Creating distance through a mastery that constitutes the object as a monument built in place of the subject's disappearance' (*An Ethics of Sexual Difference*, 215).

Jenny Saville's paint-work has a matt, but not 'dry', surface; her brush is not large, nor are her brush strokes; and in relation to the scale of the figures imaged, both brush and strokes could be considered very small. When close up to the canvas, she is not delineating the object; its borders are not in her visual control (Rowley, 'On Viewing Three Paintings by Jenny Saville', 92). She is, through an immeasurable series of small touches, building the image. We can imagine the patience with which she does this, 'urging it to unfold without a show of force' (*An Ethics of Sexual Difference*, 214). There is also an identification between Jenny Saville and the body she is painting, whether as self-portrait or not: the image of the woman she paints can thus never fully be her object.

I think something is happening here, something akin to love, which is important not to miss. I read Saville's act in making this painting as she does as a gesture of attending to the interrelation of subjectivity and body, and of restoring touch to sight, through the mediation of paint. Jenny Saville is restoring beauty to that *which has been regarded as* surplus substance by returning through the imaging of body and subjectivity, making a gift-space/object necessary for intersubjectivity and for mediation between women. There is a particular morpho-logic at play between the technical applying of the paint and the deferral between the substance of

Propped by Jenny Saville. Courtesy of The Saatchi Gallery, London.

the paint and the substance of the image, which pivots upon the qualities that Jenny Saville has required of the paint and the countless touchings she makes.

We can understand this as a particular morphology at play that is beginning to be productive of its Symbolic syntax. It is a morphology that is discernible in the relationship between the technologies selected and the imagery produced. It is discernible also through attempting to

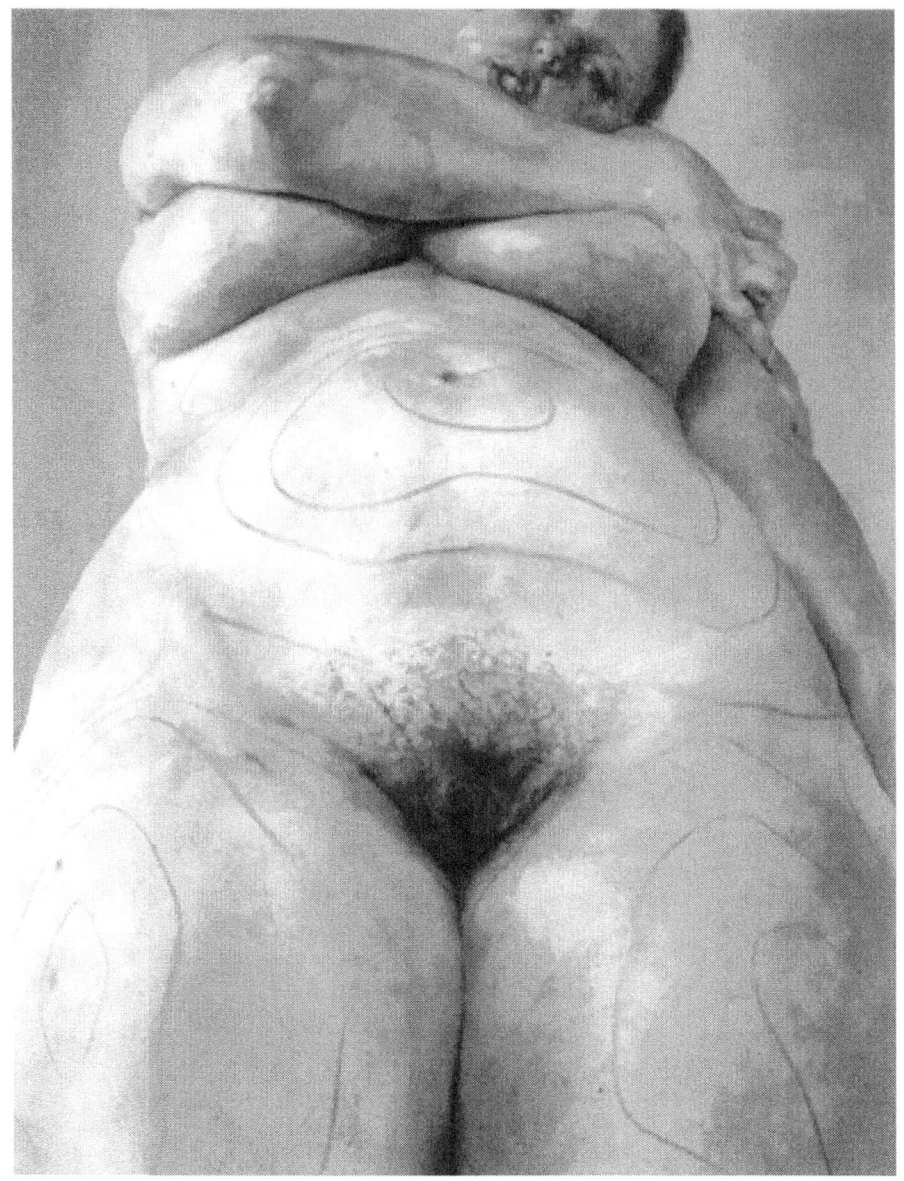

Plan by Jenny Saville. Courtesy of The Saatchi Gallery, London.

develop a practice of thinking through it: attending to the possibility of mediation through the morphology of the mucous.

HILARY ROBINSON
University of Ulster at Belfast

BIBLIOGRAPHY

Irigaray, Luce, *An Ethics of Sexual Difference*, London-New York, Athlone-Cornell University Press, 1993, translated by Carolyn Burke and Gillian C. Gill from the French *Éthique de la différence sexuelle*, Paris, Editions de Minuit, 1984.

Irigaray, Luce, *Je, Tu, Nous, Toward a Culture of Difference*, London and New York, Routledge, 1993 translated by Alison Martin from the French *Je, tu, nous, Pour une culture de la différence*, Paris, Grasset, 1990.

Irigaray, Luce, 'The Limits of the Transference', in *The Irigaray Reader*, edited by Margaret Whitford, Oxford, Blackwell, 1991, 105–117, translated by David Macey and Margaret Whitford from the French 'La limite du transfert', in *Parler n'est jamais neutre*, Paris, Editions de Minuit, 1985, 293–306.

Irigaray, Luce, 'The Poverty of Psychoanalysis', in *The Irigaray Reader*, edited by Margaret Whitford, Oxford, Blackwell, 1991, 79–104, translated by David Macey and Margaret Whitford from the French 'Misère de la psychanalyse', in *Parler n'est jamais neutre*, Paris, Editions de Minuit, 1985, 253–80.

Irigaray, Luce, *This Sex Which Is Not One*, Ithaca, New York, Cornell University Press, 1985, translated by Catherine Porter with Carolyn Burke from the French *Ce sexe qui n'en est pas un*, Paris, Editions de Minuit, 1977.

Irigaray, Luce, 'Women's Exile', interview by Diana Adlam and Couze Venn, translated from French by Couze Venn, in *Ideology and Consciousness*, 1, 1977, 62–76.

Pollock, Griselda, 'Painting, Feminism, History', in *Destabilizing Theory: Contemporary Feminist Debates*, edited by Michèle Barrett and Anne Phillips, Cambridge, Polity Press, 1992, 138–76.

Rowley, Alison, 'On Viewing Three Paintings by Jenny Saville, Rethinking a Feminist Practice of Painting', in *Generations and Geographies in the Visual Arts, Feminist Readings*, edited by Griselda Pollock, London-New York, Routledge, 1996, 88–109, and *Feminism-Art-Theory 1968–2000*, edited by Hilary Robinson, Oxford and Malden, MA., Blackwell, 2001, 392–6.

Luce Irigaray's questions

Hilary Robinson approaches very interesting questions, but I am afraid her work remains incomplete. For example: Is it appropriate to speak of the 'morphology of mucous'? Morphology generally refers to an external structure and mucous to an internal one. And it seems very problematic to confuse external and internal, especially for feminine subjectivity.

Thus a certain way of using colours, materiality of colours, could evoke the economy of mucous, and also a presence of fluids or porosity. But it is not appropriate, according to me, to erode skin in order to transform it into a mucous membrane. Skin must protect the internal mucous world. It is its morphology which permits the economy of mucous to exist.

Eroding the skin perhaps is not really feminine, but rather an effect of suffering which prevents a woman from becoming herself: with a body closed up around two lips, of which only the interior is mucous. To transform all the skin into lips does not take into account the specificity of feminine being. Perhaps it expresses a state of women in a masculine economy? But it is not by eroding or modifying our skin that we will reach the in-definite of mucous, but rather by assuming and affirming the limits of our own body.

Why do so many women making art represent the feminine body as open in a manner that precisely is not feminine — with wounds, mutilations or erosions of the limits of the body? The feminine body is open, it is not necessary to open it anew, but to know how to live a body with similar morphology.

To put the internal mucous world inside-out toward a new way of relating with others is still a manner of not safeguarding and cultivating feminine identity. If woman can enter into relationships with others differently than man, it is not by using the in-definite of the mucous in external, and even public, relations. Furthermore, this would not be a way of respecting the other as such. It corresponds to a kind of generalized prostitution. And as this remains unconscious for those who are in relationships, little by little a general madness would arise.

I think that the problem of the economy of mucous is crucial in the conflicts between women, and in the misunderstanding of my work. I fear that this is not unique to Hilary Robinson, and perhaps I am partly responsible for it. But does not staying at the first part of my work signify a willingness to maintain misunderstanding? And also neglecting, or forgetting that, beginning with *Speculum*, I said that my project is to elaborate a culture of two subjects — which requires a double or triple dialectics. Certainly this forces us to radically change our ways of thinking, and even of living, in particular the relations with others. But my intention has never been to replace a culture of a unique masculine subject with a culture of a unique feminine subject, to substitute one imperialism with another.

To relate with the other(s), and already with ourselves, we have to know something about respective identities and the manner of expressing them. A simple intuition here is not sufficient. All the work I carry out on the production of discourse, particularly of sexuate discourse, has taught me more about the difference(s) between masculine and feminine subjectivities. In order to discover mediations useful for entering into relation with the other — either mother or lover, but beyond them — , it would be fruitful to consider the difference of relational identity between the genders that shows their production of language.

But to succeed in holding a dialogue with the other, a space must be kept which belongs neither to the one nor to the other. I would ask Hilary if the mediation for mucous, and the touching of the lips, would not at first be silence? Is it not safeguarding silence, including in her discourse, that woman can reach a language appropriate to her subjectivity, both external and internal? Is not silence a key of a secular mystery attributed to woman? And does there not now exist a risk of spending or destroying this mystery by willing either to be equal to man or to reverse on the outside our own internal world? Certainly I am not speaking here of a silence imposed on the woman but of an economy of silence consciously founded by woman herself. How would it be possible, according to you, to express such a silence in painting?

Hilary Robinson's response

Thank you for your very interesting questions. The first and most important thing concerning silence is, as you rightly say, that we are discussing a silence that is freely chosen, not one that is imposed. Until women have access to a syntax in the Symbolic that is appropriate to their morphology, we have to question the nature of, and reasons for, women's silence. If a certain mystery is attributed to the silence of women, I would ask: attributed by whom? In what circumstances? And can these silent women speak in an appropriate symbolic — have they chosen this silence, or is it the silence of the person who cannot communicate? Can we discern the difference between the silences of a subject-woman and a subject-man? It is possible that silence is a necessary precursor to founding a language, and it is certainly necessary in developing intersubjectivity. Discerning a morphologically appropriate language must also mean discerning its related silences: indeed this must be safeguarded.

Silence is not an absence in that situation: silence is only an absence when it is imposed or signifies a lack of subjectivity. A chosen silence between subjects can be an eloquent presence: loving, companionable, comfortable. Buddha gazed at the flower in silence: one monk amongst many understood and responded with a smile. But was the flower visually silent? Can the (non)objects to which I refer in my essay be visually silent? Can a painting be silent? Certainly a painting can be inept, where the painter has not learned the languages possible with body, brush, and paint. A painting can also be so clichéd that it carries very little of the painter's subjectivity. A painting can be hysterical in its excessive slavery to a language deemed powerful but foreign to the painter. In all these cases the paintings, for me, are silent through absence. There is no potential for those paintings to mediate the subjectivity of the painter. But can a painting retain passages of silence? I believe so, when the subject-painter so chooses. Let me try to explain briefly.

Many women in recent years chose not to paint because the languages of painting were pre-determined by patriarchal discourses. Instead they worked in other media — especially photography — consciously developing appropriate languages for representing women's subjectivities. While many other women continued painting, this strategic withdrawal did, I think, produce discourses whereby women of Jenny Saville's generation could attend to body, brush and paint with a new set of questions concerning language and subjectivity. While a student, she read work by Luce Irigaray, and knowingly also took her concerns into her studio to interrogate and develop her painting processes. She worked on founding a language appropriate to herself, one which works in a very particular way with the images she produces. Alison Rowley, in the text cited in my paper, helped me to understand this. In paintings such as 'Plan', much remains as potential in the spaces between paint and image. It refuses instantaneous consumption. The viewer, in order to understand some aspects of the painting, has to move close. At a distance of, say, 0.5m the viewer realizes that much of the painting remains potential and yet-to-speak — as do different aspects at, say, 3m distance. The subject-painter relinquished immediate mastery of the image in making the brush-marks as she did: in working like that she suggests that the viewer should move in order to understand more of the painting. Thus, when some aspects of the painting can be 'read' others remain silent or cannot be seen. This is quite different from the silencing imposed by critics who discuss the image only; and it remains just one example. Different subjects will chose different silences.

Love in Architecture

In this paper I explore how the work of Luce Irigaray can be directed towards the problems of feminism in architecture, problems that represent a crisis in contemporary architectural debates. I introduce Irigaray's project of being two, and ask what it would mean for both men's and women's expectations, what it would mean to live with aspirations towards a culture of two sexed subjects. Directing the work more specifically to architecture, I ask how architecture can both respond to and initiate modes of living that recognise a feminine subjectivity and hence a radical sexual difference allowing two subjectivities. Or, in terms of the title of this paper and that of my Ph.D. thesis, 'With Place Love Begins', how can architecture respond or initiate a different sort of love that remains unthought within the current cultural traditions. Furthermore, I ask, does this project suggest a productive means of maintaining a practice of feminism in architecture and if so, how?

Thinking 'love' shared by two subjects is a difficult theme, particularly for architecture where problems surrounding feminism in architecture risk designating the question of feminism obsolete. The possibility of a funding a feminism that attends productively to sexual or sexuate difference, opening a place for 'an energy merely deprived of the space-time it needs to unfold, inscribe, to play' — as suggested in the paper 'Belief Itself' — provides my motive to question contemporary theory in architecture (see Luce Irigaray, *Sexes and Geneologies*, 25). Love as a theme for research is not unprecedented in contemporary architectural theory. David Farell Krell, for example, referring to the work of Martin Heidegger, Maurice Merleau-Ponty, Emmanuel Levinas and Luce Irigaray, asks in his book *Archeticture*: 'What would things be like in a world where in order to make something one had to make it with that something, as though making it with someone' (15).

Within feminism in architecture, however, the recent attempt to define a new type of feminism, or a new thinking about feminism, raises a number of issues that have provided an alibi for an attempt to dismiss more practical feminist projects, in terms of their lack of theoretical engagement. Current trends have been distinguished by a certain interdisciplinarity and cite widely from philosophy and psycho-analytical theory. Jane Rendell, Iain Borden and Barbara Penner, argue: 'Feminism and gender studies have become post-modernised

made interdisciplinary and therefore have to be considered as such'
(*Gender, Space and Architecture*, 8). This characteristic of contemporary
work is illustrated in collections, such as *Architecture and Feminism,
The Sex of Architecture, Sexuality and Space, Desiring Practices* and
Drawing, Building Text, and also in the projects of theorists such
as Jennifer Bloomer, Beatriz Colomina and Catherine Ingraham.
However, despite the characterization of such work as representing
a new feminism in architecture, what is notably problematic in it,
is that, few theorists use the term feminism and only one of these
collections names its subject as feminism, a decision described as delib-
erate and also corrective by the editors of *Architecture and Feminism*.
Although the meaning of the term feminism can be confused and
frequently linked with calls for a simple equality (the criticism that
Irigaray raises concerning conventional understandings of 'feminism')
neither the absence of the term within contemporary architectural
theory nor its replacement adequately address the need to rethink
feminism within a contemporary context. For example, in *Gender,
Space and Architecture*, Jane Rendell, Iain Borden and Barbara Penner,
somewhat authoritatively, declare the major change in thinking to
have taken place in the past five years as best described as gender
studies in architecture. However, despite their claims that: 'It is easy
to be cynical and assume "gender" has replaced "feminism" ', and the
defence that, 'this editorial group advocates that to talk about gender
is to take a political position but one more sympathetic to difference',
such proposals, where refusing the cultivation of the other, refusing
'love' given to the other for the other's becoming make difference a
question of equality (7). Furthermore, as Debra Coleman, editor of
Architecture and Feminism, suggests in such a context, 'feminist critiques
and interventions can be resisted at the same time as an outward
tolerance for diversity is sustained and even promoted' (xii).

Whilst engaging with issues of gender in terms of inequality
describes the position of women within the architectural profession,
these arguments are not necessarily synonymous with contemporary
feminism, in particular the work of Luce Irigaray. The problems of
maintaining equality suggest the need for equal but also specific rights
for women, and although Irigaray argues that the deconstruction of
patriarchal traditions is certainly indispensable she also argues it is
hardly enough (see *Why Different?*, 10). The question of equality
cannot be allowed to obscure the problems inherent in conceiving
of social structures as neutral and thus able to sustain equality. To
cite Irigaray further in *Why Different?* 'if man's dealings with woman

are to be equal, he will have to face a culture of sexual desire and co-existence in difference of which he, as yet, knows nothing' (5).

The recognition of sexual difference, so that difference is not something to be overcome is Irigaray's project, as Margaret Whitford recalls in *Luce Irigaray, Philosophy in the Feminine*, Irigaray needs her readers and interpreters, which obviously I want to argue includes architects. Whitford writes, 'this is inherent in her theory (...) she cannot on her own bring about a change in the symbolic order' (5). Thus, whilst economic and housing inequalities are significant problems for architects, these are not the only forms of social injustice for architects, whether theorists or practitioners, to address. For Irigaray there is a cultural distortion that without transformation of language and culture leaves no space for 'ethical' inter-subjective relations, and no means to cultivate and protect a place of love and silence between subjects so that one can never overcome the other. Love, responsibility or ethics are still uncultured if they cannot include a recognition of woman in her specific and symbolic identity.

The question of love is thus, for Irigaray, of how and for whom subjectivity is constituted in Western cultures; it would mean not thinking the otherness of the other as merely a version of the same, the typical resort of the Western philosophical tradition. As such it demands a certain creativity; Irigaray writes: 'Out of bed or away from home we [women] somehow mysteriously become unisexual or asexual', and this disavowal, on the part of culture, leaves women in a state of abandonment, in a state of *déréliction*, or 'homeless' (see *Thinking The Difference*, viii). However, this denial bespeaks the possibility of a different sort of relation and a different sort of construction of sexual difference. If women are not given a specificity within language, and do not obey the same sexual economy as men, this also provides both means and motive to confront the Western philosophical tradition (or the philosopher) from a position in part outside his thought (25). It offers a method to disclose in a dialogue, maybe in a sort of *amorous exchange* or 'poetic-talking' (as Judith Butler writes 'usually the kind that frightens me quite frankly') a subjectivity that simply evades men (see 'The Future of Sexual Difference', 19). It allows Irigaray to explore the limits of the patriarchal tradition and a male imaginary and also to creatively modify this limit towards; she writes in *I Love to You* 'the recognition of a sexual other who will never be mine (...) turning the negative or limit of one gender in relation to the other into a possibility of love and creation' (11). This opens a door to a radical, and by definition, undefinable future. However, it is this dialogical 'method' and its creativity that has caused the most misunderstanding amongst feminist theorists.

Reference to Irigaray's work is not uncommon but few architects explore her writing in any detail, whether as papers directed specifically at architectural design, such as the recent: 'Comment habiter durablement ensemble?' ('How To Live Together in a Lasting Way?') which works to provide concrete proposals for how architects might address the reconstruction of sexual difference, or the earlier 'Où et comment habiter?' ('Where and How To Dwell?') that engages in a more intensely poetic pursuit of the question of being two. This text is cited in an early paper by Elizabeth Grosz 'Women, *Chora*, Dwelling', a paper which, although perhaps problematic, helped to introduce the critical potential of Irigaray's work to architects. However, as yet no architects have explored Irigaray's more political arguments, such as the need for cultural transformation to maintain sexual difference in her most recent publications translated into English, *To Be Two* and *Democracy Begins Between Two*, for example. Despite projects that explore Irigaray's work few have explored in any detail her philosophical engagements with those influential to architectural theory which could include Heidegger, as is the theme of this paper, or Levinas or Derrida as demonstrated in 'Belief Itself'.

In reviewing recent papers by architects that cite Irigaray's work what emerges, however, is an interest in the possibility of a 'proper' space (*un lieu propre*) for women, and a question of Irigaray's 'method', sometimes discussed as a form of mimicry, or of how to cultivate this space.[1] To explore these ideas of space and poetic method popular amongst architects, together with the question of living sexual difference or being two, I want to look at Irigaray's readings of Heidegger's 'Building, Thinking, Dwelling' in *The Forgetting of Air* and *To Be Two* in order to argue that Irigaray's engagements with Heidegger still have value to understanding both architectural and feminist debates. Furthermore, when reading Irigaray's work as an amorous engagement with the phenomenological tradition, any accusations of essentialism are revealed as simply out of context with her thinking. Existence is always 'lived existence' and the body is always the 'lived body' making problematic the need to replace feminism with 'gender studies' or to make distinct the cultural construction of gender from any accusation of an 'essentialist' theory (see Tina Chanter, *The Ethics of Eros*, 129).

In 'Building, Thinking, Dwelling', Heidegger writes that it is 'language that tells us about the nature of a thing provided that we respect language's own nature' (See *Poetry, Language, Thought*, 146). For Heidegger, language, in particular poetry, and including art and architecture, is not just a means of communication or representation but offers the possibility of 'making visible' or disclosing a world, of 'making visible' the meaning of being. Building hence portrays nothing, it discloses a world and, if we listen to what building tells us, it gives things their look and to men their outlook on themselves. Man's access to this world or to authentic existence is through listening and responding to language where Heidegger writes: 'Man (. . .) dwells in language, as the House of being: when he listens to and responds to language the world which he is; is opened up and an authentic existence becomes possible' (see 'The Origin of the Work of Art', in *Poetry, Language, Thought*, 15–89). Therefore, if we were to listen to what language tells us about building, Heidegger suggests, we would hear three things: first that building is really dwelling, second that dwelling is the manner in which mortals are on the earth where spatiality is a property of being-in-the-world, of existence or *Da-Sein*, and, finally, that building as dwelling opens into the building that cultivates things and the building that erects building (See 'Building, Dwelling, Thinking', 148). The question of what it means to be in the world and of building is thus also that of dwelling. Building as dwelling cultivates but it also constructs and both are properties of man's authentic existence. Dwelling is therefore both a characteristic of the human being and an activity, an activity described as to be at peace, to remain in peace, to be free, preserved from harm and danger, to spare, to cherish and protect or cultivate, to care for, or to return something to its own nature as 'letting-be' (*Sein-lassen*).

Hence building portrays nothing, it discloses: 'in its standing there', as Heidegger says of the temple. In the example of the bridge in 'Building, Thinking, Dwelling', Heidegger writes that 'the bridge makes location', or that is to say the bridge makes place come into presence and elements emerge as what they are. The bridge brings the stream and bank and land into each other's neighbourhood. The bridge 'gathers', a word Heidegger derives as associated with the word thing, corresponding to the thing as an assembly. The bridge as thing and location allows 'site', which he also in anticipation calls building. Only something that is a location can make space and provide site, and — he insists — only things that are locations in the manner of the bridge allow site for building. The thing as Thing and as a property of man's being-in-the-world, or dwelling, is thus location. The Thing makes space for the four-fold he describes as earth, sky, mortals, and gods, all belonging in a mirror play which constitutes the world, or in Irigaray's criticism 'his' world. This mirror-play of the four-fold is space made clear, illuminated, 'made visible', an open 'between' or a place wherein things appear as what they are. Thus, listening to what building has to say to us, Heidegger writes; 'we do not dwell because we have built, but we build and have built because we dwell, that is because we are dwellers'; but these meanings have fallen into oblivion ('Building, Dwelling, Thinking', 148). Buildings for Heidegger admit and install the four-fold and correspond to man's being in the world opening up a world and hence as things that put up locations they respond and initiate spaces. Space for Heidegger is thus neither external object nor inner experience: 'spaces open up by the fact that they are let into the dwelling of man' (157).

For architectural readers of the text 'Building, Dwelling, Thinking' and its complicated terminology, Heidegger resolves only in part the question of 'poetic building' by saying that first we must think that nature of things which themselves require building as the process in which they are made. This intensity of thinking the question is the first step to building (154). In a feminist criticism of Heidegger's discussion of architecture, numerous questions arise as to the absence of adequate thought to the body, to the nature of desire, or strange presence and absence of it, and hence to sexual difference.

Doubling subjectivity would mean a double truth, and a double world. It would mean a different sort of poetic dwelling, a different way of speaking, a dialogical way which would take into account both man and woman's way of speaking and this would initiate, perhaps, a different poetics of architecture. Such a poetry would not conform to the traditional Western logic or scientific thinking that Heidegger's criticises but neither would it conform to Heidegger's 'thinking', nor to the valorisation of poets such as Rilke, Trakl or Hölderlin. These, Irigaray writes, lack the energy of desire shared by two subjects and the energy for getting beyond the dereliction linked to death and solitude (see *Why Different?*, 133).

To work with the criticisms suggested by Irigaray's readings of Heidegger, provides the possibility of a different sort of conception of Things, a different 'rift' or open 'between' (for the four-fold) and a different *Gestalt*. It offers the possibility of creating a double 'world' or truth. To conceive Being as two, as the Being of man and the Being of woman, shifts and splits the layout and limit of a world in which living, dwelling or thinking takes place (136). Moreover, the exchange between these two subjectivities creates a third language, which unfolds between two modes of speaking; a language we still do not know, and is yet to be created (131). This is where I want to place thinking 'love' and architecture.

The event of the 'Thing' refuses the female wholly other, Irigaray argues. The location that is the thing similarly refuses a female wholly other, where 'cultivating' or 'letting-be' presumes that nothing remains outside. Irigaray's question in *The Forgetting of Air* is directed to what man is, before the Being of man already is? Before he dwells in language, before he listens to, and responds to language and the world which is his. Irigaray asks whether there a place for the feminine that is not pre-apprehended by language, something he assimilates to disclose the free space. She asks, why is there the need for a clearing, a free space opened up where authentic existence becomes possible. Where Heidegger questions the danger of modern technological or scientific thinking for man's habitation, Irigaray argues, he nevertheless remains within a patriarchal perspective. Something happens to desire in Heidegger's work, where it presumes that: 'nothing can come about unexpectedly outside the space-time that is already determined by and for the Being of man' (*The Forgetting of Air*, 25). Where the other constitutes the possibility of existence for him. Irigaray asks of Heidegger what sort of desire motivates his search, his path towards more authentic existence, and if a different sort of desire could be thought. The question arises of what sort of thinking building would locate and cultivate an intersubjective space of breath and love?

The difficulty I have with this question is its need for dialogue. Irigaray's writing and dialogical method imply a criticism of projects inspired by Heidegger's work but also of a tradition that includes the work of Derrida. Thinking architecture with sexual difference, if we were to take on Irigaray's project, requires the re-conceptualisation of *eros* or of our love stories, and of the patriarchal family within the intimate space of the home and within societal structures. Without this creative project a feminine mode of being two cannot be made tangible. Feminism in architecture is in a certain predicament about its future, with respect to a feminist practice, but perhaps women architects are more aware of their position, to disrupt and modify architectural design. They are more aware of the potential they have to change the context in which women live and to challenge the foundations of architectural design. There is a sense in Irigaray's work that this would have to be a collective project, and that her work is incitement to others to make plans and concrete proposals. Perhaps there is a certain experimental architecture that would study the expectations of women that as yet have no means of expression. A thinking architecture that stirs things up, a fluid reality that is constantly flowing, constantly transforming. On the one hand, a definitive language of words and, on the other, that of gestures, and between these two the indication of silence and a thinking that is for the most part only breathing. This would be the remaking of immanence and transcendence in touch with the things themselves and a place of love between two, a locus of sexual difference, constructed in a moment of wonder, illuminated by a different light, announced by the intertwining kiss of a wedding, of the spiritual and the flesh, and first of all of body and words.

ANDREA WHEELER
The University of Nottingham

NOTE

1 See Mary McLoed, 'Everyday and Other Spaces' (in *Architecture and Feminism*, 1–38), May Landesberg and Lisa Quatrale, 'See Angel Touch' (in *Architecture and Feminism*, 60–72), Venessa Chase, 'Edith Wharton, The Decoration of Houses in Turn-of-the-Century America' (in *Architecture and Feminism*, 130–161), Mark Wigley, 'Untitled: The Housing of Gender' (in *Sexuality and Space*, 327–89), Andrea Kahn 'Overlooking: A Look at How to Look at Site or . . . site as discrete object of desire' (in *Desiring Practices*, 174–85), Elizabeth Grosz, 'Women, *Chora*, Dwelling' (in *Any*, 24), Katerina Rüedi, 'The Architect: Commodity and Seller in One' (in *Desiring Practices*, 234–46).

BIBLIOGRAPHY

Chanter, Tina, *The Ethics of Eros*, London, Routledge, 1995.

Cheah, Pheng and Elizabeth Grosz, 'The Future of Sexual Difference, An Interview with Judith Butler and Drucilla Cornell', *Diacritics* (Special Issue), Spring 1998, 28: 1, 19–42.

Coleman, Debra, Elizabeth Danze and Carol Henderson, editors, *Architecture and Feminism*, New York, Princeton Architectural Press, 1996.

Duncan McCorquodale, Katerina Rüedi and Sarah Wiggleswade, *Desiring Practices*, Black Dog Publishing, 1996.

Grosz, Elizabeth, 'Women, *Chora*, Dwelling' in *Any, Architecture and the Feminism, Mop Up Work*, 1: 4, 1994.

Heidegger, Martin, 'Building, Dwelling, Thinking', in *Poetry, Language, Thought*, New York, Harper and Row Publishers Inc., 1971, 145–161, translated by Albert Hofstadter from the German 'Bauen Wohnen Denken' in *Vorträge und Aufsätze*, Pfullingen, Neske, 1954.

Heidegger, Martin, 'The Origin of the Work of Art' in *Poetry, Language, Thought*, 15–89. First published as *Der Ursprung des Kunstwerkes*, Universal-Bibliothek Nr. 8446/47, Stuttgart, Reclam, 1960.

Heidegger, Martin, *Zollikon Seminars. 1959–1969, Protocols— Conversations— Letters*, edited by Medard Boss, Evanston, Illinois, Northweston University Press, 2000, translated by Franz Mayr and Richard Askay, from the German *Zollikoner Seminare, Protokolle— Gespräche— Briefe*, Herausgegeben von Medard Boss, Frankfurt am Main, Vittorio Klostermann, GmbH, 1987.

Irigaray, Luce, *The Age of Breath*, Rüsselsheim, Germany, Göttert Verlag Christel, 1999, translated from the French by Katja van de Rakt, Staci von Boekman and Luce Irigaray.

Irigaray, Luce, *Being Two, How Many Eyes Have We?*, Rüsselsheim, Germany, Göttert Verlag Christel, 2000, translated into English by Luce Irigaray with Catherine Busson and Jim Moony (text reprinted in this publication).

Irigaray, Luce, 'Comment habiter durablement ensemble?' a lecture at the Architectural Association, London, November 2000, translated from the French by Alison Martin, Maria Bailey and Luce Irigaray, forthcoming publication as 'How to Live Together in a Lasting Way?' in the second edition of Neil Leach, *Rethinking Architecture*.

Irigaray, Luce, *Democracy Begins Between Two*, London-New York, Athlone-Routledge, 2000, translated by Kirsteen Anderson from the Italian *La democrazia comincia a due*, Torino, Bollati Boringhieri, 1994.

Irigaray, Luce, *The Forgetting of Air, In Martin Heidegger*, London-Austin, Athlone-University of Texas Press, 1999, translated by Mary Beth Mader from the French *L'oubli de l'air, Chez Martin Heidegger*, Paris, Editions de Minuit, 1983.

Irigaray, Luce, *I Love To You, Sketch for a Felicity within History*, New York and London, Routledge, 1996, translated by Alison Martin from the French *J'aime à toi*, Paris, Grasset, 1992.

Irigaray, Luce, 'Où et comment habiter?', *Cahiers du Grif*, 24, March 1983.

Irigaray, Luce, *Sexes and Geneologies*, New York, Columbia University Press, 1987, translated by Gillian C. Gill, from the French *Sexes et Parentés*, Paris, Editions de Minuit, 1987.

Irigaray, Luce, *Thinking The Difference, For a Peaceful Revolution*, London-New York, Athlone-Routledge, 1995, translated by Karin Montin from the French *Le temps de la différence, Pour une révolution pacifique*, Librairie Générale Française, 1989.

Irigaray, Luce, *To Be Two*, London-New York, Athlone-Routledge, 2000, translated by Monique M. Rhodes and Marco F. Cocito-Monoc from the Italian *Essere Due*, Turin, Bollati Boringhieri, 1994.

Irigaray, Luce, *Why Different? A Culture of Two Subjects*, edited by Luce Irigaray and Sylvère Lotringer, translated by Camille Collins, Peter Caravetta, Heidi Bostic and Stephen Pluhacek, New York, *Semiotext(e)*, 2000.

Krell, David Farell, *Archeticture: Ecstasies of Space, Time and the Human Body*, New York, State University of New York Press, 1997.

Rendell, Jane, Iain Borden and Barbara Penner, editors, *Gender, Space and Architecture*, London, Routledge, 2000.

Whitford, Margaret, *Luce Irigaray, Philosophy in the Feminine*, London-New York, Routledge, 1991.

Luce Irigaray's questions

I appreciated Andrea Wheeler's paper and I thank her for it. I would first explain that I have never designated myself or my work as 'feminist'. I do not very much like words that end in '-ism' or '-ist'. In my opinion, they are too dogmatic or formalist. I have, rather, talked about the liberation of women or, more generally, about the liberation of humanity, that is to say, of the human as such.

The most important intention of my work — beginning with *Speculum* — is to try to make possible a culture of two subjects, which is a culture where a part of humanity will no longer remain submitted to the other. And that, finally, means a culture wherein humans can overcome their animal instincts or primitive attractions through love, through words, through dialogues, cultivating the difference between men and women.

There are many misunderstandings about the real intention of my work. Certainly because it opens a new age of culture, a new era of History, it meets with much resistance. As a great philosopher said, sometimes it would be necessary to discover the importance of a thought in the opposition it arouses. These words have been, are still, very precious and comforting for me.

I will now add this: Women have to become who they are. That is, they must not claim the right to become men or to become neutral, but rather strive to become themselves with responsibility to themselves, to the world, to the other(s), either same or different. I hope that feminism will assume its part in order to accomplish this becoming-woman of the woman, and thus to reach a culture in which masculine and feminine values will really be promoted and shared. This would be the way to provide a home for woman inside and outside the traditional family home.

I would also explain, on the occasion of Andrea Wheeler's paper, that the use of mimicry on my part was very strategic and selective. I do not understand very well why it encounters such success. Perhaps because mimicry corresponds to a traditional behaviour of women in our past culture. I have suggested that mimicry could serve in a strategic way as a joke to overcome a past status, but certainly not as a new way of becoming woman. Mimicry is a behaviour of a slave, of someone who is dominated. It does not correspond to an affirmation of an identity of one's own.

Now, two other questions that are perhaps more decisive for the work of Andrea Wheeler:

— Heidegger talked about the bridge as the means to create, to open space. In my text that you know, 'How Can We Live Together in a Lasting Way?' — I could say, 'How can we dwell together?' — , I recall that attraction or desire are in fact bridges between man and woman. They open a space between them. More generally, they create space in our life. The question is: How can we maintain attraction and desire? How can we preserve the place opened between us and build this space? You know that this is an important aspect of my work. Do you have some suggestions about that?

— Why is it better to 'make visible' than to 'make touchful' in building? We need, so to speak, at least three rooms in order to live together, to dwell together — her room, his room, and the room opened by desire between them: a third room. It is necessary to try to partly materialize, I have not said to always render visible, the three rooms. The third room can be created, conserved and built also by a withdrawing of each one in their own room, their own dwelling. Certainly this is not enough, but it is very important in order to open or reopen space.

— A final question: You said 'before all body and words'. I would ask you: Before or after? And how will you relate the before and the after?

Andrea Wheeler's response

Thank you for allowing me some time to respond to your question: How can we build bridges between two, or how can we sustain desire between two? Heidegger uses the bridge in 'Building, Dwelling, Thinking' to illustrate how building belongs to dwelling and 'what building understood by way of the nature of dwelling really *is*' (152, Heidegger's italics). The 'bridge' does not simply connect banks already there, the banks emerge as banks, as the bridge crosses the stream (153). Similarly Heidegger's mode of existence, *Da-Sein*, stands out, ahead of itself, inhabiting the possibilities that come toward it (see David Farell Krell, *Archeticture*, 74). *Da-Sein*, is a comportment to, consisting of ' "pure" invisible intangible capacities for receiving-perceiving what it encounters and what addresses it', holding open a domain, 'to receive-perceive the significance of the things that are given to it and that address it by virtue of its own "clearing" ' (*Zollikon Seminars*, 4). For women to find themselves in their own way, to emerge as women, you suggest, however, we have to question both the gesture that constructs the 'bridge', and the nature of the 'clearing', gathered into the constitution of *Da-Sein*. Human existence is suspended between two, but Heidegger recognizes neither the *from which* or the *of what* his capacities for receiving-perceiving are made, the feminine 'other', towards which the bridge would convey, nor a mode of comportment or being-two he could cultivate in love. In part outside Heidegger's thought is a free energy not determined by the living being that he or she is from birth, nor by language, *women* understand, but living absolute difference, or being-two evades Heidegger, and a tradition of male philosophers influenced by his work. You suggest that cultivating perception, attentive to qualities both of what or who is perceived, to the invisible in the who or what, and the invisibility of the one who perceives, corresponds more to a feminine 'to be' or being-two. In *The Age of Breath*, cultivating 'breath', also corresponds to one mode of woman's 'to be' arousing a sort of energy and receptivity that similarly cannot be mastered. Thinking dwelling in architecture as an 'hospitality given to the other as other not only in one's own country, in one's own home but also in oneself—in one's own body, and in one's own breath, one's own mind or soul' (*Being-Two, How Many Eyes Have We?*, 14e) would have to be a collective project for women, a making with, so as to sustain the meaning of two. Perhaps thinking dwelling as a co-existence could be imagined as two intertwining 'bridges', and a third place of hospitality, of life and 'love' between. However, first of all it must be a matter of finding an autonomous existence, and privacy at the same time as maintaining correspondence to develop collective meaning.

Light, Colour and Sound in Cinema

In this paper I would like to introduce the signifying potentialities that an Irigarayan sense of fluids offers for inscriptions of femininity within the materiality of the cinematic medium. I am not suggesting that we track a visual register of fluids, nor excavate a perceptual pheno-menology of fluids from beneath a Metzian understanding of narrative cinema as semiotic paradigm, but that the conjunctures and dislocations that permeate the multiple layers of cinematic representation, offer new signifying potentialities for the inscription of fluid femininity.

A history of mainstream Western cinema reveals that inscriptions of feminine subjectivity have been proscribed from direct representation at the level of the narrative. Films such as *Marnie* (Hitchcock, 1964), *Don't Look Now* (Nicholas Roeg, 1973) and *Short Cuts* (Robert Altman, 1993) revolve around the effects of dysfunctional relationships between mothers and daughters, and retain their interactions within a language of dysfunction, mysticism and hysteria. Kept from direct representation, the intricacies of the relations between mothers and daughters, as a corpus of feminine subjectivities, are drawn into a symbolic and destructive metaphorics of fluids.[1] This metaphorics of fluids differs from an Irigarayan sense of the fluid femininity that would permeate these structures of representation and open new possibilities for the inscription of feminine subjectivity.

Feminist film theorists, such as Laura Mulvey and Mary Anne Doane, have critiqued both the structure of film spectatorship and the cinematic apparatus as a predominantly visual medium through which we can track processes that echo a psychoanalytic concept of subjectivity. Feminist studies have theorized sexual difference through issues of spectatorship and the 'gaze' and, in Kaja Silverman's *The Acoustic Mirror*, through the aural elements which affect the viewer's reception of a filmic event. The materiality of the cinematic medium is one of multiple layers which interact to form a series of images and sounds through light, colour, composition, utterances, musical notes and so on. Conjunctures and dislocations in the interactions of these filmic elements can be considered to operate similarly to the processes of condensation and displacement that are at work in dreams (see Sandy Flitterman Lewis, 'Surrealist Cinema: Politics, History, and the Language of Dreams'). As feminist film theory has tracked the similarities of psychic structures, cinematic apparatus and issues of film spectatorship, then the operation of repression, in the processes of condensation and displacement, similarly allow us to trace the unprocessed affect of material that is proscribed from the language of representation.[2] In sequences of film where the constituent elements of cinematic representation resist the projected illusion, then the structure of phallocentricism is questioned.

I will elaborate this discourse through a detailed reading of short cinematic sequences from Jane Campion's 1996 film, *The Portrait of a Lady*. The narrative of this film moves through a backstitching of events and conversations that are continually reconsidered through the fluctuating impositions of familial and social expectations. The character of Isabel is drawn through a narrative of moral and visual concealment. The psychic and somatic effects of these proscriptive intrusions can be traced through moments in which the material elements of the film operate in excess of the narrative. I am suggesting that a fluid movement can be traced, permeating the complex inter-actions of the material elements of cinema to resist the phallocentric proscriptions of representation. In *The Portrait of a Lady*, possibilities for the inscription of feminine subjectivity are opened up by a movement that can be traced between constituent elements which in moments of dislocation exceed and permeate the cinematic illusion as a whole. A detailed analysis of *The Portrait of a Lady* allows us to track, within the established symbolism of light and dark, and the trope of hands, touching and closeness, a trace of fluids which press upon the screen of representation. Campion's use of slow motion and accelerated sequences dislocates the materiality of cinematic elements of light, sound and colour from the symbolic forms they have been attributed. Through this process the surface, of the cinematic illusion these elements would otherwise collude to reflect, resonates and refracts the film's narrative to register a trace of fluid. This fluid movement presses upon the surface tension representation and operates in excess of narrative structures to trace the resonance of feminine subjectivity which moves against, but is irreducible to, the proscriptions of the symbolic. In *The Portrait of a Lady* 'mother' is not represented as a character located within a human form, but through the multitude of daughters in their different roles and relationships to each other, the corporeal and the sensate, which can be traced through their fluid resonance within the material elements of the film.

Luce Irigaray elucidates a sense of fluid movements that permeate and resist, but are irreducible to the phallocentric structures of representation. Through two very different texts, 'The "Mechanics" of Fluids' and 'The Invisible of the Flesh', she evokes a sense of fluids that operates within and in excess of visual and linguistic proscriptions of subjectivity (see *This Sex Which Is Not One*, 106–18, and *An Ethics of Sexual Difference*, 151–84). Within this paper I will make a detailed study of the materiality of the cinematic medium to trace a register which operates in excess of the viewer's identification with both narrative and character to open out new signifying potentialities for inscriptions of femininity and desire. This register can initially be understood through the movements that are elicited as the conjunctures and interactions of the material elements of film slough the meanings that had been accumulated and established through the semiotic structure of the film's narrative. These fluids are not an excess which is defined in relation to, and so by, the phallocentricism of representation but operate as a sensile register of a different relation within, and in excess of, language. These fluids are dislocated within established signifying chains as a trace of pre-sensate existence that continually touches upon the invisible of female sexuality through the brushing together of vaginal lips. This *continual touching upon* evokes a movement of fluids which cannot be described as a presence, which would imply a dichotomy with absence, and so mark movement in units through a chronology of time, but is the pressing of another temporality which operates within and in excess of the divisions and severance of the visible field.

A heuristic viewing of *The Portrait of a Lady* reveals the complex development of familiar iconography, such as that of light and shadow reflecting the binds and prohibitions of a more spiritual freedom and entrapment. The signification of this visual dichotomy is established through Campion's manipulation of chiaroscuro at the level of image and composition. She establishes a metaphorical theme which her use of inter-cut black and white and slow motion sequences deliberately resists by drawing attention to the act of looking within the film's narrative. This intervention within the voyeurism that is inherent in the cinematic apparatus also elucidates the psychical structures of, what is traditionally seen as, the viewer's predominantly visual identification with the screen image. In this case Campion's editing manipulates the materiality of the film to disturb its narrative illusion in a way that allows us to trace another register which operates within, and in excess of, cinematic representation.

Through the character of Isabel the repetition of this imagery reflects the social, familial and contractual influence of all that she should do, just as the slithers and patterns within the contrasting intensities of light reveal her captured figure, an object, through the outline of her form. The figurative forms of the characters within the film are displaced through each draining or replenishing of colour. Colours bleed and resonate within, and in excess of, the monochromatic and colour sequences and their differences, registering also a tainted shadow, a residue of transient colour. These fluctuations and alterations affect the proximity of sensation within the spectator to the materiality of the film. This proximity is established as the material elements of the film echo those that may be familiar within the viewer's body; the response of eyes left warm, engorged with blood, their vision refracted through tears; a blush which drains embarrassment slowly. Sequences in which the materiality of the cinematic medium resists the ideologies of touching and sight, that are prioritized through the narrative, evoke the physiological implications of seeing; for example the turn of a head, tiring of looking, or eyes washed with the sensation of tears.

The contrasts of light and dark which extend throughout the film construct indiscriminate boundaries that encompass, through the inscription of divisions, architecture, *couture*, landscape and human form. We hear Isabel calling to another, who is caught by her father's insistence in the shadow of his house. Beneath the faint shadow cast of iron railings, we see the circuitous light of a jack o' lantern clasp and bind her visible form in moments of illumination; catching and dissolving into the monochromatic pattern of her dress. As the film's narrative progresses other movements are made; a sense and touch that is hers permeates the elements that have traced the movements and appearance of her form. The trace and warmth of blood blooms through Isabel's speech to cloud and disperse light, disturbing the scopophilic elements of cinematic representation. As the film image shudders and turns through its fluorescence, the invisible of her body, these traces of sensile corporeality, disturb the limitations of form, and problematize the influence of a communication that is bound within the structure of language.

In 'The Invisible of the Flesh', Luce Irigaray tells us that:

Something would always sing 'behind' words, like the trace of the resistance of another that is irreducible to myself, that would require the unceasing practice of openness between signs. Letting flesh appear between the sign and the sign. Dehiscence of the seer in the visible and of the visible in the seer which is insurmountable between these two 'signs': masculine and feminine, living signs that, as seer and visible, will never see each other. That in which their differences consist is experienced in touch but is never 'seen'. Not even in the meeting of their flesh. Flesh, the flesh of each one is not substitutable for the other. (*An Ethics of Sexual Difference*, 167)

Within the narrative of the film we hear a conversation in which two friends, eliciting plans, are interrupted by the words that tell of the illness of another, of this someone to be near this one last time. Isabel's cousin and her friend wait, concerned for the journey, his uncle, and the coy initiatives of another. Agitated, his fingers drum invariable notes to quickly mark, as distance, the time he waits. The distant crackle of his actions beneath the form of the words they speak is marked in the accompaniment of its visible source: a glass and a hand now the visual echo of a repeated sound, of a wasp kept close by in the bell of an upturned glass. And so quickly we find Isabel waiting in the daylight frame of a window, as a perpetual dysrythmia of rain falls and traces the border of its frozen glassed reflection. Her footsteps turn in impatient response to the sounds of another, still not calling her, from the depths of the house. Isabel weaves across the camera's frame, to and from sight, to be found by a warp of banisters threaded through with light. In quiet conversation with the sounds she traces within her environment, her gestures perform the dilemma, forgotten of words, drawing her through the swell and resound of music, again toward the reflection of her seen image. Each step she makes down a scale of stairs marks the time of her movements through the volume of her destination. Her hand, which is swathed in cloth and held in touch from vision, disperses the boundaries of this reflection through her response to this music. As she moves through the curiosity of hesitation, light reaches to cover the texture of her hand, moulding the visual and aural elements of the materiality of film into form, drawing division back into representation.

In *Speculum*, Luce Irigaray's re-reading of the discourse of 'Plato's Cave' traces the development of a language which specularizes an artificial beginning: 'This set up in which the hystera is reversed fuels the confusion between a certain origin defying representation and the daylight, the good clear light of representation' (259). This privileging of light in Western philosophical discourse aligns the specular with the initiation of perception in a move that sublimates the corporeal trace of intrauterine existence from a phallocentric concept of visible flesh. However, through the writings of Luce Irigaray, we are now able to discuss possibilities offered for inscriptions of feminine desires which permeate the phallocentric and scopophilic structures of severance, division and reversibility. In 'The Invisible of the Flesh' Luce Irigaray describes intrauterine existence as within a seer and a subject, who touches and senses another before they enter the visible world, whose beginnings are pre-sensate and so can be considered to permeate the subsequent, proscriptive structures of known sensations and emotion:

Colour resuscitates in me all of that prior life, the preconceptual, preobjective, presubjective, this ground of the visible where seeing and seen are not yet distinguished, where they reflect each other without any position having been established between them. Colour bathes my gaze, sees it, perceives it more or less well, changes it in its visibility, but can never delimit it, create it, bend it to its decisions. Colour constitutes a given that escapes from the subjective realm and that still and always immerses the subject in an invisible sojourn of the visible, a sojourn that cannot be mastered: whether infernal or celestial, preceding or following a determinate incarnation into subject-object duality. This colour, the correlative of my vision, of vision, far from being able to yield to my decisions, obliges me to see. (156)

As Isabel moves across the screen her progression, reflecting the speed of the film, is sometimes slowed. Such slow-motion sequences are disquieting to the viewer in their subtle differences from the slow turn of a camera across people moving at an un-tampered speed. We see Isabel walk towards the house, passing companions resting in the garden; she greets a dog who is begging for attention, when the camera slows to re-trace, re-frame, her path through the viscous gaze of her cousin. As she heeds his gaze, her breathing drawn out, slowly unfurling into iced air, the time to look is counteracted by the effects of looking. The editing of this sequence is echoed in others throughout the film to track the corporeal and sensate affects that operate within a visible world. As these sequences disturb the film's narrative progression, so they also interrupt the cinematic illusion of 'self-generation' (see Flitterman Lewis) and question the structures of phallocentric spectatorship.

Luce Irigaray's evocation of archaic colour and fluids disrupts the solipsistic reversibility of Merleau-Ponty's descriptions of flesh, by recalling the forgotten dilemma of a language and representation that are inscribed and perpetuated by solipsistic reversibility. This phenomenon of colour is irreducible to its constituent elements or the dysrythmia of their meetings within the visible. Luce Irigaray invokes colour as a trace of archaic fluids that permeates the 'touch' of light in the visible. Colour is not a property of light nor the material ground that allows us to see, and colour can only be discerned within simultaneous relation to other colours, across the successive reflection of light. Luce Irigaray proposes that 'Red, any colour, is more in the mode of *participation* than of the solitary emergence of the concept' (*An Ethics of Sexual Difference*, 158).

In a room of sickly silence our sight is held within a hover of figures and then drawn toward the locus of their gaze. Isabel leans close to a figure swaddled in a shroud of linen, close to his open eyes and the gape of his mouth which breathes the refusal of words. A residue of words is mouthed in indecipherable form and so emitted in a hush of breath under a suffocating blue light. The inhalation and exhalation of shared space, of viscous air heavy with the disintegration of matter. Colour participates invoking the solitude of a visible world, transient within the choke and grasp of words, their response, the saturation of fluids seeping through the seams of language. Breathing the condensation of touch.

Within the context of this film, the gradual accumulation of signification, through the visual and aural elements that associate the representation of hands with touch leads to a sequence in which the marble effigy of a child's hand questions the retrospective signification its appearance invokes. The brutal shortness of this sequence dislocates the sensuousness, which like images have signified, from the represented form of a hand. This sequence is saturated with the warmth of longing and loss. Isabel's hands trace those of the child, echoing their gesture through the brush of tears and melancholy drift of sound. The blue shudder of this parenthesis is quickly lost in the surrounding film.

Luce Irigaray's essay 'The "Mechanics" of Fluids' elucidates:

Fluid — like that other, inside/outside of philosophical discourse — is, by nature, unstable. Unless it is subordinated to geometricism, or (?) idealized (. . .) Woman never speaks the same way. What she emits is flowing, fluctuating. *Blurring*. And she is not listened to, unless proper meaning (meaning of the proper) is lost. Whence the resistances to that voice that overflows the 'subject'. Which the 'subject' then congeals, freezes, in its categories until it paralyzes the voice in its flow. (*This Sex Which Is Not One*, 112)

Within the body of the film the intertwining elements, of light, colour and sound, are more constituent than constituted, an echo of the subject's misrecognition of autonomy, that is later to be reflected as symmetry imagined of the mirror image (see Silverman).

These constituent elements are imagined through symmetry with the social of the text, to accumulate in the illusion of a whole and stable representation. Here fluids are idealized, imaged, fixed and congealed into words that can be heard and 'understood' but which proscribe the dysrythmic resonance of her voice. These are words through which her meaning does not make sense. However, in some cinematic sequences the structure of this symmetry is revealed as the interrelations of constituent elements effect a movement that leaches meaning from the stability of the symbolic. Luce Irigaray elaborates this discourse as the questioning of this system's narcissism by pressing upon the scopophilic processes of metaphor. These moments trace the affect of the invisible of the flesh, as that which pre-dates what is sensible of the visible world. The fluid permeations of this dysrythmic resonance cannot be substituted, or reflected through the metaphoric structures of phallic language. The invisible of this flesh is irreversible with what is sensible in the realm of the gaze.

Through the narrative we hear that Isabel lost an infant boy almost two years ago, an implication which carries across the cut of the film to Isabel cradling the marble effigy of a young child's hand. The caress of her fingers impart a warmth he cannot hold and articulate a conversation they cannot make: her child, her own hand, as a child, and her mother's attentive touch in memory of comfort. This short sequence of film recalls through its disturbance of the narrative, all that we have seen. In the unspoken conversation of female genealogies the potential suffocation of being watched is rendered in the harsh cuts and binds of the film. The structures of looking and its effects upon the sensuous histories of our bodies resonate through the material elements of this film.

The iconography of hands as representative of the sensations and veracity of touch is questioned throughout *The Portrait of a Lady*. We cannot speak of 'touching' a film but through an Irigarayan understanding of fluid permeability, as feminine pleasure, a resonance or trace of a history of sensations may be evoked within, and in excess of, the visible field. Thus we may find that, through another sequence of the film, the ambiguity and curiosity of what is unannounced is imparted to resist and permeate the words that forbid her from being close to the loss of her friend. The caress of his hand, once the image of affection, now marks his manipulation. The sensations of a hand brushed with the curve of her tears, which also touch, are distinct from the communication of his intent. The dissolve of tears, diffuse but not diluted, is unfixed and irreducible to his meaning. Her reflection is distorted, through warmth and evaporation from the surface tension of tears, and is diffused across the cinema screen. This fluid resonance is not dependent on the signification that surrounds its manifestation as it reveals in its movement the construction of illusions in representation. As this resonance disturbs the screen on which representation depends it permeates both the silence and sound that speak in division.

Aligned with the camera's sight, we turn as our gaze follows Isabel's journey. Drawn through the circuitous movements of a dance, we revolve though the skirted sweep of a tree, turning to heed in sight the sound of another. Snow flakes fall, turning in kaleidoscopic prisms of light to the Earth, spinning revolutions of the sun. The pulse of her blood turns through eyes engorged with its motion to press tears from the weight of expression. This gestural conversation seeps through the seams of a self defined by the visual binds of form as a fluid resonance within multiple layers of time and movement to permeate and distort the surface tension of representation. As the speed of the film slows within the narrative it resonates and refracts the image reflected of its constituent elements. Breathless, her body wrought by a language that is not hers, another relation still resonates within it. Her hand clasps the door as she turns, the hem of her skirts flaying ice from the solidity of the ground. Locked or unopened, the corporeality of the film touches upon the fluidity of feminine desire.

This sense of fluids is not a property of the cinematic medium but operates as the trace of a history of the sensuous that permeates and resists the imposition of the metaphors of phallocentric language. These fluids are not constituted by the multiple layers of representation within film, neither are these layers entirely constituent of representation as elements within the materiality of cinematic representation. However, within some short cinematic sequences, dislocations within the corporeality of film and its narrative representations, trace a resonance of fluids that is 'more in the mode of participation', as a trace of the interrelations, the conjunctures and dislocations, of mothers and daughters, as a site of sensate and subjective female genealogies (see Luce Irigaray, *An Ethics of Sexual Difference*, 158). Fluids, with this sense of permeation, offer signifying potentialities for inscriptions of feminine identity within the medium of film.

LIZ WATKINS
University of Leeds

NOTES

1 By using the term a 'metaphorics of fluids', I am referring to the trope in Western culture that aligns woman/water/death and sexual dysfunction. Cultural representations of women are surrounded by imagery of water, tears, abject bodily fluids, blood, drowning, suffocation and so on. These themes are used to 'legitimize' the silencing and display of women as objects to be looked at and as a site of exchange within patriarchal society, to exact retribution for her body that is different to their One. Examples can be drawn from a proliferation of sources such as portrayals in film, theatre, art, literature and many contemporary advertisements and promotional videos for popular music. The following are but a few examples: Ophelia, the biblical story of Susannah and the Elders and the many paintings of this scene, the shower scene in Hitchcock's *Psycho* (1960), the figure of the drowned mother in Charles Laughton's *The Night of the Hunter* (1955) and the video for Kylie Minogue's *Where the Wild Roses Grow*.

2 The psychoanalytic terms 'condensation' and 'displacement' are used by Freud in *The Interpretation of Dreams*. Sandy Flitterman Lewis refers to 'the logic of dreams' in her critique of cinema, in 'Surrealist Cinema: Politics, History and the Language of Dreams', 442–3.

BIBLIOGRAPHY

Doane, Mary Anne, 'Technology's Body, Cinematic Vision in Modernity', *Differences*, 5:2, Summer 1993, 1–23.

Flitterman Lewis, Sandy, 'Surrealist Cinema: Politics, History, and the Language of Dreams', *American Imago*, 50:4, 1993, 441–56.

Freud, Sigmund, *The Interpretation of Dreams*, translated by James Strachey, London, Penguin Books, 1991 (English translation first published in *The Standard Edition of the Complete Psychological Works of Sigmund Freud*, Volumes IV and V, London, Hogarth Press, 1953).

Irigaray, Luce, *An Ethics of Sexual Difference*, London-New York, Athlone-Cornell University Press, 1993, translated by Carolyn Burke and Gillian C. Gill from the French *Ethique de la différence sexuelle*, Paris, Editions de Minuit, 1984.

Irigaray, Luce, *This Sex Which Is Not One*, New York, Cornell University Press, 1985, translated by Catherine Porter with Carolyn Burke from the French *Ce sexe qui n'en est pas un*, Paris, Editions de Minuit, 1977.

Irigaray, Luce, *Speculum*, New York, Cornell University Press, 1985, translated by Gillian C. Gill from the French *Speculum*, Paris, Editions de Minuit, 1974.

Merleau-Ponty, Maurice, *The Visible and the Invisible*, Illinois, Northwestern University Press, 2000, edited by Claude Lefort, translated by Alphonso Lingis from the French *Le visible et l'invisible*, Paris, Gallimard, 1964.

Mulvey, Laura, *Visual and Other Pleasures*, London, Macmillan, 1989.

Silverman, Kaja, *The Acoustic Mirror*, Bloomington and Indianapolis, Indiana University Press, 1988.

Luce Irigaray's questions

Why must the feminine, or feminine genealogy, manifest themselves through a dislocation which allows fluids to permeate the whole of a phallocratic, and more generally male, representation? Why would it not be possible for the woman to interrogate the structure of a masculine culture from outside in order to liberate herself from her incarceration in it and thus to become capable of constructing her own culture? I am afraid that, remaining only in excess with respect to a masculine tradition, the feminine will continue to be a reserve for the same culture, a culture with a unique subject.

Furthermore, such a strategy is partly based on aggression, destruction of the masculine world. It is another manner of staying in this world, that is founded against the maternal or matricial beginning, without reaching a harmonious relation with feminine subjectivity. A conflict, a war which takes place inside the masculine world cannot allow women to cultivate their own subjectivity.

Affirming another subjectivity as a whole and trying to discover or create means of holding dialogues and of succeeding in exchanges with man, men, seems to me a better way for women's liberation.

In such a perspective, is it not preferable to preserve an economy of fluids as specific to a feminine identity? For woman, between women — but also between mother and son —, fluids are very present: as blood, as milk, but also and perhaps above all as permeability of flowings through mucous. Perhaps the mother-daughter relation shows a complicity with fluids, but according to me this is because they are women rather than because they are mother and daughter. In the prenatal sojourn it is not permeability but communication thanks to blood. Permeability is inside of each woman and belongs to her sexuality. But it is possible that this one is not yet completely liberated from a primitive relation with the mother.

I am asking myself these questions, and I share them with you. I have appreciated the work you did to integrate cinematic discourse in a text and I was happy to find in your paper citations of certain of my texts that are too little evoked. It was particularly interesting to confront their perspective with more recent texts that I have written: 'Being Two, How Many Eyes Have We?' and 'Dipingere l'invisible', a reading of Maurice Merleau-Ponty's *L'Oeil et l'esprit*.

I would like to put to you this question: Why dislocate the view, the visible rather than changing the way of looking at: the world, the other? I know that you are trying to realize something of this kind. But why conserve a traditional horizon in order to do that and not create another, listening differently to yourself? I could also say: Why ask discourse to fragment or change what is given to see, or ask images to break into a narrative discourse, instead of recognizing that there are two discourses and two ways of looking at: a masculine way and a feminine way?

Liz Watkins' response

May I thank you for your question and the opportunity to reply. I have found that film theorists, such as Joan Copjec, have aligned Foucault's discourse on the eye with Lacan's theories on the gaze in a move which postulated issues of spectatorship as ocularcentric. However, I have understood Lacan's 1963 work, *The Four Fundamental Concepts of Psychoanalysis*, to elicit the gaze as *objet 'a'* and as a psychic trace of a gap that fuses the register of vision with desire. This gaze does not seem to me to be a simple visual perception, but something in the visible field that is irreducible to sight. In my essay, I refer to the feminist film theories of spectatorship: viewer identification and the cinematic apparatus have allowed us to trace inscriptions of subjectivity through the cinematic medium. Thus without positing cinematic representation as ocularcentric, nor conserving the traditional specularization of identity, it is possible to trace a register of feminine subjectivity through the pathways of vision. My work does not absolutely distinguish between the masculine and feminine, but traces a fluid femininity which permeates the visual structures of representation and is, in a way, a supplementary register within film. The sense of fluid permeability which you evoke in your earlier works (*This Sex Which Is Not One* and *An Ethics of Sexual Difference*) allows us to discern, not the vision of feminine subjectivity in the cinematic medium, but a femininity which moves against, but is irreducible to the symbolic ordering of it.

Feminine Enunciation
in Women's Cinema

The question of the feminine has long dominated critical approaches to cinema, with theorists concerning themselves with issues of representation, spectatorship and authorship. Central to discussions of female authorship in the field of film studies is the role of cinematic enunciation. Enunciation in the cinema defines the spectator as a textual construct whose function is understood as a crucial element of the cinematic process and the production of meaning through exchange. The cinematic text bears meaning only in the context of it being received: in other words, cinematic enunciation depends for its validity on the spectator believing that the fantasies relayed on-screen are products of their own desire. This, in turn, depends upon the suppression of marks of enunciation within the (classical mainstream) text: the camera remains invisible throughout and attention is not drawn to its presence. This effect of this is to mystify the production of meaning. Christian Metz (*Psychoanalysis and the Imaginary Signifier*) suggests that mainstream cinematic narrative is story/history that is set in the past and that refuses an articulation of perspectives emanating from the discursive position of exchange between the first and second persons. He draws a distinction between *discours* and *histoire*[1] in order to situate enunciation in the cinema as structured through the third person.[2] Drawing on the work of Luce Irigaray, we might suggest that this is an inherently masculinist perspective on narrative cinema, privileging the ostensibly objective voice of sameness. She suggests that the project of enunciation:

is to reveal who is speaking, to whom, about what, with what means. In technical terms, this means it is a matter of uncovering the dynamics of the utterance underlying the statement produced. Beneath what is being said, it is possible to discover the subject, the subject's economy, potential energy, relations with the other and the world. The subject may be masked, bogged down, buried, covered up, paralysed, or may be engendered, may become, and grow through speech. (*Sexes and Genealogies*, 147)

This perspective on the project of enunciation allows us to suggest that Metz's account of cinematic enunciation is a limited one that is framed in terms that reinforce masculinist discourses of representation.

This mirrors the insistence of some commentators that spectatorship is framed in terms of masculine desire alone. As Irigaray has observed:

The rejection, the exclusion of a female imaginary certainly puts woman in the position of experiencing herself only fragmentarily, in the little structured margins of a dominant ideology, as waste, or excess, what is left of a mirror invested by the (masculine) 'subject', to reflect himself, to copy himself. Moreover, the role of 'femininity' is prescribed by this masculine specula(riza)tion and corresponds scarcely at all to woman's desire, which may be recovered only in secret, in hiding, with anxiety and guilt. (*This Sex Which is not One*, 30)

We might be inspired by Irigaray's perspective on enunciation to read against the grain of texts that work in this way in order to seek out what is buried and bogged down. As a feminist modality of reading, this approach is both philosophically and politically pertinent. However, I wish to argue for the potentiality of films made by women, to argue for the moments of becoming that it might be possible to discern in cinema. The cinema does not have to be read as a machine, as an apparatus of dominant discursive mechanisms. It can be read as a discursive space of exchange. I shall show that the space and time of narrative cinema is frequently aligned with fantasy and with the potentiality of imaginary identificatory processes. By drawing on films made by women, I wish to contend that there is space within narrative cinema for a discursive framework that privileges the dyadic relation between the positions of 'I' and 'you' and that this mirrors the relation of the spectator to the on-screen fantasy. As Virginia Woolf has commented:

Sometimes at the cinema in the midst of its immense dexterity and enormous technical proficiency, the curtain parts and we behold, far off, some unknown and unexpected beauty. But it is for a moment only. For a strange thing has happened — while all the other arts were born naked, this, the youngest, has been born fully clothed. It can say everything before it has anything to say. (*Contemporary Writers*, 171)

My contention is that cinema constitutes a space of fantasy in which to construct playful interrogations of structures of enunciation. I shall argue that the site of women's film-making is imbued with the potential to rework and rephrase received ideals about what it is possible to say in terms of the perceived unspeakability of the feminine. In other words, the cinema can be seen as an ideal space in which to formulate a means of articulating Irigaray's *parler-femme*. In a dual-headed approach to the feminine, Irigaray critiques the ways in which dominant ideology relegates it to an unspeakable position within the dominant symbolic realm of representation, arguing that the masculinism of the symbolic order is accountable for this. Simultaneously, Irigaray claims women's right to accede to subjective specificity on and in their own terms. In an effort to articulate a means of redress, she calls for a feminine *parler-femme* in order to show the need for a reworking of traditional ideas about how women are perceived and perceive themselves. Margaret Whitford describes this relation of women to other women as a horizontal relation, as a kind of female sociality or social contract, highlighting the way in which this notion opens up space for the specificity of the feminine and for female desire (*Philosophy in the Feminine*, 78).

For Irigaray, *parler-femme* is an effort to construct a feminine position of enunciation. She is neither setting out to define a language of the feminine nor, indeed, to create one. Her work is an attempt to show how language (in the Saussurean sense of *langage*) delimits and manipulates what is understood as femininity. *Parler-femme* draws attention to the fact that women need to address their exclusion from language. Irigaray does not prescribe a mode of feminine language. Instead, she tries to show how *parler-femme* enables women to articulate their sexed identities in and on their own terms (*par les femmes*). In the context of a discussion of the feminine in cinema, then, this article will ask whether films made by women speak (as) woman in ways that challenge our models of cinematic enunciation? If so, how and with what effects? My discussion will focus on independently produced films made by women as they often seem to take issue with the dominant ideological construction of sexual difference in ways that films emanating from the Hollywood industry may not have the power to do. There are a number of cinematic strategies in the films I have chosen to use which may be read in terms of *discours*. I have chosen to discuss these strategies in the context of four key cinematic moments.

My first example comes from the opening sequence of Sally Potter's *Orlando* (UK, 1993) in which we see Orlando (a man) pacing beneath an oak tree. A voiceover tells us:

VOICEOVER: There can be no doubt about his sex — despite the feminine appearance that every young man of the time aspires to. And there can be no doubt about his upbringing. Good food, education, a nanny, loneliness and isolation. And because this is England, [Cut to close-up of ORLANDO]
Orlando would therefore seem destined to have his portrait on the wall and his name in the history books. But when he —

ORLANDO: That is, I —
VOICEOVER: came into the world, he was looking for something else. Though heir to a name which meant power, land and property, surely when Orlando was born, it wasn't privilege he sought but company. (*Orlando*, 3)

In this sequence we witness the third person of the voiceover being interrupted by the first person in the image, and this aural/spoken disruption of patterns of enunciation is mirrored at the level of the visual in the direct look to camera. One might argue that the film is an elaborate parody of the construction of gender within the symbolic order, but this seems to miss the point. The film's opening sequence stresses the importance of voice from its outset, placing the spectator very forcefully in relation to the modes of reading that the text will require. We are alerted to the need actively to read the text, pursuing its layers of meaning and self-reflexivity in order to insinuate ourselves inside its meaning. The interruption of the voiceover by the discursive proclamation of an 'I' uttered by a female masquerading as a man calls attention to the facets of femininity that are traditionally disavowed in cinema. It mimics cinematic strategies of story-telling in order to rework them. The slippage between the voiceover and the moment of the present within the narrative allows us to reflect upon what we see and to respond (in laughter, perhaps). We recognise the subversiveness of the moment by virtue of our familiarity with cinematic language. We are simultaneously sutured into the discursive framework of a text that works against itself as it unfolds. The spectator is structured in terms of the unspeakable, and she is also forced to adopt a discursive position in relation to the space of narrative fantasy.[3]

There is a further very striking moment of feminine enunciation at the end of this text in the memorable scene where an angel appears. We are called upon here to see this as a moment of enunciation of the feminine that depends on fantasy: Orlando the mother is seen here with her daughter who runs about the garden with a video camera, recording her playful visions, when suddenly she points out to her daughter a vision of an angel, floating mid-air. It is interesting to note, here, that the opening intertitle proclaims 'Death' whilst the closing one proclaims 'Birth'. It is as though Potter is attempting to construct the subject of the text through her/his journey and experience. Subjectivity is not so much *a priori* as a process of becoming. By ending with 'Birth', Potter also returns us, as spectators, to the beginning of the text. This strategy has the effect of a flashback through the experience of our identification with the protagonist and we are irresistibly pulled into a reconsideration of what we have seen. The spectator is encouraged to rework the text in this respect, thinking through the politics of gender by reference to subsequent events that reshape and remould them. The circularity of the text is also doubly inscribed in terms of fantasy when the angel appears and we might read this as a signifier of feminine enunciation. As Orlando points out to her daughter the extraordinary vision of the angel, the image jumps and cuts from video to 35mm, suggesting that this image is one that is shared between them. This is a uniquely and unspeakably feminine moment, an example, perhaps, of *parler femme*. Moreover, as Jimmy Somerville floats mid-air, the lyric of his song encourages us to question what we have seen and to rethink the implications of our response in order to construct meaning at the point of narrative closure. In this moment of magical realism, the spectator is interpellated by the text and sutured into the birth of feminine subjectivity it attempts to announce. We might recall Irigaray's observation that: 'the angel always returns to heaven, goes home, to the other side of the ultimate veil. Unless he stands there, if only for a fragment, a flight, a detached soar that is sent, addressed, to announce what comes after' (*Sexes and Genealogies*, 36). What is more, the angel offers: 'An annunciation of more weight than any coded message, moving to and from the first and last dwellings that are withheld from present visibility or readability, to be deciphered only in the next world' (*ibid*). For Irigaray, 'angels destroy the monstrous, that which hampers the possibility of a new age' (*An Ethics of Sexual Difference*, 15). In *Orlando*, then, we might argue that the dawn of a new space for the feminine is heralded by the angel, a space of becoming that depends upon the strategies of enunciation and the dyadic relation of the spectator to the screen. We are left agog, with a sense of wonderment and awe.

A second example that might be read as echoing this disruptive play with cinematic strategy can be drawn from Susan Streitfeld's *Female Perversions* (1996, US). Once again, the sequence is drawn from the opening scene which is set in a courtroom. The cinematic strategies of this film appear, at first, to collaborate in the cinematic construction of the female body as an object of the gaze/desire. The opening sequence of the film makes this abundantly clear. Our gaze is matched with that of the camera and the court officials as they shamelessly rove across the body of Eve Stephens, a high-powered lawyer. The camera lingers on her body, fetishizing body parts and pieces of clothing and cuts to reverse shots of the men in the courtroom gazing at

Eve. The excess of Mulveyan 'to-be-looked-at-ness' is immediately striking and the movement of the camera is foregrounded throughout the scene ('Visual Pleasure and Narrative Cinema'). The marks of cinematic enunciation are made clear to us and are reinforced by the reverse shots that put the male gaze centre-frame. The ostensibly obedient camera work reveals its motivation through excess, and the spectator is repelled/distanced by the gaze in which the camera seeks to trap her. The disruption of the visual once again takes place at the level of sound as we watch the security guard turn off his hearing aid. The moment of enunciation is constructed through the disgust of the spectator who is forced to watch a scene of wilful objectification of the female form. The tone of the narrative couples with the strategies of the *mise en scène* and film form to produce a text replete with distancing mechanisms and ironic parody. At the most obvious level, the film is full of fragmented fantasy sequences that reveal the centrality of (unconscious) fantasy to the construction of female sexuality. These myriad sequences of Eve Stephens's fantasy-world attest simultaneously to the constrained and restrictive aspects of the dominant notion of femininity and to the perversely liberating sense of the feminine that emerges from it when it is pushed to its very excessive limits. This is a typically Irigarayan strategy,[4] and has parallels with her notion of mimesis. In *Female Perversions*, Eve Stephens's sexuality is constructed as perverse precisely because she is depicted as taking masochistic pleasure from the extremes of this restrictive notion of femininity—we see that she is quite literally bound by the constraints in her fantasies. Yet in the cinematic space of these fantasies, overlaid as it is with connotations of the dark and unexplored territory of female desire, there is a clear sense in which representational and formal practices are skewed and re-positioned. In this space, the perversity of Eve's body, laden with desire, is able to be articulated. The space of cinematic fantasy allows us to begin to construct a mode of representation for aspects of the feminine that are traditionally buried within discursive constructs. The sense of disturbing parody that emanates from the fantasy sequences and from the film language employed by Streitfeld allows us to resituate our response as spectators to the representation of woman in this film, which runs the whole gamut of female stereotypes. By the end of the film, it becomes apparent that each of these notions of femininity may be regarded as a perversion, trapping female desire inside the bodily limits of its excess—the epitome, perhaps, of acceptable (and representable) female subjectivity. The perversity of the cinematic space allows us to see these representations of woman as constructs to be re-worked through parody and excess. As spectators, we are positioned as questioning. The exploitation of mainstream cinematic practice around the representation of the female form demands a response. We are either left with no means of identification (through refusal of the strategies as repellent), or we must seek to rework the text in an effort to suture ourselves inside it on our own terms. The spectator here is structured as a knowing spectator, as one who enunciates, as one who reads against the grain to produce a modality of meaning that remains grounded in symbolic practice but which simultaneously refuses it. The moment of *parler-femme* is presented to us through the dynamics of the film form in this respect.

A third moment that we might appropriate comes from *Antonia's Line* (Gorris, Netherlands, 1995). The parodic scenes of exchange between mother and daughter remind us that the space of fantasy is associated with the imaginary and thus with the mother-daughter dyad. An Irigarayan modality of exchange between mothers and daughters finds a space for exploration here and the resultant humour is indicative of the femininity of the moment. The film presents to us a space of fantasy that is mediated through fertility; the maternal metaphor is celebrated and lauded; there is a huge emphasis placed on cycles of nature: births and deaths accompany the seasons and are endlessly relived. The film traces a matrilineal history of women and their relationships with one another. The specificity of female experience is heightened throughout, and this is largely premised on the centrality of the mother-daughter relation. This may be understood as a female genealogy, and thus already constitutes a representation of *parler-femme*.

However, the narrative of this film is witnessed through flashback, and we are invited, once again, to premise a reading of this text through the effects of its form. At the beginning of the film, we see an elderly woman (Antonia) who knows that today will be her last. Just as in *Orlando*, the spectator is encouraged to abandon any expectations of realism from the opening. Antonia stares wistfully through the window and we cut to a moment in her past when she and her daughter were called to her mother's death-bed. The circular structure of the film is set up for us immediately, as it is with Antonia's own death that the film will end. The spectator is left with a sound knowledge of the future to come, and this is testimony to the impact of female genealogy that is represented in the film. The female genealogy of the film rests not on patriarchally-defined blood relations, but extends to friendship between women and, arguably, to the female spectator watching in the auditorium.

The process of identification available to us in this film depends on the foregrounding of the feminine as it is mediated through the text. The emphasis throughout the film is placed heavily on female experience and on the shared nature of this. This largely remains unspoken and is perhaps best illustrated through the moments of magical realism used to underscore the sense of the legacy that is passed down from mother to daughter. These moments function in a similar way to the angelic ending in *Orlando*. Antonia is shown in these opening scenes as orienting her daughter in relation to the town (the place of Antonia's birth). There is a sense here of going back to one's roots, yet it is puzzlingly represented. Antonia is not overcome by nostalgia, as we might expect, but rather stamps her own identity on the way of life in the village inhabited by oddballs. She becomes a matriarchal figurehead in the small town, wielding moral imperatives and doling out justice on her own terms. The fact that the village is inhabited by oddballs should not go unremarked. Antonia's own oddity is marked by her femininity and her willingness to flaunt it: Gorris is effectively reclaiming the terrain of associations between femininity and madness in this respect. Antonia's inculcation of Danielle, her daughter, into life in the town goes almost unspoken. In fact, Danielle barely speaks throughout the film. Instead she sees parodic visions that make us laugh. The sense here is that somehow these visions are communicated to her by her mother: our laughter as Antonia comments that 'that's how things are around here' just as her daughter has witnessed her grandmother coming to life in order to sing at her own funeral underscores this. There is a palpable exchange of femininity going on here. This exchange takes place outside the domain of traditional symbolic practice, remaining unspoken and depending on moments of magical realism that are specified as connected with feminine experience. The centrality of female genealogy should be noted. The modality of enunciation here depends upon the relation of form (the integrated moments of magical realism that disrupt the realist text) and textual content. We are enabled by the cinematic strategies to discern the feminine as a mode of becoming. This construction of meaning depends on the engagement of the spectator with the text at the level of subjectivity and desire. The cinema as a space of fantasy at this point in the text thus allows us a glimpse of feminine specificity and it is this that enables us to reimagine the possibilities of female engagements with the cinematic image. The spectator is aligned with such moments through the play of the cinematic process. Moments of magical realism and flashback lend a mythic quality to the feminine, creating for the female spectator a sense of legacy and history. Similarly, the excessive camera movements in *Female Perversions* parallel the use of intertitles in *Orlando*, constructing the spectator through parody and excess, attributes associated with the feminine that need to be reclaimed in the name of specificity.

Finally, there are several significant moments in Jane Campion's *The Piano* (New Zealand, 1993) in which the mother-daughter relation is made central. Ada and Flora exchange symbolic gestures and share a passion for story-telling. The highly ambivalent image of a man going up in flames appears just as Flora relates the story of her parents' union, suggesting that the playful world of childish fantasy might be aligned with the discursive moment of enunciation. Flora effectively constructs a space of origin for herself in terms which centralize the importance of discourse and subjectivity. What matters in this moment is not so much the truth of Flora's tale, but rather the effect it might have on us in engaging with the narrative form. Through an act of enunciation, Flora places herself at the heart of the narrative, shaping our response to the plot and the positioning of our response to the narrative as spectators.

I have been arguing, then, that cinematic enunciation constructs us in ways that are not possible on a lived experiential level. The cinematic suspension of disbelief allows us a space and time in which to reconfigure our discursive positioning in terms that make available that which is usually left unspeakable. The process of exchange in cinema is mediated through an engagement not just with the image but also with the soundtrack and the positionality of the revelation of narrative motivation and plot. The examples from recent film-making by women discussed in this paper suggest that the cinema has a dimension of fantasy that alludes to what Irigaray has called the feminine and thus offers what is seemingly unofferable in the context spelled out in the work of Metz. I would argue that as cinematic spectators we have a transferential relation to the text and it is this which allows us to move beyond the parameters of narrative and discourse as they are traditionally framed. Irigaray has written that 'sometimes a space for wonder is left to works of art' (*An Ethics of Sexual Difference*, 33). I would suggest that the wonderment of cinema exemplified in the work of the directors I have mentioned here offers us myriad opportunities to explore the becoming of the feminine in ways that shore up political ideals about the potentiality of female authorship.

CAROLINE BAINBRIDGE
University of East London

NOTES

1 *Discours* is defined as a statement uttered in the first person in the present. In discours, the speaker is foregrounded. *Histoire* is a statement uttered as though it is in the past, in the third person. There is no sense of the presence of the storyteller. Metz refers to these terms in his discussion of voyeurism in the cinema.

2 For Metz, this lends authority to the spectatorial fantasy of the production of meaning.

3 *Orlando*, after all is a text that depends upon the over-elaborate construction of fantasy for its narrative substance. It can be read in terms of the masquerade/mimesis distinctions drawn by Irigaray in these terms, suggesting that the visual collides with the construction of a feminine mode of enunciation in order to jam the machinery of cinema so valued by Metz and other proponents of apparatus theory.

4 Irigaray often calls for strategies of the feminine to draw attention to the repressed gaps of symbolic discourse and also to expose the mechanisms by which symbolic discourse perpetuates the exclusion of the feminine from its own strategies.

BIBLIOGRAPHY

Irigaray, Luce, *An Ethics of Sexual Difference*, London-New York, Athlone-Routledge, 1993, translated by Carolyn Burke and Gillian C. Gill from the French *Ethique de la différence sexuelle*, Paris, Editions de Minuit, 1984.

Irigaray, Luce, *Sexes and Genealogies*, New York, Columbia University Press, 1993, translated by Gillian C. Gill from the French *Sexes et parentés*, Paris, Editions de Minuit, 1987.

Irigaray, Luce, *This Sex Which Is Not One*, Ithaca, New York, Cornell University Press, 1985, translated by Catherine Porter with Carolyn Burke from the French *Ce sexe qui n'en est pas un*, Paris, Editions de Minuit, 1977.

Metz, Christian, *Psychoanalysis and the Imaginary Signifier*, London, Macmillan, 1982, translated by Celia Britton et al from the French *Le signifiant imaginaire: psychanalyse et cinéma*, Paris, Union générale d'éditions, 1977.

Mulvey, Laura, 'Visual Pleasure and Narrative Cinema', *Screen*, 16:3, 1975, 6–18.

Potter, Sally, *Orlando*, London, Faber and Faber, 1993.

Whitford, Margaret, *Luce Irigaray, Philosophy in the Feminine*, London-New York, Routledge, 1991.

Woolf, Virginia, *Contemporary Writers*, London, Hogarth Press, 1965.

FILMOGRAPHY

Campion, Jane, *The Piano*, New Zealand, 1993.

Gorris, Marleen, *Antonia's Line*, Netherlands, 1995.

Potter, Sally, *Orlando*, United Kingdom, 1993.

Streitfeld, Susan, *Female Perversions*, United States, 1996.

Luce Irigaray's questions

I would like to remind Caroline Bainbridge, and other scholars in art, that my questions concern above all the use of my own work. For example, I could say that the analyses she did as a cinematographic critic are interesting but that they do not yet reach the most relevant level of my work. Certainly this results partly from the material which has been interpreted, and in any case it is better to allude to feminine subjectivity than to close up again every emergence of a world in the feminine. But I am a little afraid that women's interventions that are not decisive enough will put them back in a secondary role. Is it thus necessary for us to force the tempo of History or rather to wait for its unfolding, which unfortunately in our times is not very much in favour of women's liberation, of women's culture?

Returning to Caroline Bainbridge's paper, I could ask myself: Is it sufficient, for example, to include sequences of exchanges between mother and daughter in the film, or is the problem rather: How to modify the production of the film itself? Would that not be what will give rise to an enunciation in the feminine, to a 'parler femme' through cinematographic means? Evidently introducing some 'dialogues' between mother and daughter makes room for sequences generally neglected in our tradition. But such exchanges are also traditional in a way, even if forgotten or repressed, and they do not really open a different horizon. They can partly make this opening possible, if we do not fix our attention only on them. Otherwise we run the risk of remaining in a patriarchal or phallocentric world without elaborating another world.

No doubt it is more pleasant to laugh together than to weep alone, or to exchange with each other than to hate each other. If this remain only fantasy and does not work toward modifying social and cultural structures, then I fear that woman's life will be left unchanged. Perhaps we then will go back to cultures in which men and women remain separated. I cannot consider this as real progress. We have rather to give rise to a culture of two subjects. And such a culture requires a 'parler femme' that is truly different than the 'parler homme', an enunciation in the feminine that can construct another culture without limiting ourselves to some windows to the same culture.

Recovering fantasy, repressed or inhibited by a masculine tradition, is not sufficient in order to protect and elaborate a world of our own. This still signifies at best laughing together in the kitchen of a patriarchal family home, city, country, culture. We have to create another kind of home.

My question to Caroline therefore is: Have you any suggestions to make for establishing this new world? Have you any dreams which could inspire you to invent another world rather than being content only with exchanges, in part regressive, between a mother and a daughter? Do you not have a desire for a wider horizon? For happiness of another kind? How would it be possible to realize your dream, and to reach such happiness?

Caroline Bainbridge's response

Cinematic texts created by women can be read as opening up a space of pleasure and contemplation for the feminine in that they enable their spectators to forge new perspectives and responses to the world they inhabit. In this sense, then, one might suggest that the cinema becomes a locus in which the dream of an alternative world is momentarily tangible; it is as though it opens up a space for dreaming and re-visioning in ways that are not possible in other spaces. For me, the availability of such a space constitutes a small beginning, allowing for small gestures of the desire for change and ways of imagining it anew.

In order to establish a new home for the feminine, it seems crucial to contemplate ways of making space and time in which it might begin to emerge. For me, there is a strategic value in struggling for this from a position within the systematic machineries that seek to exclude the very possibilities of attaining such space-time. Otherwise there is little more than dereliction. Thus, it is not that I am happy to be content with regressive exchanges between mothers and daughters, but rather that my dream of a wider horizon seeks some notion of a place for beginning. The restrictions of a culture that insists on burying the feminine, on rendering it in terms of dereliction and abandonment, allow little scope for such dreams. My belief, then, is in the validity of desiring to dream, of finding moments in which to enunciate the potentiality of dreaming. This becomes a premiss, a basis upon which new dreams of happiness might be founded and explored. The cinema, for me, is a space of dreams, a space in which we actively pursue happiness, albeit fleetingly. Thus, cinema made by women would seem to be one place in which such explorations may begin.

Being Two, How Many Eyes Have We?[1]

In our Western tradition, to see generally means to see something. Thus the question related to seeing is considered as a relation between a subject and an object, whether this relation consists in perceiving or in constructing something. For centuries, on the passive as well as on the active level, on the receptive as well as on the creative level, the issue of seeing has been dominated by a relation with an object. Moreover, this object is generally assimilated with an object whose form is given by constructing or manufacturing, materially or mentally.

For us, an object is often understood as a table, as a chair, that is as something made by man's hand with a form, a 'face' imposed by man on the matter which has served to construct it: wood for example.

To conceive the act of seeing in this way approximates the manner of conceiving understanding in our culture. And to say: I understand, we often say: I see. That is: I see something, framed as and reduced to an object — conceptual, mental — for my comprehension.

Moreover our 'I see' is equivalent to 'I recognize': I recognize a form, I recognize a concept. I recognize something that already has a face according to a model, a paradigm, an *eidos*, that I have been taught.

Thus seeing as understanding generally corresponds for us with knowing again, knowing a second time, and so entering in complicity with ourselves and with the one who has already defined or constructed the form — verbal or non verbal, plastic for example. Seeing as understanding corresponds to a second time: we submit ourselves here to a model learned, and memorized.

Then what we see — through the eyes or through the mind — is not something or someone unknown that we discover, that surprises or amazes us and sometimes touches us without our being able to recognize it or to assign a name or a sense to it. Such an encounter with something or someone unknown, with what remains without form given by us, constructed by us, such an encounter we generally defer into the invisibility of a God or into the fear of a nightmare: that which evokes the time before birth, for example.

What appears familiar to us is what we have already seen, recognized, named, or what we have already captured in a form, immobilized in a structure, a formula, a discourse. And if in part we want to discover things that we do not yet know, this remains within the limits of a complicity with the already known and recognized.

Nevertheless every day we meet visible things which do not correspond to forms given by us. The living world — plant, animal, and even human — does not receive its form from us. The living world gives itself its own form, and it is in a very approximate manner that we know it again or name it again with the same word: a tree for example, or more precisely a plane tree or a beech tree. In fact usually we do not look at this tree as living. We do not see it changing, giving itself a form, forms, under our eyes. If we continue to say: it is a plane tree or a beech tree — whether it has flowers and leaves or not, of one colour or another — it is because we have learned a code and not because we observe a reality.

In a way, our language imposes on the tree a verbal construction that does not coincide with the form it gives itself as living. Language submits the tree to a permanent form that it does not have as living. Language will compel us to see it or catch only a glimpse of it through an idea of tree, a face of tree that doesn't move, and from which we will have to recognize it, renouncing a great part of our sight.

In fact, the tree is not only seen or known again by us. It gives us to see from where it lives and, as living, gives itself a form, always new. This gift of seeing sometimes will be felt as if: it looks at us.

To verify what I am trying to say, you can attempt to spend half an hour looking at a manufactured object: a table for example, and half an hour looking at a tree. Try then to test the difference between what you feel after the first and the second half hour. The effect upon you will not be the same — well it is the case for me. Approximately I could say that looking at a table takes energy from me and that looking at a tree gives me energy.

Indeed, if the table is very beautiful, if its form arouses wonder or admiration in me, if I see it for the first time and if its form perhaps is unique — if it is a work of art for example — , then it is possible that it gives me some energy, but not the same energy that I receive when looking at a tree. The form of the table is already immobilized in a face imposed on its matter, whereas the tree gives itself a face, and this one changes continually.

A tree gives me to see especially because it unceasingly creates space, a table takes seeing from me because it needs my energy to create or re-create a space for itself.

We Westerners, we lack language to express this becoming through which a tree gives itself its form as living, a form that becomes, and whose motion is not immobilized by any end, any finality, unless that of becoming itself, of blooming.

In order to find a language capable of expressing this becoming of the brightening up of its form, their forms, by the living, Heidegger converses with a Japanese: in search of a language which would be capable of expressing the motion of entering into presence of a tree as tree.

He interrogates, he questions, to know if it would be possible, for us Westerners, to say that the tree trees, or is treeing — with the meaning of: it becomes tree — as we would say: the cloud clouds or is clouding, the sky skies or is skying.

Already it would be more appropriate to what we can see of the tree, to what it gives us to see, to what we can look at, and moreover gaze at — and in a durable way — thanks to it.

Already between a table and a tree, the manner of looking is very different. What is seen, and the ground from which it is seen, appears, enters into presence, are very different.

In the case of a table, the ground itself is already dependent upon a construction. It represents an availability appropriate to what is constructed, or will be constructed, and to who has constructed or will construct. The perspective itself is distorted by the finality of the act, of the making.

In this way, to look together — being two for example — at something constructed makes us belong to a common ground by which our manner of seeing is in part mortgaged by the intention of the person who constructed it: our seeing is partly determined by their scheme, by their hand, or worse by their machine. And we lose here the possibility of a free perspective, and even of a perception of volumes. The objects constrain us to perceive their forms according to a pre-given intention.

It would be possible to apply to looking the analysis of Jean-Paul Sartre with respect to the world of technology, particularly when he talks about the tin opener and the corridor of the metro. Most of the objects that surround us constrain us to look at them in this or in that way, especially according to their use.

So we gradually lose the binocular vision, useful for recognizing volumes and perceiving the depth of a free field against which objects stand out. The only field or ground remains that of a culture which presents to us the objects in one manner or another, according to their technique of manufacture or according to their use.

Taking part in the same culture, two subjects will hardly keep an eye half open to locate, to recognize the objects necessary for their survival, and also for their cultural complicity.

In contrast with that, to look at a tree — except in a space entirely planned, perhaps with a guide that tells us what is to be seen — gives us a free field in order to contemplate the unfolding of form, forms of the living that it is, gives us back the perspective and the perception of a volume which is, moreover, in permanent evolution.

Even if they designate it with the same name, the vision of two persons who look at a tree will generally remain autonomous: they will keep their two eyes.

A tree gives us back our vision, gives us back to ourselves with a capacity of seeing, which we are deprived of by the familiar objects that surround us.

What can we say now about what we see when we look at a living human? Things then are more complicated. A human belongs both to the living world and to the constructed world.

We enjoy looking at a little child because it moves in accordance with his, or her, beginning. In a way, it is closer to a tree: it grows, it develops, it gradually forms its face. But very quickly a child also copies, on a physiological level as well as on a psychological one. It follows physiologically its parents, its genealogy. It also copies them psychologically, but not only them.

Human beings become by leaving their origins, they become themselves but they become others also, already as living. Moreover they become from two genders, from two genealogies. If they belong to a species, their pedigrees are never pure.

More, human beings move, and they imitate everything they meet. They also become what they have been taught. And education for a great part is based upon imitation.

Thus we do not feel the same pleasure when looking at an adolescent as at a little child: the adolescent is already fabricated, hesitating between nature and a construction foreign to it. The adolescent does not move only according to the forms of living.

Does it mean that human beings are less than a tree, especially for our eyes? According to what has just been said, they are. And if the tree is often considered as a religious symbol, it is perhaps because it is more purely itself than most humans.

But are most humans already human? How can we characterize human as human? As a living being, certainly, but of what kind? It seems to me that the characteristic of a human as such is not to be capable of manufacturing and of producing a world thanks to a technique, particularly thanks to a certain language. What distinguishes a human being from other living beings is the ability to create invisibility rather than to make appear, to render visible.

This dimension of the human is perhaps more familiar to a woman than to a man. Man has occupied himself constructing a world of visible objects, deferring invisibility in God (perhaps he begins to understand his mistake). A woman, for her part, knows that without something invisible, notably in herself, she cannot develop desire or love with a man, neither can she succeed in the conceiving or in the mothering of a child.

A woman knows this above all because her connection with the world fulfils itself through relations with another subject more than through relations with one or more objects. She also knows this because, in love as well as in maternity, woman is confronted with the problem of difference. She must not only allow the other to survive — which often appears as ethics for the masculine subject — , she must let the other live and grow according to his or her difference, a difference which of course is not only biological but above all psychological.

The respect of difference, particularly of sexual difference, does not correspond to the respect of something visible but of something invisible which results from a relation with oneself, with the other, with the world peculiar to each gender.

The respect of the invisibility of the other, this hospitality given to the other as other not only in one's own country, in one's own home but also in oneself — in one's own body, and one's own breath, one's own mind or soul — , corresponds, for me, to a human becoming, a human being.

It is not possible to reduce such a gesture to a moral imperative, it requires an availability of energy which allows us to realize it without ruining ourselves. And if, in my book *I Love to You*, I explain that, to recognize the other as other, I must use negativity with respect to myself — and in another way to the other — , to this new dialectical process I have to add a cultivation of energy that the Western tradition lacks.

The accomplishment of a human does then not consist only in entering into presence according to his or her own forms. He cannot realize this as well as a tree, as a flower: he is too hybrid. Nor can he manufacture as well as a machine, in a way.

The ground from which a human can enter into presence as human is a third ground: not that of the simple living, nor that of a simple constructed thing, but one where, beyond what is simply living or simply constructed, a human gives to himself a free energy, an interior energy not univocally determined by the living being that he is from birth nor by a learned culture.

To succeed in transforming one's vital energy and one's cultural energy into a free energy, available, not already determined nor finalized, would be for me the characteristic of a human being.

Becoming human in part has been perceived in this way, the part which concerns the transformation of vital energy. But the end or the means proposed for this process was to transform vital energy — in particular sexual energy — by submitting it to a defined culture, by manufacturing objects corresponding to this culture. It would consist as it were in going from one determination to another, from one submission to another.

Such a becoming was not necessarily more human, as our History taught us yesterday and teaches us still today. The reason perhaps may be found in the fact that our culture is dominated by some paradigms, some models, some faces which do not represent the whole human but only one gender, the other one being constrained to conform to so-called universal norms or forms.

Western models are also dominated by genealogy, by a biological determinism that does not allow a living human to enter into presence, or to bloom, as freely as a plant.

Some of the most recent philosophers of our tradition have supposed that something was wrong in it, and they have questioned our Western culture in its foundations. Some of those philosophers have turned to the culture of the Near or the Far East to revive forms or norms which allow greater place to life, subjective as well as objective. Thus Nietzsche puts more emphasis on the becoming of the subject,

Heidegger on the becoming of things and of the world, if I may caricature their positions.

But those philosophers have not sufficiently considered that turning back to the East implies a gesture which is not only mental and internal to language but concerns also an economy of energy that we, Westerners, do not have or do not have any longer.

Neither the practice of Buddha nor even the practice of Christ may be understood only through words, through texts. They are inhabited by breath, by the energy that breath awakes, arouses in us, in a way forgotten by us, Westerners, perhaps because we have gradually departed from cultures more inspired by feminine identity.

So the primary meaning of 'soul' is 'breath', but we also forget that through substituting for this primary meaning more speculative, more abstract meanings.

Breath ensures the joining between body and soul, between the living and the properly human. The breath is necessary for entering into the presence of a human as human, more than language and in a different way. Indispensable for life, breath is also the means, the medium to accede to spiritual life as an irreducible dimension of human subjectivity.

This breath is not given at birth, nor can it be assimilated to a constructed object. To breathe is a conquest for a newborn, and the spiritual life of a human must also correspond to a conquest, in which breath remains the matter and the vehicle.

Too often we, in the West, have forgotten the breath necessary to life and even more the breath indispensable to culture, confining it in concepts or forms, in a language, verbal or not verbal, already constructed, already fabricated.

The breath, as vital or spiritual matter of a human being, corresponds to this third ground from which we can appear as humans and cultivate relations between us.

This breath remains invisible, except indirectly. Those who cultivate their own breath often have greater presence, even corporeal presence: they radiate, they have an aura. They also continue to become and they do not decline, having barely achieved their growth. They become from a second life, a life that the subject gives himself or herself, born again in an autonomous way, as Eastern masters say.

From this rebirth — giving us a third ground — , the invisibility of the other is no longer felt as a lack of seeing but as an invisible source of seeing. To contemplate the invisibility of the other gives, or gives us again, life, including the life of sight, even more than contemplating the unfolding of the visible forms of a tree. We are nourished by an energy emanating from him, or from her, an energy which touches us in a mysteriously luminous manner.

The third ground can exist for he or she who is born again but it can also be generated between us in an infinite, indefinite way.

This generation of an invisible light is perhaps most fertile in sexual difference. Escaping the physiological or cultural imperatives of genealogy, it is supported by the desire and the respect for the other as other. Contemplating the one who remains invisible in his, or her, difference becomes a source of energy and of light if each one feeds it by a reserve of free energy, available for sight itself as well as for the becoming of each subject and of the relation existing between them.

How many eyes do we have then, being two? Certainly we each keep our two eyes. But we probably have more eyes, one or two: to contemplate invisibility in the visible, in the light of the day, but also to perceive in the night of interiority.

The way of looking will be more contemplative, passive as well as active, capable of discovering an other or a world always unknown. What it is to see is not already defined, and our eyes can thus remain open upon an infinity of views, of sights.

Our way of looking, our look itself can unceasingly be born again if we consider the other as other, with respect for the mystery of the difference existing between us. Indeed it prevents us from reducing him, or her, to an object or to an image that we can appropriate, take as a part of our own world, of our own self. A gesture that paralyses the becoming of each subject and finally brings death to the two subjects, the looked at and the one looking, including the death of sight.

LUCE IRIGARAY
Translated by Luce Irigaray
with Catherine Busson, Jim Mooney,
Heidi Bostic and Stephen Pluhacek

NOTE

1   This text was first published in a French, Italian, English and German version by Christel Göttert Verlag, Rüsselsheim, 2000. The copyright belongs to Luce Irigaray.

BIBLIOGRAPHY

Heidegger, Martin, 'On the Essence and Concept of *phusis* in Aristotle's *Physics* B, I', translated by Thomas Sheehan in *Pathmarks*, edited by William McNeill, Cambridge, Cambridge University Press, 1998, 178–276. Translated into French by François Fédier as 'Ce qu'est et comment se détermine la *phusis*', in *Questions II*, Paris, Gallimard, 1968, 178–276. Without referring directly to it, this text partially corresponds to a critical reading of this Heidegger essay.

Heidegger, Martin, 'A Dialogue on Language, Between a Japanese and an Inquirer', translated by Peter D. Hertz in *On the Way to Language*, San Francisco, HarperSanFrancisco, 1982, 1–54. Translated into French by Jean Beaufret, Wolfgang Brokmeier and François Fédier as 'D'un entretien de la parole, Entre un Japonais et un qui demande', in *Acheminement vers la Parole*, Paris, Gallimard, 1976, 85–140.

Irigaray, Luce, *I Love to You, Sketch for a Felicity in History*, New York-London, Routledge, 1996, translated by Alison Martin from the French *J'aime à toi, Esquisse d'une félicité dans l'Histoire*, Paris, Grasset, 1992.

Irigaray, Luce, *To Be Two*, London-New York, Athlone-Routledge, 2001, translated by Monique M. Rhodes and Marco F. Cocito-Monoc from the Italian *Essere Due*, Turin, Bollati Boringhieri, 1994. The French version has been published as *Etre Deux*, Paris, Grasset, 1997.

Sartre, Jean-Paul, *Being and Nothingness*, New York, Philosophical Library, 1956, translated by Hazel Barnes from the French *L'Etre et le Néant*, Paris, Gallimard, 1943, reprinted Tel, 1992, see in particular 475–6.

FEMININE IN THEOLOGY AND
PHILOSOPHY OF RELIGIONS

The Woman at the Gate: Access or Barrier to 'Goddess Talk'?[1]

> Was it your tongue in my mouth which forced me
> into speech? Was it the blade between my lips
> which drew forth floods of words to speak of you?
> And, as you wanted words other than those already
> uttered, words never yet imagined, unique in your
> tongue, to name you and you alone, you kept on
> prying me open, further and further open. Honing
> and sharpening your instrument, till it was almost
> imperceptible, piercing further into my silence.
> Further into my flesh, were you not thus discovering
> the path of your being? Of its yet to come?
>
> And I was speaking, but you did not hear.
>
> Luce Irigaray, *Elemental Passions*

Luce Irigaray's words from *Elemental Passions* (9) do not allude only to experiences with masculine discourse (that is, phallogocentric, centred on the phallus as centre of the world). Luce Irigaray's words allude also to women's discourses — the words of those who, attempting to include the feminine in male-dominated theological discourse (that revolves around a masculine *logos*), turn to celebrate the 'Goddess'. But, we must be careful here, for in attempting to include 'woman' in God/word-centred theological language, many end up using the same properties that masculine discourse has used about (and attributed to) women.[2] In other words, what happens when men's words become women's words that misrepresent 'woman'?

'Goddess Talk', or the way women seek divinity,[3] teaches us much about the misrepresentation of woman. Western philosophy perpetuates a definition of 'woman' that collapses her into masculine discourse. Following this, theology relies on the notion of a feminine Goddess that reflects a masculine God, and Goddess becomes metaphor for the feminine divine. This Goddess doubles masculine constructions of 'woman', once again reducing her to a nurturing, maternal figure.[4] Such an assimilation is structured according to oppositional, parallel, and linear thinking that alludes to the centrality of 'one'. In a superficial attempt to subvert this oneness, theologians often move from a singular 'Goddess' to the contemporary plural 'goddesses'. This move only takes us closer to another preferred (masculine) model of relationships between the 'one' and 'many'. (For more about this paradigm, see Luce Irigaray's *Why Different?*, 77–8.) Desiring to access the feminine divine, the language of Goddess Talk, instead, erects a barrier against her.

Attempting to include the feminine divine in theological discourses, Goddess Talk blends the 'divine' and 'feminine', placing them at the forefront of daily life. Contemporary culture exemplifies the incorporation of the goddess in the mundane world, and it becomes difficult to get through the day without coming into contact with her. Her commercial presence replicates her material presence, and she drives (or is driven by) cultural attitudes toward the feminine divine. Bumper stickers on autos forewarn of a goddess's power—both behind the wheel and in the passenger seat. Appearing in the media, in advertisements, in offices, in markets, on street corners, these goddesses demand worship. But, what kind of divinity is it that demands to be worshipped so? And, how disgraceful is this, to speak of the feminine, of the divine as such?

Allow me to put this another way: Lord, 'Was it your tongue in my mouth' the day you pulled down your *majuscule* 'God' and put up a *minuscule* 'goddess', changing an upper case 'G' to lower, and singular to plural? If I never knew who or what God was before, did you expect your G/goddess to serve me better? And, whose G/goddess is she? Certainly, not mine. Then, what tongue is this, whose *logos* is it, that resides in my mouth?

Filled with faith that rebellion need not preclude divinity, my own tongue aches as questions cascade from my mouth. What are these strange and unkempt words? To whom or to what do I turn when disconnected from any theological representation with a gendered subjectivity to which I am supposed to relate? And if I speak this way, does this mean I no longer believe in God? Tired of contemporary representations that juxtapose G/goddess against God, I turn to the work of Luce Irigaray.

Laying body over word, and word over body, Luce Irigaray's works lend themselves well to theology with its focus on the 'Word'. Evoking her own style, Luce Irigaray poignantly points to the exclusion of women from Western patriarchal discourse. But, if woman's exclusion from Western culture is not difficult enough, it magnifies a hundred-fold when examining the role of a masculinized *logos* in Christian theologies. After all, the theological 'Word' supposedly speaks to all.

Luce Irigaray investigates the role of discourse in the construction of women through three stages of work. In the first stage of her work, she offers a critique of 'auto-mono-centrism', the formation of a singular subject according to Western patriarchal or phallocratic standards. In the second stage, she attempts a second subjectivity, a subjectivity that includes the feminine. In the third stage, she seeks new relationships between, now, two subjects and supports relationships that are horizontal in nature rather than hierarchical. Following the chronology of Luce Irigaray's work, I first critique the Goddess Talk of a theology that bases itself on a masculinized *logos*. Second — similar to existential theology's death of an irrelevant God — I suggest the death of an irrelevant G/goddess and call for her (re)birth through a different discourse. Finally, I return to an 'other word' — 'a silent word, a living mystery, [an exchange] beyond words' — asking what the quieting of Goddess Talk might bring (Luce Irigaray, *To Be Two*, 8).

Linking body and word, the metaphor of mouth as 'gate' figures prominently in this reading. In Part One, the gate of patriarchal discourse stands completely closed, denying women access to the feminine divine. In Part Two, woman's capacity for both birth and death reveals her own gatekeeping capabilities, arousing the hope that we might remove the patriarchal gate. In Part Three, the gate disappears with the appearance of an 'other word'.

A woman's journey toward the divine is much like setting out on a path toward herself. Unable to be mandated by the words of another, she creates her own. Cautiously approaching both herself and the feminine divine, she steps lightly, on guard. The undoing of Goddess Talk that I suggest does not equal the end of the feminine divine. Rather, the seamlessness of body and word elicits a new beginning: a new talk. Carefully honing my own words, then, I seek to show how Luce Irigaray's work — that integrates body and word, that rewrites the feminine by auto-eroticizing one's own tongue — changes the theological conversation, always already grounded in the 'Word'.

Writing a path to feminine subjectivity, Luce Irigaray reminds us of the qualities of irreducibility, inappropriability, and forgiveness. As body and word, we are irreducible because we can never be known, inappropriable because we can never be owned, forgivable when we fall short and recline once again on the singular permanence of a word. She writes 'If I go astray, it is not so much because of an ambiguity or an equivocation (...); if I lose the way, it does not happen because of (...) confusion (...), but rather because I wonder how to sustain a relationship between us, between two facts of body and language, between two intentions constituting an incarnate relationship which is realized by flesh and words' (*To Be Two*, 28). This, then, is how I begin.

I. The Gate: Logos Word Tongue Talk

> *Trust me*, you
> say, you have
> come and gone,
> *I can't I'm falling*
> the whole way down
> where goddesses
> grope blind
> where the earth eats
> our friends
> and we are like
> oceans sounding
> their names
> *where, where*
> the ground is
> next to me
> going up and down

Susan Griffin, 'The Gates'

The themes of *logos*, 'Word', 'tongue', and 'talk' are aligned as one might align the posts of a fence: vertical, repetitious, and linear. But, these linguistic fences eventually lead to gates that act as points of access or barrier. This gate, or the point at which the feminine attempts to enter theological discourse in search of the feminine divine, is Goddess Talk.

On the surface, the notion of gate suggests greeting and encounter. We approach gates hoping to gain entry to something, but gates deny access as often as they allow it. Similar connotations of entry and exit get embedded within Christian theological discourse. Carrying a number of meanings, the gate signifies both death and (re)birth, as entry 'into the heavenly Paradise' (George Ferguson, *Signs and Symbols in Christian Art*, 174). The gate has similar connotations regarding both the 'expulsion of Adam and Eve from the Garden of Eden' and as 'the dividing barrier between the righteous and the damned in scenes of the Last Judgment' (*Ibid.*). And, concerning the feminine? Whereas the 'gate of heaven' symbolizes the Virgin Mary, a closed gate (representative of her 'unblemished virginity') just as often identifies her (see J.C.J. Metford, *Dictionary of Christian Lore and Legend*, 107 and George Ferguson, *op. cit.*, 95–6, 174).

As metaphorical gate, a woman's body suggests passage to 'mystery, secrecy, abyss, uterine darkness' — that which is unfathomable and unknowable (Barbara G. Walker, *The Woman's Dictionary of Symbols and Sacred Objects*, 15). Represented as 'the Holy Door of birth', a woman's genitalia simultaneously signify heavenly and creative powers (40). However, this gate is also assigned negative connotations, for she has the capacity to 'devour men' (328). As both 'gateway to heaven' *and* 'gate of hell', woman possesses both capacity for life and for death (11, 136, 328). The gate exists as entry and exit, then, to heaven and hell, to life and death, to 'woman'.

Goddess Talk, connected to the feminine, also signifies blissful entry to heaven, the holy, the divine, herself. Similar to the gate that protects a woman's womb, her mouth (a gate) accepts or rejects the seed of a new word. But, too often, an old seed/Word ('God') appears disguised as a new seed/Word ('Goddess'). When I ask, then, if it is God's tongue that pulled down 'God' and put up 'goddess', I refer to the notion of a well-seeded *logos*.

A commonly accepted contemporary philosophical term, *logos* was ripe for use by the early Christians. With its linguistic link to the Stoic 'word' and the Platonic 'divine mind', *logos* as both 'word' and 'thought' fits easily into pre-existing categories. One of these categories was a masculine engendering. This is a crucial insight for contemporary theology, for discourses appearing to be universal (or even feminist) often are not. Rather, they are encoded masculine and reflect a system based on oneness, unity, balance, and proportional equivalence.

The root of *logos* (*leg*), meaning 'to gather' or, more precisely, 'to pick out things which from some standpoint are alike' points to the term's attempt to unify (E. Hoffmann, 'Die Sprache u. d. archaische Logik,' 77, as cited in Gerhard Kittel, *Theological Dictionary of the New Testament*, 71–2). Such attempts at unification also imply dualisms that, from an Irigarayan perspective, continue to allude to the logic of the same.[5] For example, the dichotomies of 'word' and 'thought' signify a relationship based on union. Whereas 'word' (speech, discourse, narration) and 'thought' (account, logic, reason) are supposedly dissimilar in meaning, the symbiotic nature of their relationship suggests reflection. One complements the other to the point that each becomes an accomplice in sameness.

In Christianity, these notions of gender, oneness, like-mindedness, and unity lead to a presence that, among other things, attempts to connect the 'like-minded' concepts of the Hebrew Scriptures (*dabar/sophia*) and Greek philosophy (*logos*) (See, for example, work by Philo Judaeus). This is particularly apparent in early Christianity when 'word' and 'thought' unite (as *logos*) and become Jesus Christ. More concretely, Jesus (as *Logos*) links strongly varied cultures, religions, and languages, suggesting unity. The implications for a masculinization of power are immense when the vehicle, *logos*, becomes simultaneously male *and* the Word of God. Such notions rest on a belief in the centrality of *logos* and lead to accusations of phallogocentrism.

Hence, when Luce Irigaray asks 'Was it your tongue in my mouth', she links the tricky notions of 'tongue' as *logos* or Word with 'tongue' as fleshy protrusion. The flexibility of the tongue facilitates her move, since the meaning of 'tongue' (*langue*) alludes to both word and body. Meaning 'language', the tongue also sustains us through the taking of nourishment. These links between word ('tongue' as *langu*-age) and body ('tongue' as organ) allude to both the *logos* and phallus in Western tradition. Phallogocentrism, a prominent word in Irigarayan studies, suggests a linguistic culture that relies on the phallus as the centre of the word. Masculinities of meaning are revealed.

Circumnavigating the masculinity of discourse, Luce Irigaray considers the relationship between flesh and word. This, indeed, presents good fodder for an investigation of the feminine materiality of 'Goddess Talk', a term I borrow from the obscure 'God-talk'. Having moved from *logos*, word, and tongue to talk, I present first God-talk, then Goddess Talk: two discourses erected upon a questionable logic.

The ambiguity of 'God-talk' comes, in part, from the origination of the term. In the 1960's, God-talk emerged as a way to respond to contemporary existential 'Death of God' philosophies. Earlier, of course, Friedrich Nietzsche had also suggested the 'death of God', by which he meant (not atheism, but) the loss of God's relevance to humanity. The existential theological schools of the 20th century retrieved the notion of God's irrelevance, arguing for new ways to articulate the non-objectification of God. On the one hand, they advocated the use of ordinary language to talk of God. Terms like 'concrete', 'particular', 'finite', and 'secular' began to attach to language about God as a way to explain human experiences with the divine (see work by Rudolf Bultmann and Paul Tillich). On the other hand, they used God-talk as a way to explain the disappearance of God.

Such notions elicited negative connotations concerning talk about God. Implying informality, the term 'talk' already depreciated language about a mysterious and unknowable God. Speaking frivolously about

God suggested inauthenticity, and inauthentic talk about God defied divinity. In a religion founded on the notion of *logos* as 'Word', the sudden unreliability of words concerning God signified the discursive death of God. Alluding to this in her work, Luce Irigaray asks, 'Does the "death of God" not mean, therefore, the end of the security lodged with, or the credit accorded to, those who suspend meaning in the letter?' (*Marine Lover, Of Friedrich Nietzsche*, 169). The arrival of God-talk, then, articulated the arrival of a time when even talk about the absence of God qualified as God-talk. On the other hand, the arrival of God-talk signified blasphemy.

Replicating the obscurity of God-talk, Goddess Talk slips into non-subjectivity when theologians, attempting to include the feminine, exact not only the obscurities of masculine God-talk, but also patriarchal representations of the feminine. It seems that trying to escape the 'letter', leads back to it. Hence, the contemporary 'feminist quest for the Goddess' (Rita Nakashima Brock, *Journeys by Heart*, xv).

II. The Woman at the Gate

> *believe me*
> I'm not who I
> thought I was but
> truthful
> so much comes to me
> *I was wrong*
> the day I pulled up
> grief thinking
> myself bereft
> *everything is here*
> falling alongside me
> through the air
> into my hair like
> Shiva, into my
> fingers touching
> the dead

Susan Griffin, 'The Gates'

Women excluded from talk based on a masculinized *logos* rightly desire a feminine model for the divine, and often turn to the notion of a feminine God. We are asked to celebrate a tongue with the word 'G/goddess' emblazoned on it, and the feminine divine begins in name by mirroring God. This quality of reflection implicates other qualities, and characteristics attributed to 'woman' attach to the Goddess.

Searching for difference, many argue that the terms 'God' and 'Goddess' are dissimilar. Whereas God is absolute, a G/goddess image merely articulates the divine aspect of humanity as well as of divinity. But, too often these representations of a divine nature refer back to the construct of 'woman'. Such a patriarchal linguistic gate that permits or denies entry based on mimicry leaves little room for the discourse of the 'other'. In other words, what roles do the notions of 'woman' and 'G/goddess' play in patriarchal gatekeeping?

Often placed in the roles of mother and caretaker, 'woman' finds herself a 'gatekeeper', capable of allowing or disallowing particular things to get through. Although she protects self and home, preventing dishonour from entering, what she has not been taught — because such teaching would be subversive — is the omission of her own name. And, if 'woman' has been denied, how many others also? Incapable of preventing such atrocities because she remains unaware of them, G/goddess as 'woman' stands as a barrier to her own linguistic liberation.

The ease with which the contemporary 'G/goddess' slides off both feminine and masculine tongues suggests a simplistic view of 'woman'. Links between 'woman, body and nature' often reduce to the maternal, and accompany other distinctly 'feminine'[6] qualities of caring and nurturing (Rosemary Radford Ruether, *Sexism and God-Talk*, 259). For example, both 'Earth mother' and 'Mother earth' link mothering with the globe, signifying aspects of creation. But, this creation often appears as much a token of masculine discourse as of feminine divinity. Even the G/goddess 'as warrior' implicates 'seductive' rebellion, often at the whim of the Father, and often sacrificing another feminine.[7] Goddess Talk that relies on such patriarchal constructions denies the fullness of the feminine divine. Addressing logocentric dualisms inherent within Goddess Talk, Rosemary Radford Ruether writes:

In the contemporary feminist reaction to patriarchal religion, the revival of the Goddess of antiquity as an alternative manifestation of the divine is much discussed. But both those who appropriate this idea and those who oppose it often incorrectly project modern dualisms on the ancient Goddess. The dualisms of nature/civilization, sexuality/spirituality, nurturance/dominance, immanence/transcendence, femininity/masculinity are taken for granted, and the Goddess is espoused or repudiated as representative of nature, sexuality, nurturance, immanence, and the feminine. The result is the creation of a Goddess religion that is [merely] the reverse of patriarchal religion (*Sexism and God-Talk*, 52).

The attempt to extricate the feminine divine from dualisms that continue to be based on a model of 'one' leaves us with linguistic bones of divinity, as yet incomprehensible. Desiring to comprehend, I decide to disengage from such themes as matriarchy, mythology, mysticism, spirituality, 'thealogy', 'herstory', oral tradition, and the geometry of cyclical repetitions (for more on these themes, see work by Barbara G. Walker). When I do (disengage from these), I have not defected from my gender, nor have I committed a traitorous act.

Attempting to deny the constructed 'woman' does not mean she will be absent of her feminine subjectivity. Rather, the desire to remove the linguistic gate that denies her access to herself implies a desire *for* the feminine. In other words, the process that commences the feminine divine begins by undoing Goddess Talk. But, what comes is divine.

Paradoxically, the gate of a woman allows her entry to a self beyond herself (as 'woman'), but to achieve this she must remove the patriarchal gate that bases itself solely on the Word. Doing so requires the integration of body and word. The biological implications of a woman's capacity for life and death, in turn, suggest her capacity for the life and death of linguistic seed. Other body openings present other passages: eyes and ears, nostrils, the mouth. The mouth, its own gate, becomes an entry-way to many pleasures. It is the home of the tongue, an organ that creates its own body by way of word. Without a tongue, a woman is left speechless; created by another's, she remains unknown. And, *with a tongue?*

In a woman's search to connect with herself and with the divine, it is not unusual for her to turn to herself, to turn to the interior. She has grown weary of being invisible, and grows fatigued of male dominion over herself and others, over all others. Perhaps, this is because 'man generates and loves outside of himself' (Luce Irigaray, *To Be Two*, 76). He looks at woman as 'an object, not (. . .) a subject. He is unfaithful to an intention, to an interiority, to a gaze which we can share' (42). Woman, on the other hand, 'allows all becoming in herself: of woman, of child, of man. If she does not produce (like) man, if she does not go outside of herself and reduce herself to nothing, woman becomes herself in herself' (76).

Accompanying the turn to interiority is the interiority of the word. For Luce Irigaray, however, the turn to the word does not equal a masculine reliance on the letter, but includes the notion of the feminine body. Having been structured only according to masculine discourse, in reality, woman (as word and body) does not yet exist. This sense of 'not yet' offers the feminine striking opportunities for her own kinds of subversive discourse, and a feminine return to the interior signals a turn to uncharted territories, incomprehensible at best. Luce Irigaray writes 'The properties of the feminine identity remain yet to be thought, not beginning from the violent actions of the masculine' (*To Be Two*, 72). In her interior, a feminine subject cannot be owned by another's tongue, for she is indefinable, indescribable, as yet unwritten.

Returning for the moment to God-talk, we should recall that, in part, conversations concerning the death of God initiated God-talk. Could it be similar for Goddess Talk, the talk that arises from a masculinized *logos*? In Goddess Talk, do we see the demise of an irrelevant Goddess as we saw the demise of an irrelevant God? Would not the death of the Goddess also declare the death of 'woman' as we have known her, as she has been constructed? Invoking the death of the Goddess, the end of solely relying on a masculinized *logos*, the Word — could this be joyful?

Were her words to be the words of an as yet undefined feminine divine, the collapse of Goddess Talk would signify both death and birth. A reliance on her word, on her tongue, would allow a life of equal measure (feminine *and* divine): not merely Word, but word with body, captivated by its own interiority. Yes, the death of the Goddess suggests the disappearance of 'woman' as we have known her. But, what would (re)birth, a new birth, look like? Will we know her by her words?

III. Silence

I do
what you say
I do not hold I
caress what
passes you
would be surprised
what has happened
the sky is
inside me now
the earth a
falling body
like mine and I
am everywhere,
Could it be you

taking down
the gates?

Susan Griffin, 'The Gates'

Luce Irigaray's work calls for a model of discourse based on a horizontal, rather than vertical, plane. That is, she puts the accent on dialogue between two subjects — man and woman — who respect both intersubjectivity and irreducibility. The rule is that they speak with each other.

A notion of duality exists implicitly in this notion of speaking with one another. But, the duality of which Luce Irigaray speaks is not the same as the dualisms that form the constructed 'woman' of Western patriarchal culture. As a way to reach other forms of diversity, Luce Irigaray begins with the duality of masculine and feminine — *two* subjects — as yet unconstructed in Western discourse. For these two subjects (masculine and feminine) to speak with one another would, indeed, involve difference. Non-reflective in nature, their words would stand separately in their own spaces as an encounter with the divine. Luce Irigaray explains: 'Man and woman are irreducible one to the other, and the difference between them cannot be evaluated, calculated and appropriated' (*Why Different?*, 84). Such difference, she continues, is 'insurmountable, like the mystery that some blindly call "God"'.

Such discourse between these two also includes the notion of silence, formed according to a view of non-appropriation. Understanding that women seek the feminine divine because of a lack of feminine representation in theology, many turn to notions of her that, in turn, appropriate and objectify her. Allowed many faces rather than one, she is projected according to function, another kind of appropriation. This goddess gives me this, another gives me that. Continuing to be spoken of in terms of property, she is divided, separated, and claimed according to boundaries that lead to fences that lead to gates. Although her control may be represented matrilineally and/or matriarchally, she continues to be objectified, which means that she is not free.[8]

Such notions never stray far from the discursive properties of a masculinized *logos*. Excluded and denied, the silence of the feminine divine remains as yet inaccessible. However, the interiority of a woman's word offers potential for seed, for new word. Outside of *logos*, as yet unwritten, not yet formed by grammar or representation, the divine 'other word' leads us to the feminine divine.

Following Luce Irigaray's suggestion that the culture of two subjects can 'become a model for [other] relationship[s] in their diversity', I want to suggest the irreducibility of two modes of discourse: this word as 'other word', that Word as the one we have known (*Why Different?*, 91). As separate divinities, they remain distinct: two different tongues structured according to different worlds, presenting an authentic opportunity for dialogue. And, beyond . . .

Recall the development of 'God Talk' as reaction to contemporary 'death of God' philosophies. Recall also 'Goddess Talk', unwittingly constructing a feminine divine according to a patriarchal paradigm. Then, consider how the 'death of the Goddess' might parallel Nietzsche's 'death of God'. The appropriation of Luce Irigaray's words articulates this desire for the feminine divine as 'other word':

The cries and words of the last philosophers, of Nietzsche and Heidegger, about the 'death of God' are a summons for the divine to return as festival, grace, love, thought. Contrary to the usual interpretation made of them, these philosophers are not talking about the disappearance of the gods but about the approach or the annunciation of another parousia of the divine. Which involves the remolding of the world, of discourse: another morning, a new era in history, in the universe. (Luce Irigaray, *An Ethics of Sexual Difference*, 140)

When Luce Irigaray says that 'women's traditions are more concerned with weaving the body and words together[,] hence they're more respectful of incarnation and personal singularities', she suggests a theology of sexual difference (*Why Different?*, 174). This new theology focuses on the integrity of a divine 'other word' that weaves body with word. No longer focused on dogmatic discourse that defines the G/goddess according to God's reflection, a theology written by a divine 'other word' will differentiate and, by its differentiation, not withhold. This word desires memory and time. Its silence requires space.

To arrive at this place, I must unwrite myself. I must unwrite all that I have been taught, the Word that I have been called, rewriting that Word again with many others: words that are indistinguishable, indescribable, unstayable — and by their indistinguishability, indescribability, unstayability, we will be.

How do I tell you that I unwrite, and then write again, these words with joy? That this divine 'other word' that accompanies them sees by way of its own light, forgives before it is able, and challenges the limits of any tongue. That it is not a fence, a line, a winding, but an unwinding, an undoing. That these are the words I want to remain on my tongue: woman's words, from woman's mouth. That it takes a long time to unwrite and then rewrite anew, to extricate another's tongue and to replace it with one's own. That I have far to go.

Joyful and fearful both: the unknown. From now forward, we name ourselves. From this place filled with questions, from this place with which I am both familiar and unfamiliar, I ask: Will my words fill the spaces I desire? Or, will they conjure images I do not intend, provoking dishonour rather than grace? Will they fail the divine 'other word' as other's words have failed me?

There is a hunger in me today, a sadness. I ran too far yesterday and lost myself in the view of the bay. At sunset. The memory of her turning to see what I was gazing at. Empty tide, thousands of leggy beaks pecking at the marsh, supposedly, an arm to the sea. Where did the water go? And, how can I write, how can I make a link to the divine when I am so sad?

In the garden, I watch his fingers as they turn the soil — this land that smells of pleasure — and I am filled with longing. Lord, I am not forsaking you. I only ask that you know her, too. And, how I wish she were here, that you both could know this with me: this centre of this divine earth.

Some will say that (cyclically) we are only back where we began, with an organ in my mouth. But, this is not so. Both tempered and taught by her tongue, I arrive with my own in my mouth. Seeded within — fruit-bearing, fruit-dying — is it the phallic Word with which we were born, is it the tongue that attaches by sheath to my own bone of contention, is it another opening: my heart, lungs, eyes, ears? What is this divine pleasure that welcomes me home? The silence of a G/goddess? As she began with word, so will she end. And start again, 'a whole new poetry beginning here' (Adrienne Rich, 'Transcendental Etude', 76).

LAINE M. HARRINGTON
Graduate Theological Union, Berkeley

NOTES

1 I have more gratitude than words can express for the assistance of many people. Among others, I want to thank Luce Irigaray for her work, and for

this opportunity to dialogue with her work, Amber Straus for her assistance as editor, and Corinne Allen for her assistance with translations.

2   Luce Irigaray refers to this type of discourse as a 'speaking-among-women that is still a speaking (as) man', comparing it with 'the place where a speaking (as) woman may dare to express itself' (*This Sex Which is Not One*, 135).

3   I use the term 'divine' with Luce Irigaray's definition in mind. She writes 'For me, divine designates a process that permits passing from here-and-now to perfection, for spiritualizing body and nature (inseparable in their relationship), for other humans (each according to his/her being and freedom), for establishing a continuity between human nature and divine nature' (*Le Souffle des femmes*, 223, translated by Corinne Allen and Laine Harrington).

4   Luce Irigaray explains 'It is abusively that one speaks of the great Goddess [in the singular] . . . as exclusively maternal. The Goddess, known only as Mother, is already a patriarchal paradigm: she figures the mother of a son, of sons, the most legitimate and prolific spouse of patriarchy' (*Le Souffle des Femmes*, 237–8).

5   *Logos* scholarship often relies on the articulation of numerous other dualities (for example, human/divine, external/internal, immanence/transcendence).

6   As defined by masculine discourse.

7   Luce Irigaray writes, 'The ambivalence the god feels for the mother, the woman, is incarnate in the character of the goddess. What will henceforth be called women's deceitfulness. Which is merely a projection of the Father. Adorned, femininity — the father's thought appearing over female authority. By taking over maternal power, by swallowing it, introjecting it, he engenders, produces, this daughter who (only) gives herself out to be what she is not: a simulacrum borrowed by the God to help him in his work, establish his empire. A semblance that claims to do without body, death. Seduction rules in appearance — *truth*. Also needs beauty, but as a decoy. That touches, therefore, only to achieve some — virile — objective. That no longer affects, is no longer affected by, anything "within herself". Always already standardized according to the father's desire alone. Knowing nothing but the master's jouissance' (*Marine Lover, Of Friedrich Nietzsche*, 102).

8   For example, David Kinsley writes that 'research has recently shown that no strong, positive relationship exists between matrilineal and matriarchal societies and the relative freedom and power of women, or between women's economic contribution and their relative status' (*The Goddesses' Mirror*, xviii).

BIBLIOGRAPHY

Brock, Rita Nakashima, *Journeys by Heart, A Christology of Erotic Power*, New York, Crossroad Publishing Company, 1992.

Ferguson, George, *Signs and Symbols in Christian Art*, New York, Oxford University Press, 1961.

Griffin, Susan, 'The Gates', in *Unremembered Country, Poems by Susan Griffin*, Port Townsend-Washington, Copper Canyon Press, 1987.

Hoffmann, E., 'Die Sprache u. d. archaische Logik', *Heidelberger Abh. z. Philosophie u. ihrer Geschichte*, III, 1925, 77, in *Theological Dictionary of the New Testament*, edited by Gerhard Kittel, Michigan, William B. Eerdmans Publishing Co., 1967.

Irigaray, Luce, *Elemental Passions*, London-New York, Athlone-Routledge, 1992, translated by Joanne Collie and Judith Still from the French *Passions élémentaires*, Paris, Editions de Minuit, 1982.

Irigaray, Luce, *An Ethics of Sexual Difference*, Ithaca-New York, Cornell University Press, 1993, translated by Carolyn Burke and Gillian C. Gill from the French *Ethique de la différence sexuelle*, Paris, Editions de Minuit, 1984.

Irigaray, Luce, 'Je-Luce Irigaray, A Meeting with Luce Irigaray', in *Women Writing Culture*, edited by Gary A. Olson and Elizabeth Hirsh, Albany, State University of New York Press, 1995, translated from the French by Elizabeth Hirsh and Gaëtan Brulotte.

Irigaray, Luce, *Je, tu, nous, Toward a Culture of Difference*, London and New York, Routledge, 1993, translated by Alison Martin from the French, *Je, tu, nous*, Paris, Grasset, 1990.

Irigaray, Luce, *Marine Lover, Of Friedrich Nietzsche*, New York, Columbia University Press, 1991, translated by Gillian C. Gill from the French *Amante marine*, Paris, Editions de Minuit, 1981.

Irigaray, Luce, *Le Souffle des femmes, Luce Irigaray présente des credos au féminin*, edited by Luce Irigaray, Paris, ACGF, 1996.

Irigaray, Luce, *This Sex Which is Not One*, Ithaca-New York, Cornell University Press, 1985, translated by Catherine Porter with Carolyn Burke from the French *Ce Sexe qui n'en est pas un*, Paris, Editions de Minuit, 1977.

Irigaray, Luce, *Thinking the Difference, For a Peaceful Revolution*, London-New York, Athlone-Routledge, 1994, translated by Karin Montin from the French *Le Temps de la différence, Pour une révolution pacifique*, Paris, Librairie Générale Française, 1989.

Irigaray, Luce, *To Be Two*, London-New York, Athlone-Routledge, 2001, translated by Monique M. Rhodes and Marco F. Cocito-Monoc from the Italian *Essere Due*, Torino, Bollati Boringhieri, 1994.

Irigaray, Luce, *Why Different? A Culture of Two Subjects: Interviews with Luce Irigaray*, translated from the French by Camille Collins, with Heidi Bostic, Peter Carravetta, Stephen Pluhacek, New York, *Semiotext(e)*, 2000.

Kinsley, David, *The Goddesses' Mirror*, Albany, State University of New York Press, 1989.

Metford, J.C.J., *Dictionary of Christian Lore and Legend*, London, Thames and Hudson Ltd, 1983.

Rich, Adrienne, 'Transcendental Etude', in *The Dream of a Common Language: Poems 1974–1977*, New York and London, W.W. Norton & Co., Inc., 1978.
Ruether, Rosemary Radford, *Sexism and God-Talk, Toward a Feminist Theology*, Boston, Beacon Press, 1983.
Walker, Barbara G., *The Woman's Dictionary of Symbols and Sacred Objects*, San Francisco, Harper & Row Pub., Inc., 1988.

Luce Irigaray's questions

To talk about Goddess in a general sense raises questions. It could be a simple matter of giving a gender to God without changing anything. Now the subjective relation with God or with Goddess is not the same. It is not the same matter that is in question. The problem for a woman is not to affirm the right to say Goddess instead of saying God. God and Goddess represent another reality for the woman, but also for the man. And if today we use Goddess without changing the context in which our subjectivity pronounces this word, such a gesture does not have great meaning. It is necessary to interrogate the epoch of history in which Goddess represented the divine for humanity. And if one then talks of Goddess alone or Goddess with God, and also of Goddess in the singular or in the plural.

I could recall here that the use of Goddess in the Eastern tradition of India does not signify the same thing as the use of Goddess in the beginning of our Western tradition, in Greek culture for example. And I could add that it would be opportune to interrogate some of the Presocratic philosophers, in order to understand something about the gradual forgetting of the Eastern tradition by the Western tradition.

It would also be fruitful to recognize that men, and not only women, in these times, worship Goddess and that the discourse they use is different than the discourse used to talk of God or to God.

The question of the divinity of the woman is thus very complex and it concerns not only woman herself but also man. Imposing on women the veneration of Goddess alone is furthermore perhaps not the best because women are disposed to refer to the other and not only to the same. It is even possible that women themselves have invented God ...

The question that I would ask Laine Harrington is: Have you studied various epochs in which a worship of Goddess exists? Have you considered the properties of the Goddess in these times? Is she venerated as a girl? As a virgin? As a lover? As a mother? If there are Goddesses — in the plural — is the worship the same on the part of men and women? And is the way of talking about Goddess or to Goddess the same for women and for men?

Laine Harrington's response

Initially, I want to say that I chose to work with the term 'Goddess' because contemporary Western culture's use of the term has seemed problematic to me for some time. I find your use of the term intriguing and I believe your work can illuminate the 'Goddess Talk' that occurs in much of contemporary feminist theology. Furthermore, I want to respond to those women and men who, like myself, feel disenfranchised from the feminine divine when she is spoken of metaphorically as 'the Goddess'.

Concerning pre-patriarchal cultural notions, I am aware that much of the research suggests the belief in one Goddess who manifests in a variety of ways. Here, 'nature', 'earth', the 'feminine', and 'divine' get linked together and often include notions of creativity. 'Divinity' becomes apparent through mysteries associated with the female body, procreation, and growth. Hence, we understand the importance of sexuality, fecundity, fertility in the pre-patriarchal feminine divine.

Early images of the divine were female. What becomes problematic in these early, and often contemporary, images of the feminine divine are the numerous female figures with 'exaggerated body parts' (buttocks, breasts, genitals, pregnant belly) or images that are wholly made up of these parts and 'do not always include a full body' (for more on this, see work by Marija Gimbutas). I think that something similar happens in contemporary Goddess Talk. There occurs a feminine appropriation of the female body that relies on only biological differences, or the maternal. The 'separatist' notions of such a move troubles me.

Having said this, I want to return to my text. If we think of text as body, or its figural expression, we may find that she — the feminine divine — is not that far from the earlier alluded to pre-patriarchal notions of Goddess. In other words, I have tried to present a creative text, a mysterious text, a text that can be read a number of ways — so, a text that speaks to differences — , a text with exaggerated body parts — 'woman's tongue' rather than the generally preferred masculine *logos* of theology. I attempt these moves to suggest other ways of speaking about the feminine divine. Furthermore, I have turned to your work, certainly for content, but also for style. From both the content and style of your work, we can learn many things concerning ways to speak about the feminine divine.

Finally, certainly there are numerous other cultures that rely on the notion of 'Goddess' to address the feminine divine. However, because my focus is on the Greek *logos*, I prefer not to address these other cultures' usages for fear of misinterpreting other religious/discursive practices.

Incarnation: The Flesh Becomes Word

Incarnation is a notion that speaks to the imagination of many. It invokes stories of 'God with and among us' and a yearning for God's continuing presence. And it evokes an ethical and political programme of incarnating God in the world, by working for just and right relations among human beings and between human beings and the world.

The Christian tradition does not make it easy however, to understand oneself as potentially incarnating the divine in gestures, speech–acts or body, when one is a woman. For in this tradition 'incarnation' is used to refer to Jesus Christ, who is professed to be 'verily God and verily man', the one and only human being in which the divine Word became flesh. This profession marks the definition of true humanity by the masculine and reinforces the idea that God is male. Its message is that women, that female embodied subjects, are not fully human, because they are not fully man. Their difference, and especially their different corporeality, their flesh, forms a barrier to think women as made in the image of God or to envisage the divine Word as being incarnated by female embodied subjects.

To keep open the notion of incarnation as a horizon and programme for women, it is therefore necessary to re-think this notion and especially the relation between the female body and the divine, between flesh and Word. In order to do so I turned to the works of Luce Irigaray, because her philosophy of sexual difference offers both a useful critique on the manner in which the dominant discourse stages the relation between Word and flesh, the order of discourse and the body, and because it offers the means to formulate an alternative for the staging of the relation between flesh and Word.

This text is devoted to the consequences of this alternative staging for the discourse of theology. In the first part I offer a picture of the properties of the flesh and its function in thinking and speaking, derived from Luce Irigaray's work. This picture is then followed by an interpretation of the significance of Luce Irigaray's idea that the flesh has a morphology from the beginning, for the process of flesh becoming Word. In the last part I will draw out the significance of this picture of the flesh for the discourse of theology.

The flesh becomes Word

Hysteria and the hysteric

Luce Irigaray's interpretation of hysteria and the hysteric was important for the project of re-thinking the relation between Word and (female) flesh. She pictures hysteria as a mode of relation to the other — a relation, which is expressed in the enunciations of the subject — and as a pathology (See my 'A God in the Feminine'). These two are intimately related. According to Luce Irigaray, the inscription in an order of discourse which does not know 'a generic *she*, a transcendence in the feminine, a culture of women amongst themselves', leaves the female subject no means to express her subjectivity as a female subject ('L'importance du genre', 15). This impossibility causes corporeal suffering, because this language is in no way 'continuous with — nor a metaphor for — the "movements" of [her] desire' (*This Sex Which Is Not One*, 136–7). This brings me to the interpretation that the (corporeal) suffering of the hysteric is due to the inscription of the female subject in an order of discourse which does not take into account her carnal, libidinal, sexual difference.

On the other hand, Luce Irigaray pictures hysteria as a revolt of the flesh against this alienating inscription and subjection. She formulates this view as follows: 'There is a revolutionary potential in hysteria. Even in her paralysis, the hysteric exhibits a potential for gestures and desires ...' (*The Irigaray Reader*, 47), and 'there is always, in hysteria, a reserve power (...) the possibility of another mode of "production" notably gestural and lingual' (*This Sex Which Is Not One*, 138).

The interpretation of hysteria as paralysis of the flesh by, and of resistance to, a moulding of its libidinal movements, which is strange to it, implies a conception of corporeal matter as a productive source and resource of relating and speaking, of being and becoming. It points towards a conception of the flesh as source of a different *parole* and eventually of a different *Word* — a culture of women amongst themselves.[1] This conception of the flesh is the subject-matter of the following sections.

The flesh: sensible, libidinal, tangible matter

When the passages in Luce Irigaray's work that are devoted to the flesh are taken together a picture of the flesh emerges, in which the flesh is painted as sensible, tangible, libidinal, maternal matter. It is 'a living mobility (...), that is undergoing perpetual transformation' (*The*

Irigaray Reader, 51). The flesh is moreover being's most elementary level of being, and of being in the world. It is the condition of the possibility of being and knowing.

The first range of epithets emerges directly from Luce Irigaray's work. The idea that the flesh constitutes the most elementary level of being and of being in the world as well as the condition of possibility of being and knowing arises from the interpretation of her dialogue with Maurice Merleau-Ponty and Martin Heidegger as well as from her critique of what she describes as the founding gesture of western civilization, notably 'the murder of the mother'.

In her work Luce Irigaray shows that this 'murder of the mother' returns in various discourses and guises: in stories and philosophies, in psychoanalysis and economic exchange relations, in popular culture and in theological ideas.[2] It takes the form of an appropriation of the creative power of the maternal by the paternal in reproduction, and in a displacement of origin from the mother to the father, or from earth to heaven — a child/son comes from God. It can be discerned in the privileging of the paternal genealogy and the erasure of a female genealogy. It comes to the fore in the downgrading of the body, which takes effect in the split between ideal and material, sensible and intelligible, immanence and transcendence, flesh and Word. This downgrading of the body can be interpreted as a 'murder' of mother-matter-nature, because this split between the flesh and Word can also be analysed as a gesture of displacement of origin, a displacement whereby the origin of knowledge, of truth, is located in the meta-physical rather than in the physical, the sensible, the material.

In her analysis of this order of discourse Luce Irigaray shows, however, that the intelligible, that language or the order of representation, cannot do without the sensible, without the material, without nature. She writes 'Mother-matter-nature must go on forever nourishing speculation' (*This Sex Which is Not One*, 77). And 'Language, however formal it may be, feeds on blood, on flesh, on material elements' (*An Ethics of Sexual Difference*, 127). She therefore brings to light that blood, flesh, the material and the maternal are the forgotten sources of knowledge, of language, of the Word. In other words, she illuminates and elaborates that flesh is (a) transcendental, the condition of possibility of being and knowing. She shows that flesh is our most elementary 'home', that being is always 'being (in the) flesh'. 'Being', human being, must therefore be understood as 'living, dwelling in this flesh, in a carnal body, and relating from there to the things and the living beings'.[3]

This flesh is pictured by Luce Irigaray as *sensible* matter. The starting point of all sense-making is the experience of the senses. This means that the relation to and knowledge of the self, as well as of the world, are mediated by the experience of seeing, hearing, smelling, tasting, but above all by the experience of touching the self and others and being touched by them. This view leads her to the conception of this sensible matter as above all *tangible* matter. For touch/ being touched is part of all sensible experiences, of all the experiences of the senses. Light, sound, smell, and taste touch the eye, the ear, the nose, the tongue. Luce Irigaray formulates it as follows: 'the sense that underlies all the other four senses, that exists and insists in them all, which is also our first sense and the sense that constitutes all living (*habiter*) all environment (*milieu*) (is): the sense of *touch*' (*Sexes and Genealogies*, 59, translation adapted; see also her *To be Two*, and *Between East and West*).

This conception of the flesh is also important to the interpretation of the flesh as *libidinal* matter. It illuminates, first, that the tangible flesh mediates all relations to the self and to the other, by touching and being touched. And secondly, it implies that desire must be understood as a touching/being touched in the flesh by the other, thus as a movement of, and in, tangible matter.

In turn this picture sheds light upon the epithet 'living mobility' which Luce Irigaray uses to picture the qualities of the flesh. For touch/being touched induces a movement of the senses. This movement travels through the flesh turning the flesh into moving, vibrating matter, elucidating that the flesh must not be understood as solid matter but as matter-in-flux: mobile and undergoing a perpetual transformation in response to the experience of touching/being touched.

This interpretation of the flesh as sensible, tangible, libidinal matter, the primary home of the subject, 'the *hulé* or primary matter that she is' ('A Natal Lacuna' in *Women's Art Magazine*, 12), suggests that Luce Irigaray's notion of *the sensible transcendental* makes clear that the integral structure of connexion between human beings and the world is a sensible structure.[4] It brings to light that the sensible is the condition of possibility of being and knowing, and that identity and subjectivity are rooted in this flesh, in the sensible, libidinal and tangible matter of the body.

The flesh is formed: birth means the entry into a morphology

Of this flesh by which human beings relate to the world, Luce Irigaray asserts that it is not neutral but female or male. This view stems from her understanding of birth as the entrance into a morphology ('A Natal Lacuna' in *Women's Art Magazine*, 13), into the morphology of the female or male sex. It highlights the irrevocable character of sexual difference, criticizing those discourses which depart from the idea that humanity is one, or which present (human) difference in terms of the many. Both gestures efface sexual difference.

The conception of the flesh as formed from its very beginning takes issue with the dominant hierarchy between matter and form. In this system of hierarchical oppositions, primary matter is represented as a-morph, unformed, not predicated, feminine, the silent substratum of all things. Form, classified as masculine, is either represented as pushing itself energetically in matter towards its 'telos', its essential existence, or it is seen as a pre-existent, immaterial idea which functions as the formative power in and of the material, sensible reality.

The idea that primary matter is formed clarifies that 'becoming' must be thought of as giving form to the morphology of the living mobility into which one is born. It entails exploring the many possibilities of being (a) woman or man in and through the life-work of becoming (a) woman or man. This exploration entails discovering, acknowledging and assuming the limitations to these possibilities due to this morphology, which implies the renunciation of the phantasmatic desire to be all and become all.

This assertion that the flesh has a morphology from the beginning, that it is sexed and sexuated has important epistemological implications. For as I have argued above, the flesh as the condition of possibility of being and knowing must be seen as the material substratum of thinking. This implies, first, that all thinking is material and displays traces of this materiality and, secondly, that thinking displays traces of the sex of this flesh. It suggests that knowledge — but aesthetics as well — is gendered, or better, that there are two genres or styles of knowledge, a feminine and a masculine one.[5]

'Morphology' in the process of flesh becoming Word

This interpretation of the implications of the idea that the flesh has a morphology from the beginning can be easily misunderstood as reaffirming an essentialist understanding of sexual difference. I use the word 'misunderstanding' for such a reading of the notion of 'morphology' for two reasons. First, such a reading passes by that the expression of 'the morphology of the female sex' does not refer to the corporeal morphology alone, but also to the morphology of the imaginary, and, last but not least, to the morphology of language, the morphologies of words and sentences. In my view, the notion of 'morphology' functions on all these levels in the process of flesh becoming Word, but takes on different significance on each level. And although there is a certain correspondence or connexion between these levels, this is not one of cause-and-effect nor of metaphorization, but rather one of contiguity and transfiguration.

My second objection is based upon my own understanding of the notion of 'morphology', notably as a defining *parameter* to the process of sense-making, the process of transformation of the sense-perceptions of the flesh into a perception of self and of the relation to the world and others. I have borrowed the notion 'parameter' from chaos theory,[6] where it points to a distinctive mode of reaction of a system to a disturbance, without determining the outcome. I turned to chaos-theory, because I found it useful to think through both the relation between sexual difference — understood as an irrevocable and irreducible difference — and the diversity among women, as well as the relation between stability and change in the constitution of identity.

Chaos theory studies processes of self-organization of natural systems and explores the non-linear reaction within these systems. These processes of self-organization are interpreted as processes of the generation of order out of chaos in and through the formation of 'dissipative structures'. These are formations of communication between particles in a natural system, in which the energy of a natural system is dissipated along the lines of this structure. When the system is disturbed and brought from an equilibrium situation into chaos, it will generate order out of chaos, although the dissipative structure will be a new, different one. In this process the defining parameter determines the reaction of the system to the disturbance, but not the outcome, the structure itself.

In my view, the flesh as sensible, tangible and libidinal matter might be understood as such a natural system which is studied by chaos-theory.[7] When the flesh touches, or is touched by, an other — be it an object, a sentence or another person — , this touch moves the flesh and brings about a chaotic whirl of sensations, from which emerges a structure, dissipating the energy of the sense-perceptions generated by the touching/being touched; and such a structure is bound by the morphology of the body of the subject.

I would like to compare this structure to what in other discourses is called an *imago*: an image or map of the body, constituting a certain coherence within the disparate and fragmented experiences of the flesh (Sacks, *A Leg to Stand on*; Grosz, 'The Body', 35–40, and *Volatile Bodies*). This imago is not an outline of projection of the real body, but an imaginary mapping of the body and of its relation to the world, generated by the sensations of touching/ being touched, and diffused with affect, with experiences of pleasure and non-pleasure. This imago reflects not only the morphology of the body, but also the relation of others towards this body, and the cultural valuations attributed to this particular body (Grosz, 'The Body', 37). These are transmitted in and through touch, but also in the speech-acts of the other.[8] This interpretation explains both the generation of identity as well as the processes of change of this sense of self and other. It illuminates that the touch of the other can throw the female subject off balance, move her so deeply that her sense of self and of her relation to the other and the world is changed. It, moreover, explains that, although the process of the generation of identity is bound by the morphology of the body into which the subject is born, this process is different for each one, rooted as it is in her or his personal history.

This imago, this imaginary mapping of the body is called imaginary, because the constitution of this structure is the stuff of the imaginary, this realm in which the unconscious and the conscious, the individual and the collective intersect. This means that the morphology of the imaginary and the morphology of thought-processes are not divorced but rather correspond to each other. This interpretation is based upon Luce Irigaray's critical remark that western discourse 'shows a certain isomorphism with the masculine sex' ('Women's Exile', 64, and Whitford, *Luce Irigaray*, 53–74). As the imaginary stands at the crossroads of flesh and Word, the morphology of the imaginary is central to the process of the transformation of the perceptions of the flesh into conscious bodies-of-work. In the realm of the imaginary the imagos of individual subjects are transfigured in images and bodies-of-thought in and through interchange with others and collective bodies of thought. These images and bodies-of-thought subsequently display a morphology in which traces of the morphology of the flesh, of the imaginary mapping of the body of the subject which generated these images and thoughts, can be discerned. It accounts for my statement above that all thinking is material and displays traces of the sex of this flesh. It explains, moreover, my contention that there are two genres or styles of knowledge, including two modes of experiencing and imagining God and the divine, a feminine and a masculine one.

Thinking and speaking God: a *poiesis* of the world

My interpretation of the flesh as the condition of possibility of being and of thinking and speaking, as well as the idea that this flesh is sexuated from the beginning, has important epistemological implications, especially for the discourse of theology. To begin with, this interpretation undercuts the dominant hierarchical opposition between flesh and Word, between matter and mind, and between the sensible and the intelligible. It rather asserts that all thinking and speaking is rooted in the flesh, is produced by the flesh in response to touch/being touched. This implies that the Word or the intelligible is not cut off from the flesh or the sensible, thus that the intelligible is not meta-physical nor transcendental. Although this position holds true for all discourses, it has grave consequences for the discourse on God, because Western philosophical and theological discourse has a long history of associating God with the metaphysical, especially in the theistic interpretations of the figure of God. However, my picture of the relation between flesh and Word undercuts such an understanding of the figure of God. It rather leads to a post-theistic understanding of the figure of God, in which the notion 'God' does not refer to a metaphysical presence nor to an ultimate — material — ground of being. God's existence becomes understood as an existence in the symbolic, thus as a linguistic sign. Or 'God' is interpreted as a *site* in the structure of discourse, notably the site of the absolute or the ultimate. The figure of 'God' is then interpreted along Feuerbachian lines, as a projection or externalization of the qualities that a (collective) subject sees as the ultimate.

Although I used the term 'projection' in my explanation of this post-theistic reading of 'God', I prefer another term derived from Luce Irigaray's work, notably *poiesis* — making and creating (*An Ethics of Sexual Difference*, 5) — , because this term illuminates that speaking, thinking, imaging 'God' means at heart a poietic act of giving shape to the world or expressing a world view, and of calling this world view into being. This interpretation of 'God', and especially of speaking 'God', corresponds in my view with Mary Daly's assertion that naming the self and the world implies *a naming toward God* (*Beyond God the Father*, 33). It calls to mind that speaking or thinking 'God' entails a risk, the risk of venturing into the not yet, into the future. I also prefer the word *poiesis*, because it underlines that the process of flesh becoming Word is not a linear process, but one of transfiguration. It recalls that, although speaking, thinking and imaging 'God' has a projective element in it — how could it be different when it is rooted in the movements of the sensible, tangible flesh — , it entails a working through, a labouring upon, a transformation of the sensible, tactile experiences of the world and the other which lie at the basis of the images of and the stories about 'God'. It is therefore a (self-)critical, creative and transformative activity which has nothing to do with setting up 'God' as a flat mirror of human desire.

This reading of 'God' proceeds from my interpretation of Luce Irigaray's text 'Divine Women' (*Sexes and Genealogies*, 55–72). In this text she draws upon Ludwig Feuerbach's *The Essence of Christianity*, in which Feuerbach argues that God is the absolute essence of man (generic); that 'consciousness of God is self-consciousness and that knowledge of God is self-knowledge' (12). He arrives at this statement by saying that man is the only species — or gender[9] — which is conscious of and relates to his own essence. It is a species — or gender — which can turn his own essence into an object outside himself. This object, which is infinite, unlimited, not bounded by limitations of individual beings, is called 'God' by man. He helps man to become conscious of himself, of his own essence and of the goal or purpose of his existence.

Luce Irigaray uses Ludwig Feuerbach's interpretation of 'God' to argue that women need a 'God' in the feminine gender to become autonomous, sovereign and free subjects (*Sexes and Genealogies*, 62). Playing with the polysemy of the word 'gattung/genre/gender', she shows that Ludwig Feuerbach uses the generic as a cloak for the masculine subject in his discourse on God. But she also uses his interpretation of the figure 'God' to assert that women need to externalize those qualities, attributes and values they hold to be essential for female subjectivity and identity in order to become female subjects themselves. In her view, women have to think of a quality or an attribute — of qualities, attributes and values — of female being-in-the-world, which they would call divine, that is to say a quality, attribute, predicate, or value they would see as a perfection, essential for the existence of women as female subjects. In other words, Luce Irigaray asks women what qualities of their gender they would externalize and project upon God, or — in different words again — what qualities would make them divine women.

I understand this call upon women to imagine a God in the feminine in a twofold way. First, I see the call upon women to imagine their God as a lever to change, as a call upon women to liberate themselves of their subjection to the ideals the masculine subject has erected for them. In my view, the very process of imaging a God in the feminine is in and of itself a liberating gesture or enterprise, because it calls female subjects to introspection, to becoming attentive to the experiences of the flesh, to the sensations of touching and being touched, to listening to their desires, yearnings, dreams. It calls them to take seriously their qualities, attributes and values as possibly worthy of the predicate divine. It also asks for a self-critically working through and labouring upon these desires, yearnings, dreams, by sifting through the range of qualities and values, by engaging into a dialogue among themselves in this process of speaking and thinking 'God'. This process must therefore be seen as a path to become a female subject, because it asks women to think of themselves as (potentially) embodying or incarnating the divine in their speech-acts and gestures.

Second, I interpret this call upon women to imagine their God as a summons to claim this discursive site of the absolute for themselves and for their gender. This reading stresses that women have to appropriate it and fill it with female imagery, with stories that portray those values that they deem to be essential to the being-in-the-world of female subjects. The appropriation of this site is part of the creation of a house-of-language in the feminine, which women need to become subjects of their speech-acts.

I read Luce Irigaray's argument for the necessity of a God in the feminine as emblematic of her view that women need a house-of-language to become subjects of their speech-acts. She describes 'God' as 'a horizon of accomplishment of my gender', as 'the objective without which women cannot fulfil her subjectivity', the 'ideal that would be her goal or path in becoming' (*Sexes and Genealogies*, 62, 63–4, translation adapted). Especially the idea that God must be seen as a 'horizon' suggests that the notion 'God' functions as the symbol of this house-of-language, which women need. The notion of 'horizon' evokes, first, the idea of a symbolic universe or that of a house-of-language of and for women, and second, the idea of a point on the horizon that offers the subject orientation and direction in the process of becoming. This means that 'God', that images of and stories about 'God', function as the objective of the process of the constitution of (a) feminine identity, directing the process becoming woman of women.[10] They direct the female subject in the process of realizing, of incarnating, the quality or value embodied in that particular image of God, thus in becoming divine and woman, or a divine woman.

This brings me back to the beginning of this text, in which I wrote that due to the masculinity of the Word and a certain understanding of the relation between Word and flesh, women cannot incarnate

God in their speech-acts or gestures, at least not as female embodied subjects. I conclude this text by describing the possibility that women incarnate God, that they 'become woman and divine' together, or divine women. But this possibility is viable for female subjects only when the images of, and stories about, 'God', which female subjects try to realize in their being-in-the-world, are generated in the process of female flesh becoming Word in the feminine. Only then will they not lose themselves in the task of incarnating an ideal that is imposed upon them. To speak positively of incarnation as a programme and horizon of 'God with and among us, women' rests therefore upon the presupposition that the Word which has to become flesh in female embodied subjectivity is in turn a female flesh become Word.

ANNE-CLAIRE MULDER
University of Utrecht

NOTES

1 This ought to have been formulated in the conditional because, in order to make this happen (the experiences of sensible and libidinal), flesh ought to be taken seriously, in the sense of perceived, listened to etc. I would like to argue that the practice of yoga is one of the paths Luce Irigaray recommends in her later work to come to this awareness of the flesh as a source of different *parole*. See *I Love to You, To be Two* and *Between East and West*.

2 See Daly, *Beyond God the Father*, Radford Ruether, *New Woman, New Earth* and *Sexism and God-talk*, Mulder, *Divine Flesh, Embodied Word*.

3 Vincenot, Agnès, *Een mythe aan de horizon*, unpublished paper presented at the conference *Festival der Utopieën* at the Katholieke Universiteit Brabant, Tilburg, the Netherlands, January 18–19, 1996.

4 Agnès Vincenot developed this interpretation in *Voor Denise*, a paper presented at a colloquium of the University of Humanistic Studies in Utrecht.

5 Elisabeth Gross illuminates Luce Irigaray's play upon the full resonances of the term 'genre/gattung', notably upon 1) genre as 'genus/gattung/gender': the general idea of a group of beings or objects presenting common characteristics, 2) genre as 'gattung/gender': as a linguistic category expressing the gender of words, 3) genre as 'gattung/genre/style': as kind, manner, or sort, imposition of categories, thereby pointing to the field of epistemology, 4) genre as 'gattung/genre/style': as style and aesthetic achievement (*Irigaray and the Divine*, 12).

6 Lorraine Gauthier has been the first to elaborate Luce Irigaray's reference to the book *Order out of Chaos* by Ilya Prigogine and Isabelle Stengers (*An Ethics*

of Sexual Difference, 124, and in *Parler n'est jamais neutre*, 314) in her thesis *Citing, Siting Irigaray*. I have further elaborated the correspondence between Luce Irigaray's work and the chaos-theory as developed by Ilya Prigogine and Isabelle Stengers in my thesis *Divine Flesh, Embodied Word*.

7   Although Luce Irigaray refers only twice to the work of Ilya Prigogine and Isabelle Stengers (see note 6), their work has probably informed her text 'The "Mechanics" of Fluids' (*This Sex Which Is Not One*, 106–118). From the recurrent theme of the fluid, of fluidity and of movement I have drawn the conclusion that she would also see the flesh as a natural system in flux.

8   It explains moreover that although the flesh is the source of all thinking and speaking, and that the revolt of the flesh is the source of change of discourse, it pays off to work for change by consciously subverting grammatical rules and received conceptions, as for instance the conception of God.

9   Ludwig Feuerbach uses the German word 'Gattung' to refer to the human species. This is a polysemic word, though, because it signifies not only 'species' as in 'the human species', but also 'gender' as in the male or female gender. See also note 6.

10 In the light of Luce Irigaray's assertion that 'the most valuable goal of becoming is *becoming*, infinitely' (*Sexes and Genealogies*, 61) this interpretation implies that in the course of the process of becoming a female subject might change direction, thus that she needs an other image of 'God' to go on becoming. And also that the point on the horizon/God is not the same for every woman.

BIBLIOGRAPHY

Daly, Mary, *Beyond God the father, Toward a Philosophy of Women's Liberation*, Boston, Beacon Press, 1973.

Feuerbach, Ludwig, *The Essence of Christianity*, Buffalo-New York, Prometheus Books, 1989, Facsimile edition, translated from the German by George Eliot 'Das Wesen des Christentums', *Sämmtliche Werke VI*, neu herausgegeben von Wilhelm Bolin und Friedrich Jodl, Stuttgart, Fr Frommanns Verlag, 1903.

Gauthier, Lorraine A., 'Citing, Siting Irigaray', Ph.D., Toronto, Ontario, York University, 1989.

Gross, Elisabeth, *Irigaray and the Divine*, Local Consumption occasional paper, 9, Sydney, Local Consumption, 1986.

Grosz, Elisabeth, 'The Body', *Feminism and Psychoanalysis, A Critical Dictionary*, edited by Elisabeth Wright, Oxford, Blackwell, 1992, 35–40.

Grosz, Elisabeth, *Volatile Bodies, Towards a Corporeal Feminism*, Bloomington, Indianapolis, 1994.

Irigaray, Luce, *Between East and West*, New York, Columbia University Press, 2002, translated by Stephen Pluhacek from the French *Entre Orient et Occident*, Paris, Grasset, 1999.

Irigaray, Luce, *An Ethics of Sexual Difference*, Ithaca-New York, Cornell University Press, 1993, translated by Carolyn Burke and Gillian C. Gill from the French *Ethique de la différence sexuelle*, Paris, Editions Minuit, 1984.

Irigaray, Luce, *I Love to You. Sketch of a Possible Felicity in History*, London-New York, Routledge, 1996, translated by Alison Martin from the French *J'aime à toi, Esquisse d'une Félicité dans l'Histoire*, Paris, Grasset, 1992.

Irigaray, Luce, 'Importance du genre dans la constitution de la subjectivité et de l'intersubjectivité', Paris, Larousse, *Langages*, 111, 1993, 12–24.

Irigaray, Luce, 'A Natal Lacuna', *Women's Art Magazine*, 58, May-June 1994, 11–13, translated by Margaret Whitford from the French 'Une lacune natale, Pour Unica Zürn', in *Le Nouveau Commerce*, 62–63, 1985, 39–47.

Irigaray, Luce, *Parler n'est jamais neutre*, Paris, Editions de Minuit, 1985.

Irigaray, Luce, *Sexes and Genealogies*, New York, Columbia University Press, 1993, translated by Gillian C. Gill from the French *Sexes et Parentés*, Paris, Editions de Minuit, 1987.

Irigaray, Luce, *Speculum*, Ithaca-New York, Cornell University Press, 1985, translated by Gillian C. Gill from the French *Speculum*, Paris, Editions de Minuit, 1974.

Irigaray, Luce, *This Sex Which Is Not One*, Ithaca-New York, Cornell University Press, 1985, translated by Catherine Porter with Carolyn Burke from the French *Ce sexe qui n'en est pas un*, Paris, Editions de Minuit, 1977.

Irigaray, Luce, *To Be Two*, London-New York, Athlone-Routledge, 2000, translated by Monica Rhodes and Marco F. Cocito Monoc from the Italian *Essere Due*, Turin, Bollati Boringhieri, 1994. The French version has been published under the title *Etre Deux*, Paris, Grasset, 1997.

Irigaray, Luce, 'Women-Mothers, the Silent Substratum of the Social Order', *The Irigaray Reader*, edited by Margaret Whitford, Oxford, Blackwell, 1991, 47–52, translated by David Macey from the French 'Les Femmes-Mères, ce sous-sol muet de l'ordre social' in *Le corps-à-corps avec la mère*, Montreal, Editions de la Pleine Lune, 1980, 81–9.

Irigaray, Luce, 'Women's Exile', *Ideology and Consciousness*, 1:1, 1977, 62–76.

Mulder, Anne-Claire, 'Divine Flesh, Embodied Word: Incarnation as a hermeneutical key to a feminist theologian's reading of Luce Irigaray's work', Dissertation, University of Amsterdam, 2000.

Mulder, Anne-Claire, 'A God in the feminine', in *Towards a different transcendence: Feminist Findings on Subjectivity, Religion and Values*, edited by Kune E. Biezeveld and Anne-Claire Mulder, Bern, Peter Lang, 2001, 49–73.

Prigogine, Ilya, and Isabelle Stengers, *Order out of Chaos, Man's New Dialogue with Nature*, with a foreword by Alvin Toffler, London, Heinemann, 1985.

Radford Ruether, Rosemary, *New Woman, New Earth: Sexist Ideologies and Human Liberation*, New York, Seabury Press, 1975.

Radford Ruether, Rosemary, *Sexism and God-talk, Toward a Feminist Theology*, Boston, Beacon Press, 1983.

Sacks, Oliver, *A Leg to Stand On*, London, Duckworth, 1984.

Whitford, Margaret, *Luce Irigaray, A Philosophy in the Feminine*, London-New York, Routledge, 1991.

Luce Irigaray's questions

I would first remind Anne-Claire Mulder that the utterance 'The flesh becomes word' is a pontifical one. Perhaps she will not be satisfied with this but it is true. The Supreme Pontiff who preceded John Paul II recalled to us that the word has become flesh and now the flesh must become word. A religious friend said this to me after the death of the Pontiff. And he added that I am working in a pontifical perspective. Thus I transmit to Anne-Claire this message, this compliment, with a little irony. I imagine that a Protestant theologian does not very much like obeying the messages of the Supreme Pontiff. But we are in an epoch of hospitality to all traditions and it is worthwhile recognizing what is good in everyone. This represents an ethical way which the becoming of humanity needs.

Thus after passing on to Anne–Claire Mulder these congratulations, because of her interest in this aspect of my work, I shall formulate a question about her text.

You have spoken about incarnation starting from feminine corporeal morphology. You know that I have insisted on the importance of the two lips in feminine morphology. I have insisted on this beginning with *Speculum* and I have tried to introduce the first occurrence of such an utterance in the middle of the book. It is the place around which the book closes, like the feminine body.

I would ask you the question: How do you imagine the passage from this closing up of the feminine body to being-two? In other words: How can you pass as woman from auto-affection, from the return to you, in you, to the relation with another?

I could explain or specify my question in still different terms. It seems to me that, in your talk, you develop mainly a perspective of auto-engendering, perhaps in the masculine way — the word becomes flesh — but above all in the feminine way — the flesh becomes word. In order to present this feminine perspective, you have inverted the order of the utterance. And, in a way, the direction of the genealogy. Masculine genealogy would be more descendant and feminine genealogy more ascendant. This point of view is interesting but we remain in auto-engendering and in genealogy. We remain in a vertical auto-engendering which goes to the earth or to the sky, which goes lower or higher.

I would ask you: How can we — according to you — engender one another? How can we engender the divine between us thanks to our difference(s)? In particular our sexual difference? Is not this horizontal way of conceiving the divine more feminine? More independent of an inversion of a divine in the masculine?

Anne-Claire Mulder's response

Let me start with your remark that Pope John Paul II has also spoken of the necessity that the flesh becomes Word. With this expression the Pope situates himself in a long tradition of theologians, who all affirmed that 'The Word became flesh, so that the flesh becomes Word'. They thereby interpret Christ's death on the cross as salvation for humankind: his death would have unified God and humankind again. This interpretation is accompanied with an ethics of *imitatio Christi*, of imitating Christ in word and deed.

However, I would like to reformulate this expression of the Christian tradition as follows: 'the flesh becomes Word so that the Word becomes flesh'. This formulation encapsulates the dialectical relation between flesh and Word I have tried to elaborate in my presentation. It reflects the different relation between flesh and Word I have argued for; a relation in which the Word is rooted in the flesh, or, in which the sensible perceptions and experiences of the flesh are transfigured in images, bodies-of-thoughts, bodies-of-work, gestures of love. This Word, generated by the sensible flesh, in turn touches the flesh of the subject, moves it, and thereby engenders the process of flesh becoming Word (again).

With respect to your second question (whether the picture I have given of incarnation as flesh becoming Word is not primarily a picture of the auto-affection of the female subjects, directed at the emergence of feminine identity and female subjectivity), I would like to say that you are right to some extent. I have focussed in this paper upon your assertions that women need a house-of-language of and for themselves to become free, autonomous and sovereign subjects, and that this house-of-language ought to be continuous with her desire, or show a certain isomorphism with her sex. But in my picture of the process of flesh becoming Word, I grant an important role to the experience of touching/being touched by the other. For by, in and through this touching/being touched, the movement of flesh becoming Word is engendered. This touch is able to destabilize hardened patterns of the imaginary or to undo the ties and knots of the imaginary, so that the creative productivity of the flesh is mobilized again. The question becomes then who the other is, who might bring about this change in the imaginary of the subject. In your text 'Communication linguistique et spéculaire' you write that the word/the touch of this other, by whom the subject is touched in this way, may be that of a psychoanalyst, but also the touch of a lover (m/f) or the words of a poet. Each can effect change in the imaginary of the subject (*Parler n'est jamais neutre*, 15).

In my dissertation I distinguish three different shapes or figurations of the other, whose touch might engender the process of flesh becoming Word: a) the word of the poet or works of art in which female subjectivity is expressed. I call this figuration 'the horizon of her gender' and b) the other of a different sex and c) the other of the same sex. Here I would like to say that the words of poetesses, of feminist thinkers have effected the most change in my sense of self and relations to others. Among the words which have touched me deeply are your words on the love of the other of different sex, but I experience them first and foremost as a point on the horizon which evoke a yearning for different relations between the sexes and which function as a beacon offering orientation to effect these changes — and not as a lived reality (yet).

Divine Love

The work of Luce Irigaray resonates with references to God, goddesses, the divine, and the need for women to find and express integrity and desires in a way that affirms a love that is divine. This paper will be an exploration of this aspect of Irigaray's work, with particular reference to her more recent work, *I Love to You, The Age of Breath, To Be Two* and *Between East and West*.

For Irigaray, what is of most importance is that a woman must be able to experience her own existence in ways that attest to her own fullness of identity, or, as Irigaray deems it, to divinity. This mode of 'becoming divine' is portrayed differently in various of her works, but it is in 'Divine Women', in *Sexes and Genealogies*, that Irigaray first develops the idea of women realizing their own divinity. And while Irigaray acknowledges the need for a divine element that corroborates one's identity, her use of the term 'infinite of becoming' certainly places this divine entity on a different plane than the traditional static and transcendent categories of the male symbolic, such as Being/Idea/Unity, which she addressed in *Speculum*. In 'Divine Women', Irigaray also associates love with the divine when she states, 'The belief in the love of God is the belief in the feminine principle as divine' (*Sexes and Genealogies*, 70). Irigaray's next step is to acknowledge that it is only if a woman has realized her own divinity, especially with its resonance of love, that she is capable of entering into a relationship.

The fecundity of God would be witnessed in the uncalculating generosity with which I love, to the point of risking myself with the other. A loving folly that turns back the other's ultimate veil in order to be reborn on another horizon. Together, the lovers becoming creators of new worlds. (*An Ethics of Sexual Difference*, 205)

Initially, it seemed that this might indicate a relationship with either sex, but it is Irigaray's move endorsing a felicitous meeting of female and male genders that marks a distinct development in her work. Indeed, since *An Ethics of Sexual Difference*, and especially *I Love to You*, where she undertakes an extended dialogue with Hegel and the notion of negativity, she has been concerned with establishing a right order of relationship, of ethics, between men and women. For Irigaray, this fulfillment of the two respective genders both separately and together is a charged task — one that could spiritualize humankind. It involves a labour of love, 'a taking of the negative on oneself', that supports an affirmative recognition of sexual difference that enhances life. This process replaces what Irigaray understands as the imposition of sacrifice or death on women by denying their access to self-determination. She states: 'Hegel knew nothing of a negative like that' (*I Love To You*, 13). It also respects the irreducibility of the other, while allowing what Irigaray describes as 'a positive access — neither instinctual nor drive-related — to the other' (13).

Such a restructuring of human relations does not require an externalized alienation from oneself, but instead, an internal differentiation. 'I thus differentiate myself within myself through the facts of my being a particular individual and of my belonging to a gender. This process enables me to make a pact with a person of the other gender without the mediation of the object' (145). In Irigaray's depiction of the relationship between the two sexes, there is insistence on two distinct gendered universals (106), and the task of each to realize, both separately and together, the fullness of life.

Irigaray also posits that this ethics will involve moving beyond the state of the couple as it exists within Hegel's privatized domestic realm — with its marital and reproductive duties. '[W]e need to establish an ethics *of the couple*, a place, a bond, where the two halves of the natural and spiritual world can be and change' (*Sexes and Genealogies*, 132). And though the ethical ideal that Irigaray promotes is a love relationship between women and men, it is not to be confused with conventional heterosexuality, nor with a facile fusion of romantic sensibilities, and its associated sensual pleasures. The latter are simply indicators of self absorption which do not acknowledge differentiation, where the other gender is the irreducible token of exteriority (*I Love to You*, 145). This necessary encounter with the other gender establishes the moment of recognition as an exemplification of a new form of relationship between a man and a woman, based on the 'transfiguration of desire *for* the other (as an object?) into desire *with* the other' (139).

It is a love expressed in this way — with care, with respect, in a mode of intransitivity towards the other — that Irigaray depicts in her words 'I love to you'. For Irigaray, carnal love between a man and a woman thus becomes divine. 'Love, even carnal love, is thereby cultivated and made divine. The act of love becomes the trans-substantiation of the self and his or her lover into a spiritual body' (139). This co-existence of corporeal and spiritual reflects Irigaray's seemingly paradoxical proposal of a 'sensible transcendental' which functions as a refutation of traditional dichotomies such as immanence/transcendence, nature/spirit, body/soul. Irigaray also distinguishes her appreciation of spirit from that of Hegel's *Geist*, especially with her reference to the mode of 'becoming one's gender' instead of Hegel's abstract and neutral idea of Absolute Being/Spirit.

The process whereby gender might become perfect is lacking in Hegel, and indeed in ourselves. If gender were to develop individually, collectively, and historically, it could mark, *the place where spirit entered human nature*, the point in time when the infinite passed into the finite, given that each individual of a gender is finite and potentially infinite in his or her relation to gender. (*Sexes and Genealogies*, 139)

This is no neutered *Geist* unfolding in History, but a form of real-ization of love that appreciates that both women and men, separately and together, can achieve not only the perfection of their gender, but the redemption of humanity. Irigaray is no less exultant than Hegel in her claims:

[W]e need to realize History — or at least continue it — as the salvation of humanity comprised of men and women. That is our task. In accomplishing it, we are working for History's development by bringing about more justice, truth, and humanity in the world. This is the task for our time (...). It is a task for everyone. No one is beyond it, and it makes no one naturally a master or slave, poor or rich. (*I Love to You*, 29–30)

In *To Be Two*, *Between East and West* and *The Age of Breath*, Irigaray expands these deliberations in ways that qualify and refine these proposals. 'The other gender', respected as a subject, not object, remains central, specifically in its mode of sexual difference. It is the notion of breath, however, that becomes of major importance as the means by which 'spirit might enter human nature'. To accomplish this, Irigaray draws together various references that she has made to air/breath/spirit in her work. It is not as if the element of air has been absent from her work, as is obvious from her book on Heidegger, *The Forgetting of Air*. In *An Ethics of Sexual Difference*, Irigaray comments that, '*To forget Being* [as Heidegger charged Western thought had done] *is to forget the air*, this first fluid given us gratis and free of interest in the mother's blood' (*An Ethics of Sexual Difference*, 127). She also referred to this forgotten alliance of the mother and breath in 'Belief Itself' (in *Sexes and Genealogies*). In this essay, Irigaray's critical evaluation of Freud's reading of young Ernst's 'fort-da' exercise as a means of controlling the absence/presence of his mother, stresses a more significant form of absence than that of Ernst's mother's physical form. For Irigaray, 'She [woman] remains the elemental substrate of life, existing before all forms, all limit, all skin, and of heaven, visible beyond-horizon' (*Ibid*, 46). It is thus the primordial absence of woman, as well as of the divine aspect of life that accompanies it, that has been forgotten. Irigaray intimates in this article that if the divine is to be experienced again in this life, the focal role of women and her connection to breath/air needs to be brought to consciousness. To achieve this, a person needs to proceed not by clinging to encultured structures and behaviours, but by an openness to a dimension, as yet unattained, that is communicated by air/breath/spirit. It is this synthesis of air/breath/spirit that becomes the core element of Irigaray's thinking. For her, air, as natural sustenance, is related to the breath which can be both physical activity and a way of spiritual transformation that links both nature and spirit.

In her recent works, Irigaray is also describing her own spiritual quest, which was evident, though not fully developed in earlier texts. This marks a departure from her radical re-readings of the Western philosophical and religious traditions. Irigaray is now more concerned with the dynamics of personal spiritual experience, rather than simply theoretical statements regarding the way in which 'the perfecting of our gender', can foster the integration of spirit and nature.

Air/breath/spirit becomes of utmost importance, particularly in relation to the preservation of life itself—both natural and spiritual. Yet it is not just for herself that Irigaray undertakes this search — her intention is that human beings, both men and women, need to become aware of their breath and of being 'attuned to the cosmic world, and to corporeal nature', so that 'we transform our vital respiration into spiritual breath' (*I Love to You*, 123). Such a development implies a form of spiritual practice. As a result of this, there is a special resonance not just for the practice of an individual, but for a couple in this undertaking: 'Man and woman breathe together, engender together, carnally and spiritually. Their alliance is flesh becoming word' (124).

These developments are profoundly influenced by Irigaray's encounter with Near and Far-Eastern traditions. Her explorations into this area have provided her with insights that she weaves together to provide herself with alternate approaches to that of traditional Western spiritual thought and practice. As a scholar of religion, while I do find certain of Irigaray's procedures troublesome — particularly a lack of original textual study, and an absence of contemporary Hindu women's voices — , I believe that her work does have very important implications as to how God/divinity can be conceived of today in ways that honour both the carnal and spiritual aspects of our existence. Spirituality need no longer demand a separation from the body and its senses.

However, Irigaray acknowledges that she has benefited from the wisdom of certain masters or gurus, especially with regard to her daily practice of yoga. On her own admission, Irigaray does not undertake this work according to Western academic procedures:

Like some recent philosophers of the West, I needed to turn myself towards the East in order to find guides and basic principals of method. I did this differently than the Western masters. I did not claim to incorporate the knowledge of Eastern masters in my knowledge, nor even to pass from their words to my words. This type of transmission appeared to me to have become obsolete. (*Between East and West*, 6)

Nevertheless, from her reading of and reflection on certain books on Hinduism and Buddhism (71), she does not hesitate to criticize certain aspects of contemporary Eastern philosophy/religious practice. She worries, particularly in the case of yoga, that the affirmation and respect of the divinity of women themselves, and that an ethics of love between man and woman in the flesh as spiritual, have not continued to be honoured (10).

In her own practice, Irigaray has chosen a number of spiritual disciplines that support her belief that the body itself can become divine through a method of spiritual training: these practices foster the transformation/trans-substantiation of the flesh of an aspirant. Irigaray describes certain elements that she has found helpful in her own spiritual growth.

Through practising breathing, through educating my perceptions, through concerning myself continually with cultivating the life of my body, through reading current and ancient texts of the yoga tradition and Tantric texts, I learned what I knew: the body is the site of the incarnation of the divine and I have to treat it as such. (62)

In addition to yoga and Tantrism (specifically of the Hindu variety), there is also the figure of the Buddha. In *I Love to You* (25, 140), Irigaray discusses the Buddha's gaze of compassion 'as both material and spiritual contemplation' — another form illustrative of Irigaray's 'sensible transcendental' — and noted that it might supply her with a model for the appreciation of the non-duality of form and matter. She develops this idea in *To Be Two* (41–2), elaborating how perception can be trained as spiritual practice. The Buddha, with his compassionate and non-possessive gaze, reached after long years of disciplined breathing, meditation and insight, provides an appropriate exemplar of this (64). I do not believe, however, that Irigaray would agree with the fact that, in Buddhist training, these steps are regarded as merely elementary training on the way to Enlightenment (*nirvana*). The notion of 'no-self', central to a Buddhist worldview, and its attitude to the body as simply physical phenomena, does not seem to be in accord with the ideal of a fulfillment of body and spirit that Irigaray seeks. This is apparent when she depicts her understanding of the fruits of contemplative attentiveness: 'Between us, we can train ourselves to be both contemplative regard and the beauty appropriate to our matter, the spiritual and carnal fulfillment of the forms of our body' (*I Love to You*, 25).

It is in her involvement with yoga, however, that Irigaray is especially concerned with the exercises in breathing that are connected with the cultivation of energy, particularly the conscious manipulation of the *chakras*, or the seven energy centres of the body, as they are termed in Tantric yoga. Irigaray describes this process:

The person following these techniques will endeavour to bring the different *chakras* of his/her body and the dimensions of the universe into relation with one another by appropriate postures and gestures, by mastering breathing, visualizing forms and colours, and emitting sounds. Such a knowledge of energy is gained thanks to the preferably oral teaching of an experienced practitioner. (*I Love to You*, 137)

Irigaray develops this subject further in *Between East and West*, stating that it is within Hindu Tantrism that the model for an actual bodily transformation can take place. This occurs after the body and its energies have been subtly educated by these preliminary exercises.

This transformation, transubstantiation of elementary corporeal matter into spiritual flesh, is achieved particularly through the passage of energy from certain *chakras* — or psycho-physiological centres — to others: thus from *chakras* of sexual energy or of elemental vitality to those of the heart, of the throat, of the head, without forgetting the return circulation all the way to the feet. (62)

In this Tantric transformation, Irigaray is not interested in ecstatic sex for its own sake, but rather in the expression of love that reaches its culmination in an intimate relationship of a man and a woman which does not remain simply at the physically erotic level. The sexual relation thus transmutes into a spiritual relationship. As she states:

Sexual desire has generally been taught to us as a work of the flesh alone and not of the spirit. This error has paralysed the energy of man and of woman in the Western tradition ... It has made sex an instrument of possession, of perversion, of death, instead of finding in sexual difference a spiritual path, which can lead us to love, to thought, to the divine. (*Between East and West*, 83)

This same theme is treated again in *To Be To* (50), but, in this instance, Irigaray declares that she is not in favour of abolishing completely the subject/object distinction which she understands to be the goal of certain masters of the Eastern tradition. She makes this statement particularly with reference to Patañjali, author of the *Yoga Sutras*.

Abolishing the distinction between subject and object does not seem to me to be the end of this journey, as several masters from the East would have it (Patañjali, for example). Although it leads to ecstasy, such a gesture appears to me to be an annulment both of the 'subject' and the 'object', an annulment desired by these masters. (50)

For Irigaray, contemplation of nature and of the other, for example in a sexual relation, as well as the freedom 'to cultivate my subjectivity, my energy, thanks to perception itself', is central to her spiritual path. It is only in this way that '[S]ubjectivity (. . .) arrives at spirituality while remaining sensibility' (50). For Irigaray, there can be no elevation to a higher consciousness if it means leaving the body, and its specific form of sexual difference, behind.

As is obvious in her interactions with the texts and practices of both Buddhism and Tantric yoga (in its Hindu form), Irigaray is selective in her appropriations of certain aspects of these traditions. This is something that will be problematic for academic scholars, be they either Eastern or Western. Irigaray, however, has stated that she is not concerned with the traditional forms of scholarship, but with following her own spiritual insights. There is, nonetheless, another objection that could be made by contemporary critics of Orientalism regarding Irigaray's adaptation of these Eastern practices in order to change Western religious traditions. Specifically, Irigaray proposes that 'a third age of Judeo-Christianity' (*The Age of Breath*, 13e) — the age of spirit — can emerge only after the age of the Father and the Son. In that Eastern religious traditions are being integrated in Western ones (however reformulated), practitioners of these Eastern religions could interpret such actions as cultural misappropriation. These are issues that will no doubt receive attention with the publication of *Between East and West*.

Perhaps the most important aspect of Irigaray's recent work is her profound interest and respect for the role of women in this spiritual process. In this connection, she had previously discussed the role of divine women in *Sexes and Genealogies*, and the nature of woman as goddess, in *I Love to You* (135). Though Irigaray endorses the divine union of male and female, represented by the gods and goddesses in Tantrism, she appreciates that this relationship discloses 'the worship of a Goddess (worship of her body and her sex) by man' (137). Irigaray also deems that it is women and their energy/spirit/breath who are most pivotal for the work of spiritual transformation. 'This passage to another epoch of the reign of spirit depends upon a cultivation of respiration, of cultivation of breathing in and by women. They are the ones who can share with the other, in particular with man, natural life and spiritual or divine life, if they are capable of transforming their vital breath into spiritual breath' (*Between East and West*, 91).

In *The Age of Breath*, woman is further depicted by Irigaray, not only as the one most responsive to air/breath/spirit, but also as being divine from birth, in the light of a reinterpretation of the Genesis myth that she describes (*The Age of Breath*, 3e). This rereading would hold that women need not be associated with original sin and its associated scenarios of a form of knowledge that implies sin, guilt, greed, antagonism and exploitation. Only an autocratic God and his absolutist mandates could organize a world such as this. Woman, in contrast, would have to act in accordance with a type of knowledge that comes from within, from being in touch with a divine that manifests itself through inner or self-revelatory modes. The breath, as the 'vehicle of the soul' (8e) can be appreciated as the means of such communication. Such knowledge enhances life rather than suffocates it. A woman's task then becomes an acceptance of responsibility and the cultivation of her inherent divinity (4e). This, however, is not a simple undertaking, as it means being available and receptive to a form of energy which can never be deliberately invoked or controlled. For Irigaray, 'It is necessary to let grace be' (11e). But to live in this way needs the cultivation of a daily spiritual practice. Because of their spiritual affinity, women thus not only live in harmony with the cosmos, but also protect the secret of human relations (*Between East and West*, 85). This spiritual responsibility, however, is not quite the same as women's tasks as 'the angel of the house' which informed the alleged morally and spiritually superior status of the nineteenth-century domesticated woman. This is because, in the present situation, according to Irigaray, women are not deprived of their autonomy.

Irigaray even proposes that a woman, because of her connection with air/breath/spirit and the earth, maintains a type of 'psychic virginity' or spiritual virginity which does not tolerate any privation or disregard of her own growth. It does assume, however, that the other gender, also in the form of the man that she loves, recognizes and respects this dimension of her life. 'This dimension of woman's psychic virginity, kept and cultivated in love and desire with man, is without doubt one of the most extraordinary spiritual riches of humanity, a richness still to be discovered beyond the value of maternity, which is not properly human' (*Between East and West*, 68).

In making this remark, Irigaray appreciates that a woman does not achieve fulfillment solely through maternity. It is her role as (spiritual/carnal) lover that Irigaray regards as being of more importance for women (89). Indeed, she is inspired by what she believes was the case in the Eastern tradition, where 'the woman has long been the first and even the sole sexual and spiritual initiator' (81–2).

Though the female is thus the initiator of divine love, there remains both a mystery and a form of transcendence involved in the interchange of love between a man and a woman. Mystery lies in the fact that the other cannot be possessed, cannot be fathomed, and so is infinite in possibility, in becoming. 'The other, whose mystery will never be a shared secret, the other who will always remain a mystery to me, is the other of sexual difference' (*To Be Two*, 111). The relationship is also an access to transcendence. 'Between man and woman, thanks to love, including carnal love, an awakening to transcendence can take place that corresponds to the reign of the spirit as spiritual breath, as soul' (*Between East and West*, 90). Most importantly, however, this is not the transcendence of old. While the other of sexual difference is transcendent, in the sense that she/he is irreducible among other things to my desires/demands, the other is also an opening to a form of transformation. 'The other of sexual difference forces me to an elaboration, to a transformation of my inclinations, leading me to open my desire to a transcendental dimension in my relationship with the other as other' (*To Be Two*, 93). The type of transcendence that results is thus not simply a vertical form of transcendence, but a relational one — a horizontal or immanent mode of transcendence — that is in keeping with Irigaray's ideal of the sensible transcendental in breaking down old exclusive dichotomies.

Irigaray has journeyed far from her work in *Speculum* of dismantling the good old patriarchal God of the Jewish and Christian traditions as well as the binary system of Western metaphysics. It is a loving and life-affirming form of divinity that has been the inspiration and aspiration of her recent quest. A form of divine has emerged that nurtures life and that dwells in humanity and the cosmos. This is a form of divine that shatters the antiquated divisions between immanence and transcendence, and allows that humans can inhabit the earth in a way where nature and spirit are not divided or divisive; where woman and man are no longer estranged in a dance of death, but cherish each other physically and spiritually; where love has come to be experienced not as frenetic desire to satisfy a hunger that can never be satiated. Divine love asks of human beings a commitment to a life that can flourish beyond alienation and repression, a task that requires careful and constant attentiveness. It is the spiritual practice of the cultivation of the breath as the elemental spirit of life that sustains the spiritual transformation of human love.

It would be only too easy to wrangle for hours debating the theological and gender disputations that arise from these writings of Irigaray. Is this pantheism? panentheism? orientalism? ethnocentrism? utopian religiosity? heterosexism? idealized femininity? These are issues that have been brought forward, and will no doubt continue to be part of the on-going discussions regarding Irigaray's work. But what is of most importance for this colloquium, is to appreciate the importance of Irigaray's work for those who perceive religion as something other than displaced needs for security or authority, than self-indulgence in erotic or necrophiliac imaginative fantasies. Divine love is a vision of a world where both women and men, having individually differentiated their drives and energies, love and affirm this life — not an external, eternal otherwhere. Irigaray believes that this change could encourage the emergence of a 'third age' — the age of the breath/spirit where, as Irigaray writes 'the task of humanity will be to become itself divine breath' (*The Age of Breath*, 13e).

MORNY JOY
University of Calgary

BIBLIOGRAPHY

Irigaray, Luce, *The Age of Breath*, Rüsselsheim, Christel Göttert, 1999.

Irigaray, Luce, *Between East and West, From Singularity to Community*, New York, Columbia University Press, 2002, translated by Stephen Pluhacek from the French *Entre Orient et Occident, De la singularité à la communauté*, Paris, Grasset, 1999.

Irigaray, Luce, *An Ethics of Sexual Difference*, Ithaca, New York-London, Cornell University Press-Athlone, 1993, translated by Carolyne Burke and Gillian C. Gill from the French *Ethique de la différence sexuelle*, Paris, Editions de Minuit, 1984.

Irigaray, Luce, *The Forgetting of Air, In Martin Heidegger*, Austin-London, University of Texas Press-Athlone, 1999, translated by Mary Beth Mader from the French *L'oubli de l'air, Chez Martin Heidegger*, Paris, Editions de Minuit, 1983.

Irigaray, Luce, *I Love to You, Sketch for a Felicity within History*, London-New York, Routledge, 1996, translated by Alison Martin from the French *J'aime à toi, Esquisse d'une félicité dans l'histoire*, Paris, Grasset, 1992.

Irigaray, Luce, *Sexes and Genealogies*, New York, Columbia University Press, 1993, translated by Gillian C. Gill from the French *Sexes et parentés*, Paris, Editions de Minuit, 1987.

Irigaray, Luce, *Speculum*, Ithaca-New York, Cornell University Press, 1985, translated by Gillian C. Gill from the French *Speculum*, Paris, Editions de Minuit, 1974.

Irigaray, Luce, *To Be Two*, London-New York, Athlone-Routledge, 2001, translated by Monique M. Rhodes and Marco F. Cocito-Monoc from the Italian *Essere Due*, Turin, Bollati Boringhieri, 1994. The French version has been published as *Etre Deux*, Paris, Grasset, 1997.

Luce Irigaray's questions

I thank Morny Joy for her work, and I shall propose some comments on it, as I did for other texts. The aim is to put the texts back into perspective with respect to my own work and thus to facilitate dialogue.

I very much enjoyed the title of this paper because of the ambiguity of its meaning. It was possible to understand it in at least the following ways: as 'the love for God', 'the love of God' and 'love as divine'. In fact, Morny Joy did not develop these possible interpretations and she talked rather about a becoming, particularly a becoming woman, which attempts to reach the divine, including in love.

Perhaps because of this choice, she can say that I began to consider the relation of woman with her own divinity only in *Sexes and Genealogies*. Yet this argument is already present in *Speculum*, for example in the chapter 'The Mysterique'. It also exists in *This Sex*

Which Is Not One, Marine Lover, Elemental Passions, The Forgetting of Air and *An Ethics of Sexual Difference*. In fact, the divine is a dimension of our becoming human and as such it has a place in each of my books, except in the exclusively scientific texts. Re-thinking the divine is indispensable in order to refound subjectivity — masculine or feminine. This is also true in order to understand the necessity and find the means of cultivating breath, in particular in order to attain autonomy. And this dimension already appears in my text 'And the One Doesn't Stir without the Other' which was published in *Signs* in 1981.

More generally I consider it a mistake to divide my work into parts that are foreign to one another. Its becoming is more continuous and the way it develops is close to that of a living being.

Another point related to chronology but in a different manner: for my work, the *Upanishads* of yoga, for example, are more important than more recent texts, because they belong to an earlier feminine tradition. Certainly Tantric texts allude to these earlier texts and that signifies that feminine traditions are still alive in them, as Mircea Eliade reminds us. But it is better, to help the comprehension of my thought, to refer to the *Upanishads* of yoga as I did myself for the text of *I Love to You* cited in 'Divine Love'. Similar care could perhaps avoid some criticisms concerning my renunciation of working for women's liberation.

I also noted that the translation of the excerpt from 'The Fecundity of the Caress', which Morny Joy cited in the beginning of her text, is not very faithful. It should be: 'The fecundity of God would be witnessed in the uncalculating generosity with which I love, to the point of risking myself *to* the other. A loving folly that turns back *in* the other *its most* ultimate veil in order to be reborn *in* another horizon. The lovers becoming *co-creators* of new worlds'. Similar looseness prevents an understanding of my discourse about the other, and also about the divine.

I would also like to clarify something about my 'following my own spiritual insights'. Certainly, I try to follow them, and it is often difficult to discover them. But every day I bring together these insights with those of masters whom I respect: masters whom I encountered or whose texts I read. It is true that I am more interested in masters than in scholars or commentators because these masters had intuitions and they followed their way through a practice.

About my willingness to 'change Western religious tradition' by 'adaptation of Eastern practices', I would like to say that, like a few others, I am in search of how to renew bonds with the Eastern tradition. Furthermore I am not sure that there are several traditions. The accomplishment of humanity as such certainly manifests itself through different manners in time and space. But perhaps there is finally only one way to become human. We discover it little by little if we do not project the transcendental into an entity foreign to ourselves. This possibility of a unique way would be the means of avoiding wars of religion, particularly between monotheisms. It is really a pity to hear, in our time, the believers of different monotheisms credit a supposedly unique God with contradictory wills in order to maintain powers and conflicts. Doesn't that signify that believers project their own will onto a God who doesn't yet correspond to a real transcendence?

Of course, I do not want to 'integrate' the Eastern tradition into the Western tradition. But they have in common a respect for breath as spiritual. The problem is that we gradually forget the necessity of cultivating breathing. To recall that a culture of breathing is necessary — through a practice of yoga but also of singing, for example — does not correspond to an integration. The question is rather of identifying in the two traditions what is irreducible for our becoming human beings. Certainly it is the case for a cultivation of breathing.

I could continue with other remarks. But I will now ask Morny two questions:

— You speak about a 'horizontal or immanent mode of transcendence'. Is it possible to speak about 'immanence' for a reality or a process which takes place between two subjects? Did not the opposition immanence/transcendence belong to a culture of one unique subjectivity?

— According to you, is a science of religion possible? For whom? And how?

Morny Joy's response

Question 1: To conflate 'horizontal' with 'immanence' is not appropriate. 'Immanence' is not the correct word to describe a process that takes place between two people. Traditionally, transcendence and immanence are two oppositional terms operating both culturally and on individual consciousness as a way that artificially separates aspects of the divine. It is in *Ethics of Sexual Difference* that you discuss the idea that it is love itself, expressed according to an ethics of sexual difference, that mediates this false division. The 'sensible transcendental' — 'the dimension of the divine *par excellence*' — operating within an open-ended horizon of becoming promotes this form of love that is both spiritual and material. It also repudiates the static categories of Being or God that had confined the understanding of separate subjectivities within dualistic parameters that kept not just God and humanity separate, but women as subject to men.

The term 'horizontal', in contrast, is used in connection with transcendence in another frame of reference. In *I Love to You*, transcendence is redefined as not referring to God, but to a partner in a love relationship. This person is transcendent, not in the conventional absolute way of God, but as someone who is irreducible in their otherness — his/her mystery cannot be contained by another's emotional impulses, nor reduced to any anticipated agenda. To confer 'transcendence on horizontality' is to recognize this other person that is transcendent in accordance with their own spiritual worth, yet is horizontal in terms of the relationship between two people. In this relationship, both partners also respect their own spiritual worth and gendered identity. This involves an acceptance of an incarnate spirituality where the spirit can act horizontally and, in a revised sense, transcendentally within a revised relationship of sexual difference and love.

Thus, while immanence has a specific reference to a traditional theological dichotomy of separation and distinction from transcendence, which the notion of sensible transcendental mediates, 'horizontal transcendentality' pertains to a form of relationship, where separately and together men and women can love as if it is always for the first time.

Question 2: The question 'is a science of religion possible' is a troublesome one for me. I teach in a department of Religious Studies which is basically concerned with both trying to learn and appreciate the religions of the world in their variety and complexity. It is an interdisciplinary undertaking and so employs methods and approaches from different disciplines in both humanities and social sciences. In the areas in which I specialize — both philosophy of religion and women of religion — the basic approach I use is a hermeneutical one. Thus, it is not one that seeks for absolute truth, but attempts to understand why and how certain definitions and methods for the study of religion have developed over the years. I would not regard this as a 'science of religion'. One of the approaches has been termed the Science of Religion, though it goes by other names, such as the History of Religion(s) — both of which are but two translations of *Religionswissenschaft*, the German term used by the founders of the discipline. There are certain people today who still adhere to the ideals of objectivity, impartiality, truth (but of a non-theological variety) in research in religion. However, much of this work, up until recently, particularly on religions other than Christianity, have been shown to demonstrate a Western bias that has imposed its own categories on people's beliefs and practices that are not necessarily appropriate. Thus, a more critical approach has developed, whereby a self-reflective position is taken, both as regards one's own position with regard to texts, but also including a suspicion of the texts that have purported to supply non-biased descriptions or definitions, yet have often exhibited sexist, racist or other unconscious projections that mar the work. From this position, if by science of religion is meant an objective evaluation of beliefs, practices, peoples in the tradition of rationalism, I do not believe that a science of religion is possible.

Conclusions

I would first like to say that I am grateful to all participants in these *Dialogues* for their work. I would also like to recall that each of them chose the subject of their contribution and expressed herself or himself with complete freedom. The requests by Judith Still and myself were only about the length of the text, correction of language and formal details of presentation. Even here, we finally accepted some diversities, for example in the way of presenting references. This international gathering has proven to be problematic particularly on this point: how to present bibliographic references. I can understand that he or she who starts from French, Italian or Spanish wants to refer first to texts in his or her own language. And I considered it more important for an intercultural dialogue to accept this, rather than imposing a particular formal habit. Even if it has become more complicated: some have preferred to refer first to their own language, and others to conform to the requisites of *Paragraph*. After three months of discussions about the manner of presenting references, I have better understood that most international conferences, scientific or political, revolve around 'how to do references', that is to say, turn around formal questions which prevent approaching the real problems. I hope the readers will share my preoccupation for considering, rather, real problems.

The diversity among the contributors to this volume is very interesting. They belong to different fields of traditional culture, being in a way transversal with respect to it. This represented an institutional question: how to carry out such a crossing of limits of university Departments, for example. The problem is theoretical — especially in a time of technical scientific methods like ours — , it is also economic. But it demonstrates that everything is organized in our educational system in order to prevent dialogues between subjects. A common object seems necessary in order to converse. This in fact submits the subject to the object, and the exchanges are conditioned upon the same. This does not correspond with a dialogue between subjects as such. It was thus interesting to discover that in order to treat the questions approached by my work, we had to pass through already structured fields and discourses — as did philosophers in the past. This does not create difficulties for understanding between us, although it arouses resistance from academic structures and their way of transmitting knowledge. We have to change our habits of thinking, focusing our attention on subject(s) more than on object(s). We then can reopen paths and perspectives for dialogues, if we do not transform the subject into an object as it is too often the case in human sciences, particularly by putting feminine subjectivity once again in a defined place.

Thus interdisciplinarity has not prevented our exchanges. Nor has the diversity of languages: we had to speak only in English! But we have treated the different ways of expressing gender in languages and the difficulties which can arise from that. However, he or she who is capable of holding a dialogue will not be precluded from doing it in spite of the diversity of languages. And they will succeed also across cultures even if, in this case, someone will put the accent more on one aspect and someone else on another: rights, language, labour, religion, for example.

He or she who interposes here as an objection the diversity of cultures, languages, scientific fields etc. manifests his or her resistance to consider what really is at stake in our dialogues. And in fact he or she shows above all an opposition to dialogue itself. These two points correspond: to be opposed to reflecting upon the status of sexuate identity and upon the relation between genders signifies refusing to succeed in holding dialogues. Why? Because the relation between man and woman is the only universal one which is, or which should be, not hierarchical, where language is indispensable to join nature and culture, and dialogue necessary to communicate between two different worlds. Without this kind of exchanges, man and woman, men and women, do not yet attain their humanity. To insist on diversity — of cultures, languages, traditions etc. — still represents a way of cancelling a more decisive problem: how to be two and to converse with respect for our differences? How would a dialogue be possible between us without submitting one to the other?

Why is it so difficult to recognize the importance of and to attain such an end? Probably because all our behaviours are still hierarchically organized. And we have not yet emancipated our cultural habits from the patterns of our traditional natural genealogies or families. Thus we remain dependent upon the intellectual father, perhaps more recently upon a mother, without being able to go out of hierarchical structures. But dialogue needs that. It wants an horizontal relation without any submission of the one to the other. Both faithfulness to myself and faithfulness to the other are indispensable for a dialogue. If I submit myself to the words of the other, I am not yet capable of conversing with him or her. Nor can I do it if I appropriate their words, consciously or unconsciously. Holding a dialogue requires being two and remaining two, each keeping one's own relation to life, to world, to the self and to the other(s), to discourse. It enjoins us to preserve difference between us.

On the contrary, our tradition has taught us to model our speaking according to a unique truth, to the same patterns of thinking, of producing discourse. This has precluded any dialogue between us. The famous Platonic Dialogues are not in fact dialogues. They are a pedagogic way of bringing the disciple to the truth of the master, a truth supposed to be unique and universal. Then there is no longer any dialogue, nor is there any speaking of one's own by each one. To speak has become only to know how to pronounce a common language, how to memorize it, how to repeat an already defined meaning in an appropriate context. This is not yet to speak. And if it is possible, in this way, to take part in a community of supposed human beings, in fact it is not yet to become a human on one's own.

Teachers, the educational system have generally introduced us to a matrix of discourse, of culture, which substitutes for the mother's womb. In such a place men speak together, but such speaking together is not yet a dialogue, it is a complicity in the same discourse, a discourse founded in part on the impossible representation of their origin, of the mother's womb, which unconsciously determines their horizon.

Thus men talk and talk together to share needs, to survive, to protect themselves from turning back to a natural or maternal beginning, to try to reach their own being men. They still lack the space or the time to breathe, to grow and to bloom as humans. Attaining such a stage requires leaving the original matrix, stepping into the open air, encountering the other, the different other(s), including the mother, and learning to listen to him, or to her, and speaking words appropriate to the one and to the other, words appropriate to each time, singular and unique, of their encounter. This could finally be or become a dialogue. But we are far away from this happening. We have just begun to sense that it would be possible, that it is necessary for our being human.

Waiting for such a new stage of our becoming, we approach, hobbling along, the possibility of holding a dialogue. We pave the way to prepare for it. The most awakened, rather, try to restore the opening of the path in all dimensions and directions. Then they remain alone and in a way naked, taking care of their life, their growth, stepping in open air, where sometimes they happen to encounter an other. Now they have forgotten the language which they inhabited, and they are capable of providing for their needs themselves. Perhaps they discover desire, but they lack words for sharing it. They are still mute, or still in another stage: still submitted to a master's discourse, still appropriating his discourse, claiming to become master themselves.

In order to attempt such a purpose, we kill those who have taught us, in reality or in a symbolic manner. We have recourse to criticism or to a multiplicity of masters, even if they belong to different horizons. We barely care about that, we want to become the first, the most competent, he or she who knows the whole, he or she who makes it to the top, who has amassed the most knowledge, the most abilities. We stay at the top, barred against the approaching of any other, holding always the same discourse alone. We have a vision of the world, and we would like to impose it as unique. In such an horizon constituted once and for all, we repeat, we are guardians of tautologies with authoritarian instruments, we use language as a weapon. Not in order to communicate, except for transmitting information, which we already know and are proud to impart to others: we become teachers in information. We do not attend to the fact that our language — thought to characterize our humanity — becomes poorer and poorer, only utilitarian, unless it confines itself to a ciphered code. Perhaps, the two are finally the same. And what seemed for centuries to be at the service of ideas, of the ideal, reveals itself as a simple means of appropriation.

Since communication between us has not been put at the centre of our becoming human, we have become a little mad. For example we say that something is the very truth but we do the opposite, divided in this way between saying and doing, perhaps because we do not produce a discourse of our own. We repeat, on the one hand, and we act, on the other. We have become the slightly schizophrenic offspring of a truth which is developing, leaving its origin, its source, its relation to the real: leaving he or she who has perceived and taught this truth.

But without assuming a truth born in the relation with another, another different from ourselves, we clone the truth, or the discourse of someone — a master, man or woman — , and we generate a society of clones speaking a formal but unreal language. We are moving and speaking in a dream, completely elsewhere, without knowing it. Furthermore, the clones are incapable of holding a dialogue. They multiply, each for their own part, elements of the original truth. The relations between them are only competitive: who has generated the greatest quantity of words, of culture, with respect to this truth, is supposed to be the best. And when the entire horizon is saturated by such a proliferation, it is necessary to kill the clones and to discover another master with cells still available to found a new cultural generation. Then a family of sames is born again. But there is not yet dialogue, and the process of becoming humans remains paralyzed.

For women, the problem is a little different and still more complicated. But it depends on them that not only they but also men could succeed in holding dialogues. As already said, the discourse of men and between men takes place in a matrix which is in large part a substitute for the mother's womb. To have access to her own language, a woman must be able to not fulfill such a function for man, for men. It presupposes that she leaves her past status in culture. She no longer has to provide a natural pole for men, and she has to discover a language appropriate to her subjectivity, including the natural dimension of it. Woman has to elaborate a language to speak the singularity of her birth, of her body, or her relational identity. It is not sufficient for her to speak as men or to speak against men. She has to speak a language of her own and, faithful to herself, to attempt to hold a dialogue with the other, this one who does not belong to the same identity. As our culture has been based on both inclusion and exclusion of a subjectivity in the feminine, the woman has to overcome the economy of such a culture in order to become capable of speaking by herself. The possibility of a 'parler femme' or 'parler entre femmes' can exist beyond the interpretation of, and women's coming out of, their position in Western culture. If this does not happen, I am afraid that the language of women will remain the same as in masculine culture: a naturalistic, emotional or imaginary language which fills up the spaces opened by the masculine symbolic order. This is not yet a language in the feminine, capable of dialogue, particularly with the other gender, but remains a complement of men's discourse. And even a 'parler femme' or 'entre femmes' will then take place inside of a masculine culture. Perhaps it will be more permitted, publicly permitted. But this is not the principal change necessary for reaching a feminine subjectivity. This could even remove women from discovering it, above all in its transcendental dimension, a dimension indispensable for becoming really autonomous with respect to men's world.

Talking only in the place assigned to them in masculine culture, or talking only as men, women contribute to impoverishing discourse, because their speaking little by little departs from any meaning. It does not correspond to a necessity for constituting feminine subjectivity and its content is nothing, in a way. Perhaps it takes the place of singing, sometimes singing together? Otherwise it represents a kind of labyrinth in which woman runs the risk of losing gradually the internal or external traces of the path toward her subjectivity, her discourse, and the possibility of a dialogue with the other gender. Talking together also becomes more difficult with their own gender because it is competitive, appraised, as it is the case between men, according to the more or less, according to quantity and not real differences. Unless these remain only empirical: then the discourse stops narrating. We have not yet reached here the possibility of a dialogue. Each one gives information about their own life, and the other at best listens with politeness but without interest, except to appropriate some details.

To hold a dialogue is another thing. And it is manifest that, for most of us, we have hardly attained such a kind of exchange — for example, many participants have changed their papers after knowing my questions, accepting with difficulty my own liberty. But, at least, we have tried, and we have begun to understand the difficulty of holding a dialogue, also and perhaps above all between subjects of the same gender. I hope that we will go further on this path, each for their own part and also together. And thus discover little by little what it could signify to communicate between us taking into account our respective differences. Then we will search for words, for syntax, for gestures — also talking gestures such as keeping silent, listening to, praising, offering beauty through speech, etc. — capable of giving and receiving meaning, not only about things or an already-existing world, but about ourselves, and one another — with our bodies, desires, hearts, souls, thoughts, ideals . . .

This could happen precisely thanks to our differences, the difference between genders being the most universal and the most capable of opening a horizontal transcendental space between us. If we succeed here in holding a dialogue, the world will be changed: we will discover the way for living more awakened, more loving and more happy. This was my wish when working on these *Dialogues*. I am sure that it does not correspond to a simple utopia but to the difficult bringing into the world of a new stage for our humanity.

LUCE IRIGARAY
December 2001

EU Authorised Representative:

Easy Access System Europe Mustamäe tee 50, 10621 Tallinn, Estonia

gpsr.requests@easproject.com

Printed and bound by CPI Group (UK) Ltd, Croydon, CR0 4YY

22/04/2026

02095383-0005